DANGEROUS SCOT

The Life and Work of

an American "Undesirable"

DANGEROUS

SCOT: *The Life*

and Work of an

American

"Undesirable"

by JOHN WILLIAMSON

INTERNATIONAL PUBLISHERS
New York

.

Library of Congress Catalog Card Number: 74-86082
Manufactured in the United States of America

◆657

Foreword: Our "Dangerous Scot"

This book was written in exile. John Williamson was decreed *persona non grata* by the U.S. Government because of his thoughts. The banishment of the author and his American-born wife and two sons was added as punishment to a long term he served in a federal prison.

There were reasons for this vindictive persecution against the man who was never charged with anything more serious than "thinking." For "dangerous thoughts" was the essence of the charge the government brought against John Williamson under the infamous Smith Act.

What were the reasons? His thoughts were political and of a nature that disturb those in power who reap their fortunes by despoiling the great mass of our nation. John Williamson is a Communist, a Marxist: his thoughts are clearly related to action—they are behind his tremendous organizing skill. This sturdy Scot is among those who believe the purpose of thought is not only to observe, but to change what is harmful to humanity. His "crime" is the conviction that life can be much better, that civilization can move to higher plateaus if the vast national treasures high-jacked by the industrial-financial complex were transferred to the public domain. Williamson was exiled because he firmly believed that socialism, through which the people can operate such publicly-owned industries, is a far superior system of society than all that has gone before. He was driven from the United States because he never compromised one iota in his lifetime struggle against racism and white chauvinism. He is firmly convinced that civilization has arrived at a moment when it can, and it must, abandon this left-over of barbarism. Human progress can be measured by its rejection of the poison of racism.

The lords of the military-industrial complex regarded Williamson as a danger for additional reasons: not solely because he was an angry workingman, nor because he was an individual in rebellion. Yes, he was all that, but fundamentally they moved against him because his rebelliousness was related to a revolutionary social science. His anger was the anger of his class.

Natural science makes clear that nuclear energy which is not controlled and directed, is energy wasted. The social science of Marxism kept Williamson from wasting his political and organizing energies. It related them to the masses of workingmen in motion in the popular upsurges against capitalism. Thus his rebelliousness contributed to the chain-reaction of the mass struggle. It gave his "anger" a maximum relevance and direction, a meaning beyond his own personal powers. It illuminated his road in the class struggle on which he never faltered.

Because of this relationship to mass trends, the Communist Party—and John Williamson as one of its national leaders—became an important factor in giving the class struggle this mighty power of the chain-reaction that has molded America. There is a transmission of power from the early struggles of workers against the first imperialist war of 1914, to the militant mass rebellion of the unemployed during the 1930s and to the struggles against racism and Scottsboro-type frameups. It is evident in the organization of trade unions in the mass production industries resulting in the Congress of Industrial Organizations; in the big sitdown strikes in the rubber and automobile plants, the steel strikes in 1937. It is transmitted to the present upsurge of the struggle for black liberation and to mass revolts against U.S. imperialist aggression. It is developed further in today's grass-roots rank and file movements, in the Black caucuses in the trade unions. This is the chain reaction leading to people's and working-class power.

What nuclear science is to nuclear power, the science of Marxism is to people and working-class power. Without this relationship the "rebellious Scot" would have been just one man in rebellion. It is his mastery of the science of Marxism that has made of him a "dangerous Scot," dangerous in the eyes of the industrial-military Establishment.

It was my good fortune to work with John Williamson on many levels. The man is a superb organizer. He has never lost the sense of working-class discipline he learned as a youngster in the shipyards of Seattle and the machine-shops of Chicago. From his earliest years, his life is marked by a deep working-class sense of personal and collective responsibility. He is a working-class intellectual, schooled from youth in the struggles of the Young Communist League, in the trade union world, in the Communist Party. He regards that party as dear as life itself, for it embodies all that his life has held worthwhile and precious.

The "dangerous Scot" is part of the class struggle as it has unfolded. John Williamson is a modest man. He has not overstated his own important contributions to the struggle. As a social scientist and a leader of the Communist Party he has contributed greatly to charting the class struggle and social progress in the United States.

As a working-class revolutionist he has prevailed over the penalties capitalism imposes on such men: brutal terms of imprisonment, daily personal hardship. He has shown his mettle in many ways, primarily in the long, unsung, hard haul of organizing masses of men — not dramatic but driving to the essence of our modern-day life. And he has, when need be, engaged in such necessary drama as the Ellis Island hunger strike to focus national attention on the crimes committed by the Establishment against workingmen and their families. It is vividly told in this book.

The forces that banished John Williamson and his family confront us all. They are the forces of the ultra-right and fascism that stalk our land. Democracy in America cannot be assured unless these forces are overcome. The henchmen of big business who run the government should be forced to rescind the decree of exile against John Williamson and his family. Such men as he can do our nation a great deal of good.

The "dangerous Scot" is no danger to our people. He remains an unfaltering champion of people's and working-class power.

—Gus Hall

Contents

Author's Preface

For many years I have hoped vaguely that time might be found in the future to record the rich and varied experiences of a lifetime of activity and struggle for socialism. The opportunity came much earlier than I expected.

In the midst of a very active Communist party life in Britain, I suffered a serious heart attack on April 1, 1963. After I recovered, the medicos laid down strict rules that forced me to relinquish for a while the active life I was used to, and to limit myself to work within normal hours, without major strains and worries.

It was then that many old friends and comrades in the United States—especially Henry Winston, Carl Winter and the late Elizabeth Gurley Flynn—urged me to write of my life in the working-class movement and my participation in its struggles. Over the many months of my convalescence I got started nicely, but during the subsequent year I was able to write only at odd hours over weekends, since even limited assignments in the Communist movement have a habit of expanding.

When I began to plan the book, I soon realized it would have to be about a man with two countries. After living the first ten years of my life in Scotland, the next 42 years were spent in the United States and, since 1955, I have been back in Britain as a result of deportation by the United States government.

When I was returned to Britain in 1955, I had a basic decision to make—should I sit out the remaining years of my life as a political exile awaiting the possibility of re-entering the United States, or should I pitch into work as an active member of the Communist Party of Great Britain? I chose the latter course, and as each year passes it confirms how correct that decision was.

Karl Marx, in *A Contribution to the Critique of Political Economy*, wrote: "It is not the consciousness of men that determines their being, but, on the contrary, their social being that determines their consciousness."

It was my good fortune to reach maturity at a time when the greatest event in the history of exploited peoples occurred—the

Russian Revolution of 1917. Its impact on the working-class movement in the United States, subsequent political and economic struggles in America, and the role and development of the American Communist Party throughout these years — all influenced me and helped shape my life.

My generation has witnessed unquestionably the greatest convulsions of world history: two world wars; the rise of fascism; the spread of socialism beyond Russia to eastern Europe, to China and other parts of Asia, and to the Caribbean; the breaking up of the colonial system; the development of atomic energy and the nuclear bomb and the exploration of outer space.

Whatever I contributed to the Communist Party was given back to me a hundred times over by the movement. My knowledge and ability came from a combination of experience, self-education and participation in party life. Those thousands of hours spent in smoke-filled rooms and halls taught me lessons that I have absorbed, tried to learn from, and tested in daily struggle.

The purpose of this book is to offer an insight into the many-sided activities of the American class struggle as I have experienced it, together with comments on some of the participants and contributions of the Communist Party. It also deals with my own background and how I came to the working-class movement 51 years ago, the last 47 of which have been spent as an active Communist.

Space considerations have resulted in substantially reducing the original script. Nevertheless, I believe it still provides an account of a crucial period in the labor movement of the United States and the role of the Communists in its history.

I can only hope it will help to acquaint the younger generation and others with these developments, and, incidentally, also make clear why the economic royalists and their government declared me and others "undesirables." Perhaps my story can also be of some value in showing that Communists are human beings with joys, sorrows and personal problems like anyone else.

During the writing of the last chapter and the ensuing years, some of the comrades closest to me, about whom I have written here, have died — Elizabeth Gurley Flynn, Ben Davis, Jack Stachel, Bob Thompson and Leslie Morris. Their names are added to that long list of friends and comrades like William

Z. Foster, Eugene Dennis, James Ford, Robert Minor, Ed Strong and Israel Amter, whose deaths were all hastened by the persecution of American reaction. But each of them died as they had lived — in the midst of struggle.

Without the help and encouragement of my wife, Mae, as well as her untiring help in typing the entire original manuscript, this book would have taken much longer to produce.

For the difficult job of editing and cutting the original manuscript, my sincere thanks go to a good friend in New England and James S. Allen of International Publishers. For reading the manuscript and suggesting changes, I am thankful to my old friends, Carl Winter and Hy Lumer.

While originally completed in 1965, more urgent matters in New York delayed its publication till this 50th anniversary year of the CPUSA. While this Preface is updated to 1969, the book itself is only updated to 1966.

I write this in Britain, where the Williamson family remains united and relatively acclimatized. To Bob and Neil, their country of birth is essentially a memory, while — without detracting from our life and activity in Britain — to Mae and myself, it is a vital part of our being.

January 1969, London — John Williamson

1

From Scotland to America

When I opened my eyes on the morning of June 23, 1913, I felt a swaying sensation and the thud-thud of engines. My nose immediately recoiled at a peculiar and offensive odor. A glance through a small round window rewarded me with the sight of continuous water that eventually merged with the skyline. This was the way my tenth birthday began — in mid-Atlantic, aboard the old *S.S. California*, bound for the United States. Until then I had lived in Glasgow, Scotland, where I was born. Those first ten years have significance here only insofar as they tell something about my forebears and describe the impressions registered in childhood from a life of poverty, and their consequences in later life.

As an only child, my life up to then was relatively sheltered — all the more so because my father sustained an injury when I was 18 months old and was permanently hospitalized two years later.

My father, for whom I was named, was born in Glasgow on March 31, 1872, of a working-class family. He was a marine engineer, having served a six-year apprenticeship in Henderson's in Glasgow, on the Clyde. On the day that he completed his apprenticeship, he went to sea as an engineer on the Anchor Line ship, the *S.S. Furnesia*. A few years later, in 1897, after successfully passing various examinations and receiving his chief engineer's certificate, he became at 25 the youngest chief engineer to sail from the Clydeside. As soon as he got his "chief's ticket," he married. He seems to have sailed to all parts of the world. I can still remember the showpiece of our house — a glass case about six feet long by two feet square which held a variety of beautiful ornaments from many countries in the Far East.

Like other sailors, my father, at the end of 1904, considered he was lucky that his ship had reached home port in time for the New Year's holidays (most important, in Scotland). After a few days at home, however, his company called upon him to substitute for an engineer who had been suddenly taken ill. He was disturbed at this upset of his holiday plans, but it was to be only a short trip to Spain and France for iron ore, and the marine craftsmen shared a community of interest even though they had not yet reached the degree of understanding to organize a union.

The *S.S. Kathleen* sailed from Glasgow on Hogmanay, 1904, to the great disappointment of my mother. Down the Clyde only a short way, it collided with an incoming ship. The *Kathleen,* cut almost in two, sank in three minutes. My father was among those rescued, but he was badly burned and shocked. He had probably been hit by some heavy object when all the engine-room crew scrambled up the narrow ladders to try to reach safety. This resulted in the paralysis that incapacitated him two years later. He died April 23, 1911, in the hospital where he had been confined for about five years.

My father's father had also been a marine engineer for the Anchor Line. He was originally from the town of Montrose, and his wife came from Greenock. Her family name was Knaggs, and I can still recall hearing, when I was "a wee shaver," what I would now regard as chauvinist remarks about her having some "foreign" antecedents.

My mother was born on November 14, 1875, in Glasgow. Her family name was White. She was raised in the Anderson Cross area, and in her teens went to work as an upholstery weaver. She married in 1897, when she was 22 years old. Seemingly it was a happy marriage, although, like all sailors' wives, my mother was lonely much of the time. I never knew what it was to have a father. I vaguely remember his being taken from the house in an ambulance, then visiting him in the hospital, and finally attending his funeral. My mother was both Dad and Mom to me during my childhood and youth.

My grandmother on my mother's side was born and raised in Eaglesham, a village about 10 miles from Glasgow. She had been a weaver in the textile mill of that town, where her father was a tester. As a girl, she went to school half a day and worked in the mill for the other half. I remember my mother telling me that when I was only four years old my grandmother taught me to say "I am a Scot to the backbone and inch in the marrow."

My mother's father, who died before I was born, went to sea in his teens. Later he became a sailmaker, which remained his trade throughout a lifetime. His family came from Irvine, Ayrshire. His grandparents were named Bigbie, and were friends of the immortal poet, Robert Burns. In Burns' poem, *The Ordination,* reference is made to the Bigbies. It seemed they owned a tavern that was frequented by Burns and his friends.

After my father's accident, our family's economic circumstances became very bad. In those days there was no system of workmen's compensation from either government or company, and no social security or death-benefit system. The steamship company never paid my mother a farthing. Until my father's death we received from an insurance company amounts that diminished from ten shillings and sixpence to three and six per week. One of my earliest memories is of tramping streets and climbing stairs (there were no individual houses, only three- and four-story tenement houses) with my mother, who tried to make a living by selling Cooper's tea and coffee from door to door. When this did not bring enough, she moved to a larger house where she took in boarders, and continued selling tea and coffee to a selected number of good customers.

As long as I live I will never forget that brown handbag that smelled of coffee when it was packed neatly for our rounds. From contact with the boarders in our house, many of whom were Anchor Line engineers, I developed a yearning for the sea.

My mother was always kind to me, and in fact sheltered me too much. Of these early childhood years, only a few general impressions remain. The entrance to each tenement was called a "close" and it was usually dark. In the backyard the designated spot for ashes and garbage was called the "midden." I remember the all-cement backyards, divided off by spiked fences. The more hardy jumped over the spikes, which took its toll in torn clothing and occasional injury. The less hardy, like myself, looked for spaces where the rails had been bent to squeeze through. It was a rule that if the space was big enough for your head, your body always could come through. There were exceptions, however, with accompanying punishment.

Since house space was always at a premium, even the kitchens had built-in "holes in the wall" where a regular size bedspring and mattress were fitted in to supply one more bed for the ever-growing working-class families.

At school the leather strap was still the means of punishment. Books were carried back and forth each day in schoolbags strapped to one's back like a knapsack. A half-hour each day in school was devoted to religious teaching, especially the Ten Commandments.

I was sent to the Sunday school of the Presbyterian church in Partick, a red stone building. I also belonged to a church organization for children called the "Band of Hope." My ambition was to be old enough to join the "B.B.'s" (Boys Brigade), with its uniforms, bands and parades.

As I got older, I went through the normal stages of imagining myself in various roles, going to sea having a high priority. An interesting variation was to play at "minister." I would line up all the chairs as an audience, stand in front of them and preach sermons, interspersing them with hymns on my harmonica. My favorite was *Onward Christian Soldiers*, which I bellowed forth at the top of my lungs. My fluency with extemporaneous sermons appears from this distance to surpass some of my speeches of later years, when I tended to follow the text perhaps too slavishly.

Every child lives part of the time in a dream world. The harsh realities of poverty intrude on the vision and cut down the flights of fancy, but they still retain their enchantment.

When we sailed in 1913 on the 3,000-mile trip to America, there was implanted in my mind the dream that had led countless others to make the same trip—the dream of a better life. I carried in my memory a calendar picture, called *Going West*—golden corn swaying in the breeze, the rich earth, the eager face of the homesteader and the train rushing by. To me, going to America meant a new and different life—no more tenements, no more tea-selling, lots of play and sunshine, and a place where my mother would not have to work so hard.

We were going, on the basis of an oral agreement, to a family in Newport News. In exchange for paying our fares and underwriting our arrival as immigrants, my mother was to become their housekeeper. The wife in the family was a permanent invalid, the husband a superintendent of a shop in a large shipbuilding firm, and the children already in their late teens.

Only after considerable hesitation did my mother make the difficult decision to tear up all roots, leave all kin behind and enter the unknown. At my age, however, it was all thrill and adventure. To crown my dream of a new land, I was promised by the old lady, whose relatives we were going to work for and who had negotiated the trip, that when I got there I would have the use of a pony and cart which I could learn to drive by myself. This really promised to be heaven for me, and I talked of nothing but that pony, my equivalent of fairyland and the golden sidewalks.

Numerous pictures of our arrival in New York are recorded in my memory—meeting the pilot ship at Ambrose Light, the Statue of Liberty, the examination by Immigration, Health and Customs, the hustle and bustle of longshoremen unloading the ship. But two things stand out: the skyline with its skyscrapers, of which the Woolworth building was readily identifiable as the world's tallest, and the day we spent sitting in the Pennsylvania Railroad station waiting for a train that was to depart that night.

We didn't leave the station because my mother was afraid of the bustle of New York City and thought we might get lost. How long that day seemed! To be in a new world and not see it! To sit all day on those hard benches! I kept running up and down the flight of stairs from the men's smoking-room to the basement. In later years, on the innumerable occasions when I traversed those stairs, the memory of July 2, 1913, always returned, and I often thought of the hundreds of thousands of immigrants who must also have had their first impressions of America in that station.

That night we boarded the long-awaited train, and next morning took a ferry to Newport News, Virginia. The excitement of arrival in a new land was mingled with timidity and apprehension of our new surroundings. It was the day before July 4, and terribly hot. After we were met, taken to the house, given a meal and shown our room, I immediately began to wonder, "Where is the pony?" By the next day my ten-year-old patience was exhausted, and my mother inquired about the promised "heaven." I then suffered my first great disappointment in America: they had once had a pony and cart, but disposed of it several years before. All the proffered firecrackers and Coca-Cola on that July 4 could not alleviate my bitter disappointment.

When autumn arrived, I was enrolled in the Stonewall Jackson School. All the children made fun of my Scottish accent. (While there were many Negro children in Newport News, I never saw any at my school. My American education thus began with an introduction to Jim Crow.) School books had to be bought, which ate up several weeks of my mother's wages of $2.00 per week.

We stayed in a house in a middle-class neighborhood. My mother and I had a room inside the house but the Negro servants lived in a shed in the yard. Nearby flowed the historic James River.

After a short time, my mother was made to understand by the head of the household that he expected her to be more than a housekeeper to him. She was horror-struck. I was too young to be taken into her confidence, but somehow got to know something of the situation. The family had signed for our entry into the country, and we knew absolutely no one here except a family in Seattle, three thousand miles away, but my mother was determined to leave.

She answered several want ads in a Philadelphia paper that sought a housekeeper. Finally she was offered a job as housekeeper at $4.00 a week plus our board. Off we went again, just five months after landing in the United States, to settle in West Philadelphia.

The head of the O'Neil household was an old matriarchal witch with two middle-aged daughters, one of whom was married. These three women worked full time editing the cooking and baking section of a well-known women's magazine printed by the Curtis Publishing Company. Their work included initiating and commenting on recipes, holding national contests on new recipes, and making photographs of the finished products. Their large, old-fashioned, three-story turreted house was fenced in by a yard covering half a block. My mother had to clean the many rooms all by herself, serve the meals, and help in the kitchen.

We arrived in Philadelphia in December 1913 and the ladies decided there was no use in my going to school that term. I was given chores to do, cleaning the yard and taking the two dogs walking several times a day. My main job was to open the avalanche of several hundred letters the ladies received daily, in answer to recipe contests and such. I had to pin each letter to its envelope. The skin of my forefinger and thumb was worn off, but with bandages and glove I continued.

That terrible household nearly ended my liking for dogs. They had two Boston bulls, each with special clothes, its own beautiful bed, its own blanket to be put on before I took them out. It is no exaggeration to say that these dogs lived much better than my mother and I. We were given a big attic without heat. When it became bitterly cold, we received an old-fashioned kerosene heater.

After the first month, my mother's wages were cut $1.00 a week. The explanation was that "the boy eats too much." When indoors, I was told, when not opening envelopes, to stay in one of three places—the attic, basement or kitchen. I will never forget those months in Philadelphia.

Sunday evenings my mother and I would walk through the streets. On one such occasion, it started to rain and, coming upon a church, we decided to go in. It chanced to be a Negro church. In our innocence we didn't know there were separate churches. The congregation was more surprised than we were. Our presence seemed to cause a stir, so we got up to leave. We were then approached by a couple of men—probably elders or ushers— who explained that this was not a white church, but if we wished to stay it was God's house. Probably as a result of unconscious influences absorbed during the five months we had spent in the South, plus the apparent embarrassment we caused, we excused ourselves and left. My mother was completely nonpolitical in her thinking, and neither of us was aware that there was a race problem. But I still remember her comment: "If God made us all, Negro and white, it's darn funny they have to worship in separate churches."

After three months of exploitation by the O'Neils, we were ready to pick up and go back home. My dream of America was nearly completely shattered. But my mother had been writing her friend in Seattle, who urged her not to give up but to come out West. I must again commend my mother's courage. Seattle was only a name, and was 3,000 miles distant. Nevertheless, she said, "Well, here we go again, but by God, if this doesn't work out, back home it's going to be."

After a row with the O'Neils, we left. We borrowed money from the Seattle friends and, buying the cheapest through-tickets, we were on our way. In later years I traveled to Seattle from New York by train in 54 hours or by plane in 12 hours. But in early 1914 it took us five days and nights to travel there. We didn't know that such a thing as a Pullman existed, nor would it have made any difference. For 120 hours we sat up in a day-coach, with one change at Chicago.

In those days the railway company gave you a coupon for transportation in the Parmelee Co. coach from one station to another in Chicago. As we walked out of the station, we were surrounded by cab drivers and hangers-on. Sizing us up correctly as greenhorns, they told us that the Parmelee coach had left, but that one of them would take us. Instead of driving us to the other railway station, where we had intended sitting up until morning, he dropped us at a flophouse on or near Adams Street. After being fleeced for the cab fare and "hotel" rent, we didn't even get a night's sleep. There were so many rats running back and forth that we sat up all night on our suitcases chasing them away. Finally morning came, and by walking no more than two blocks we reached the railroad station and entrained for Seattle.

Seattle was the metropolis of the Pacific Northwest. By 1914 there was no more frontier and the gold rush to Alaska was over, but this region still retained vestiges of these periods. The bulk of the state of Washington lies between two mountain ranges, the Cascades to the east and the Olympics to the west. East of the Cascades, which are covered with snow the year round, lies Spokane in the north, and to the south the rich fruit and farm country of Yakima and Wenatchee.

The cities west of the Cascades were surrounded by rich timber country, mainly fir and spruce. Hundreds of logging camps and sawmills were scattered throughout the area, carrying out vast and complex operations: felling the trees, stripping and sawing them into logs to be transported — either by being floated in the streams or piled on flat cars — to the mills. These logging camps were moved from one location to another each season. The lumberjacks lived in camps with bunkhouses, and each camp had its own "cookie" who prepared the meals. Families were left behind.

Prior to World War I, the main industries of Washington were fishing, shipping, agriculture and lumber. Lumberjacking was "a man's work," and the men, hardened and tough, were herded and driven by gang bosses. As the companies planlessly and ruthlessly cut down the rich timber, the territory left behind was sold or rented to families who wanted to farm. Because the land was covered with tree stumps, these farm were referred to as stump ranches.

The social background of the Northwest — the recent frontier, the gold rush to Alaska, homesteading, the specific characters of such industries as lumbering and fishing—all contributed to and influenced the individualistic but militant character of the people and especially the workers.

Seattle was the key city. Founded in 1852, it still had only 3,533 population in 1880. But with the Klondike rush in 1897 the town mushroomed to 80,000 in 1900, then to a quarter of a million in 1914. The city contained a large Chinese population but less than 500 Negroes. Located on Puget Sound, Seattle had a large modern harbor and ships plied between the city and the Far East, Alaska, Canada and other Pacific points.

It was a beautiful city, built on seven hills and traversed by quaint but effective cable cars. The center of the city was then the Totem Pole, at the foot of Yesler Way. Nearby was Washington Street, nicknamed "Skid Road," lined with employment agencies, flophouses and coffee shops.

Into this bustling city, my mother and I arrived in early 1914. We lived with our friends on Graham Street, Brighton, in Rainier Valley. Through the windows we could see picturesque Mt. Rainier. Our friends made their living by breeding, raising and exhibiting English bulldogs and Scottish terriers. (I seemed fated to associate with dogs.) They also boarded other pedigreed dogs. The dogs and the big garden became my substitute for the punctured dream of the pony and cart of nine months earlier.

In that city, there opened up for me a new life, not a daydream, but days of happiness in which I was to grow up, mature physically and mentally, and start a road in life that I have never regretted.

2

Labor Movement in Seattle

After being accepted into the fourth grade, I attended the Brighton Public School. Within a month I had an after-school newspaper route for the Seattle *Star* from which I earned 25 cents a week. This was duly turned over to the family funds; my candy allowance was two cents a week, but later increased to five cents.

I soon made friends with other schoolboys on the same street. We used to gather every evening about suppertime to watch the autos go by. The number of motor cars then in use can be judged by the fact that we knew how many to expect. The central attraction and the subject of much debate was the big Stanley Steamer. Other cars were the Overland, Sterling, Maxwell and Metz. The main roads where we lived were made of 12-inch-wide wooden planks laid in a V-shape, so no great speed was possible. To outrun these cars, at least for a stretch, was a daily challenge to us.

In the summer we went swimming in Lake Washington or picnicking in Seward Park on the lake. In the winter, sledding on the half-mile-long hill of Graham Street, with no wagons, cars, fences or telephone poles to interfere, was great fun. At Christmas we would go into the nearby woods and chop down the tops of firs, which made fine Christmas trees for our homes. A few extra were sold.

Soon after our arrival in Seattle, my mother got a job as housekeeper and cook with a couple who lived in the swank suburban area of Laurelhurst. Theirs was a beautiful house, with a lawn of several levels that gradually sloped to Lake Washington, where the owners had their own wharf and boat. Aside from being political opportunists, they were pleasant people. Our employer was a lawyer and a Republican state senator. He paid my mother $25 a month — the highest wage she had ever earned.

I remained with our friends in Rainier Valley and my mother came to see me once a week. In the middle of 1915, my mother's employers went on a trip, leaving her in charge of the house. It was arranged that I would stay with her and that nothing would be deducted from her wages.

But this meant changing schools again. Furthermore, the prosperous area of Laurelhurst had no public school—residents sent their children to private schools. The nearest public school, three and a half miles away, was a two-room affair, covering all classes through the sixth grade.

At the end of that school year, my mother decided we had to have a house of our own. She quit the housekeeping job and we moved back to the Graham Street area of Rainier Valley, and I returned to Brighton School. Along with school and studies, I led the usual teenager's life. I also went to the Sunday school of the local Presbyterian church and later became secretary of a Sunday school club. I was well known at the local library, two miles away, as an eager reader of all their adventure books. During this time I worked as a delivery boy every Saturday at Schuman's Butcher Shop. For a 12-hour day I was paid $1, which seemed like big money to me. When not delivering packages, which had to be carried in two big baskets over a distance of many miles, I helped kill and pluck chickens.

The first house of our own was a yellow, two-room shack located on a lot about 150 by 35 feet for which we paid $4 a month. It had no electricity, and an outhouse at the foot of the yard. We stayed there until early 1920, during which time I shingled the roof and built a wooden sidewalk, a chicken coop, a rabbit hutch and a doghouse. (My wife and children can hardly believe this because of my apparent helplessness at home during the busy days of my political life.) Our firewood was bought cheaply by the cord and supplemented by my sawing up old telephone poles.

We had a garden with potatoes, sweet corn, lettuce, carrots, peas and turnips. We kept chickens and had fresh eggs to eat and sell, but I never was successful at raising rabbits. Everything would go all right for five or six months, and then they would all die on me. After experiencing this twice, my rabbit-raising came to an end and I have never eaten rabbit since.

To maintain our own house my mother got a job as a cleaner in the Haight building downtown. This meant working from 6 to 11 P.M. Sometimes I went with her and helped dust and empty wastebaskets. To leave servant status behind was a great relief to her.

When I was in the eighth grade at school, our living problems became very critical. I had to leave school, much against the opposition of my teachers. My first job was in the West Seattle Box Co. factory. It was a 10-hour-a-day job, sawing and planing wood. The pay was $4 for a 55-hour week. After two months' time, I was cut by one of the saws and had to be treated by a doctor. The boss, probably worried that I was not yet 14 years old, laid me off.

My mother, supported by the school principal and teachers, insisted that I go back to school. This I did, and I graduated from the eighth grade in June 1917, when I was 14 years old. There was no thought of going further in school. I had to turn seriously to finding a steady job. I first landed in Seattle's largest printing shop, Lowman and Hanford's. I began learning to be a press-feeder, working on a Gordon press. A journeyman pressman set up the job, and all I had to do was to insert paper and withdraw the printed sheets, carefully and quickly. I handled mainly envelopes, letterheads, advertising or calling cards. When I got a job of 25 or 50 thousand envelopes to do, I thought the monotony would kill me. Because the machines were electrically driven, you had to be alert all the time or else your fingertips could get crushed. The job paid $6 for a 48-hour week and it promised an opportunity to learn a trade.

Lunch hour at this job was a pleasant interlude for me. Since the shop was located only a few blocks from the waterfront, I would go from pier to pier watching the ships while eating my lunch. My family's maritime background still influenced me, and I had a longing to go to sea as an engineer. The busy harbor, with its miles and miles of waterfront and the ever-present, pungent, salty smell of Puget Sound helped me float through each day with dreams of the future in my mind.

Before World War I, Seattle had one ship-repair yard—the Seattle Drydock and Repair Co. My school chum's father was the dockmaster and his tales fascinated us. With the war, Seattle became a boom town. Not only did the old repair company expand into new shipbuilding, but even larger steel shipyards— Skinner & Eddy, J. R. Duthie and Ames—opened up.

Along with this went a boom in building and construction. The wooden streets and sidewalks soon disappeared. The "tallest building west of Chicago," the 42-story L.C. Smith Building, was constructed; and, next to it, the new County-City Building.

The shipping and lumber industries also expanded rapidly and, when the United States got into the war in 1917, the lumber industry became indispensable in the rapid building of airplanes.

As these and other industries blossomed forth, they attracted tens of thousands of new workers. The shipyards, with their better-than-average wages and lots of overtime, were a magnet for local workers as well. Futhermore, employment in an essential industry served to secure many deferments from the draft.

The menfolk in most of the Scottish families we knew worked in the shipyards, usually as skilled craftsmen. Arriving at a compromise with my mother, who was bitterly opposed to my going to sea, I decided to be a ship's draftsman and designer and got a job in the J. R. Duthie Shipbuilding Co. According to custom, an apprentice started from the bottom, and I was assigned to the blueprint room. At night I took a course in ship designing at the Franklin High School. (In later life I learned that Eugene Dennis — destined to become secretary of the Communist Party — attended the same school and had the same teacher, only he was a day student.)

After a few months, early in 1918 I decided to change my job and I transferred to the pattern shop as an apprentice. This was considered one of the skilled crafts of the yards, and journeymen pattern makers were being paid $1.50 an hour. I started at 25 cents an hour (considered big wages for a boy of about 15) for a 48-hour week. We worked on the dayshift, from 7 A.M. to 3:30 P.M.

In the shop, I started with shellacking patterns and core-boxes, but soon I was given simple jobs to do under the direction of a journeyman. A requirement was to read blueprints and then lay out in full scale the job you were to do, using special shrinkage rules for different metals. So I changed my high-school night course to mechanical drawing. Later I took an International Correspondence School course in pattern making.

For the next three years I learned pattern making in that shipyard. Wage increases were given every six months. While the Duthie shipyard employed 4,000 to 5,000 workers, the pattern shop never had more than 50, basically composed of old-time trade union craftsmen, some of them from England and Scotland. The local union president, an Englishman named Castle, worked in my shop. The foreman, another Englishman named Bonner, had been a business agent of the local union. The assistant foreman, McDonald, another Scot, was a former local union president.

All this led to a conflicting situation. There was no question as to everyone's being a union member and adhering to union conditions. Yet the relatively high wages of these "aristocrats of labor" and the former local union officials in foremen's positions, tended to place the pattern makers well behind the forefront of struggle. I hasten to add that they loyally participated in every strike. But they failed in that they always left the organized picketing to the large unions.

This craft attitude was reflected in my own union status. The local union president signed me up, but since I was an apprentice, told me not to come to meetings. Later, I stayed away (for incorrect political reasons); therefore, unfortunately, I never played any real role in the Pattern Makers Union.

Our yard was located far out of the city. It took me one and a quarter hours to travel there by streetcar, although for a time the government ran special railroad trains for shipyard workers. This cut 20 minutes off the trip. Nevertheless, it meant getting up at 5:30 every morning—a habit of early rising that has stuck with me throughout life.

With my mother working at a variety of jobs and my wartime wages, we were able to make our two-room house more comfortable by installing electricity. We also saved enough money for my mother to fulfill a dream that she shared with all the other Scottish families I met in the United States—a visit to the "auld country." This she did in late 1919, returning in the spring of 1920. We then moved to Ballard, at the other end of Seattle.

During this period I tended to move more among adults than young people. Many were Scots. I became acquainted with Scottish songs, especially those sung by Harry Lauder. With these friends, I would attend the one legitimate theater, the Orpheum, and hear or see such singers or actors as Chauncy Olcott, Feodor Chaliapin, Sarah Bernhardt and John McCormack. With my younger friends, I went to the movies of the day. First, the nickelodeons; then the serials with Pearl White as the heroine; the Wild West movies with Bill Hart, or the comedies with Chaplin, Arbuckle and Keaton.

In 1920, the process of closing down the shipyards finally reached my yard. The war was over; the replacement of ships was no longer necessary. Finally came the last day of work, with

my apprenticeship uncompleted. Neither the company nor the
union did anything about it. Like tens of thousands of others,
I was now on my own.

I found out that in Vancouver—about ten miles from Portland, across the Columbia River—the Standifer Shipbuilding
Co. was still operating. (This became the site of one of Henry
Kaiser's big yards in World War II.) I got a job as a fourth-year
apprentice, or improver. The pay was approximately $43 a
week—more than I was to make at any time during the next
25 years. Vancouver was a very small town, whose population had been inflated by the influx of shipyard workers.

Founded in 1820 by the Hudson Bay Co., and in those days
used by the Indians as a trading post, Vancouver's population
before the war was about 10,000. Its only other industry was the
Oregon Packing Co., a subsidiary of the California Packing Co.,
where 400 to 500 women, many of them young girls, tinned
and packed Italian prunes. The bulk of this fruit consumed in
the domestic market came from this area.

With the shipyard workers crowding in, housing was impossible to obtain and prices were prohibitive. My mother and I
landed in a room behind a shop. I commuted several times a
week to Portland, but never struck any roots or found friends
there.

Standifer also ground to a halt in five or six months. Again I
was out of a job, so we went back to Seattle. Hard times had set
in; there was an exodus from the city; unemployment was growing rapidly. No such thing as unemployment insurance existed.
You either lived on your savings or went on charity, while wearing out shoe leather looking for another job.

During these years, from fellow-workers who became firm
friends I learned not only about life, but about trade unions,
politics and socialism. A few of those whom I met as a boy were
my first teachers and played decisive roles in influencing the
course of my entire life.

Hardly a person living during the years 1916-1920 could escape the impact of events. The entire world was ablaze with wars
and revolutions. The United States had entered World War I on
April 6, 1917. The great economic struggles and strikes, which
had been growing in number, were officially blocked by a combination of imperialist jingoism, government oppression, terror,
wholesale arrests, and the labor officials' agreement not to con-

duct strikes during the war. In 1917 there were 4,324 strikes, while in 1918, only 1,515.

One strike stands out in my memory, because of its proximity to Seattle, although I was not a participant. On June 1, 1917, the Industrial Workers of the World called a strike of all lumber workers in the Northwest. The first men walked out at Cle Elum, just a few miles from Seattle. The government dispatched troops and arrested and interned the strikers for several months at Ellensburg, Washington, without any charges. Despite this, the strike continued, and by July 15 there were 50,000 lumber-jacks out on strike for the eight-hour day and better conditions in the camps.

Side by side with the effects of the United States' entry into the war came the impact and tremendous repercussions of the Russian Revolution, November 7, 1917. It aroused great excite-ment and high hopes among many advanced workers—and cor-responding hate and fury among the employers.

Broad sections of the American people were beginning to question the social values of the past and were reaching out for new ones. Nowhere was this more true than in Seattle, con-sidered by many as the most advanced city in the nation, so far as ferment, activity and struggle were concerned. This was due to its historical background and its special character. It was the last area of the frontier days, with the individualistic tendencies that go along with stump-ranching, lumberjacking and fishing; with the radical traditions of Greenbackism, free silver, munici-pal socialism and a strong IWW. The Socialist Party had been consistently left-wing. The best-known leaders were Hulet Wells and Sam and Kate Sadler—the latter a middle-aged woman whose fiery and fearless manner drew sizable audiences at public gatherings.

Seattle had a municipal light and power plant which supplied most of its residents with the cheapest power in the country. This was the outcome of strong anti-monopoly sentiment, aimed particularly at the Boston-owned company, Stone & Webster, which made constant efforts to strangle municipal ownership.

Of great significance, too, was the founding in 1917 of the Seattle *Union Record*, the only daily trade union-owned news-paper in America. It was the official organ of the Central Labor Council, which owned 51 per cent of its stock; the balance was owned by various local unions.

Edited by the left-winger, Harry Ault, the *Union Record* played an important role in establishing the solidarity and the left outlook that characterized the Seattle labor movement. Its highest circulation was 112,000; it lasted till 1928, but it was a difficult job to keep it alive. The strongest force behind it was Ault, ably assisted by Anna Louise Strong and a staff drawn largely from the local labor movement.

The atmosphere of the city was most conducive to my developing a heightened responsiveness to events, a consciousness of my position in society, and a desire to contribute my "wee mite" to changing and bettering the world. Of course, all this was a gradual process. I had come to work in the shipyards without any working-class political consciousness, but I was conditioned for it by the hard life and struggle for existence that I saw my mother experience during my first 14 years, and by being one of the thousands of shipyard workers who were 100% unionized. (The great majority belonged to Local 104 of the Boilermakers Union.)

The workers were astir with a new feeling of strength, and with the realization of their own power they won substantial improvement in their economic conditions. They didn't hesitate to use job action and to strike if need be. Indicative of the spirit that "Seattle is a 100% union town" was the decision that every union should issue monthly a different-colored button or badge to be worn on coat lapel or dress, with the month stamped plainly on it. Woe unto the worker who didn't wear an up-to-date button!

In the shop, at lunchtime, and coming and going from the job, many subjects were hotly discussed and debated. Friends inside and outside the shop developed my understanding, directed my reading, argued with me about events and finally convinced me to enter the revolutionary socialist movement.

Workers of that day who were responsive to radical proposals and who wanted to learn had certain advantages over workers in the post-World War II era. The distractions of television and radio, with their narcotizing effect, did not exist. In those early days many were self-educated, widely read, and capable of expressing themselves in a convincing fashion. Lectures and public gatherings were available and popular; the worker with intellectual curiosity could find a going movement that stood for opposition to, or criticism of, capitalism. All this was in striking con-

trast to the recent McCarthy period (not yet dead) in which
Marxism became *de facto* illegal, while the facade of *de jure* legality remained on the books.

A friend and neighbor of mine, McCallum, a Scotsman, and a
rigger by trade, was a strong "Wobbly" (IWW) adherent, and he
explained everything from that viewpoint. The IWW had been
organized in 1905, with the Western Frederation of Miners as its
biggest constituent. It had the support of the Socialist Labor
Party, large sections of the Socialist Party, including Eugene
V. Debs, the Socialist Trades and Labor Alliance and most of the
radical industrial workers. By 1908, the IWW had split because
the majority rejected political action and adopted a syndicalist
policy. The Socialist Labor Party and others withdrew and
waged war against the IWW.

Nevertheless, the IWW played a militant role in the West.
During the years I am discussing, it bore the brunt of an attack
by employers and the government for its antiwar stand and
strike activity. Its strength in the Pacific Northwest was primarily
among the lumber and agricultural workers, not in Seattle.
Traditionally, however, it had much influence in all radical circles in Seattle. IWW headquarters and open-air meetings in the
Skid Road were a fixture.

While the bulk of its members and leaders were sincere, militant and honest, their opposition to political action, their advo-
cacy of what they called "direct action" (which opened the door
to employers' provocateurs) and their general scoffing at theory
never attracted me, and I could not identify nor join with them.

A Scotsman by the name of Harris, who worked in the pattern
shop with me, had a decisive influence on my thinking and associations. He had emigrated from the Clyde. From him I heard
all about the shop stewards' movements and about McManus,
Gallacher, McLean, Maxton and many other socialist leaders in
the land of my birth, even before I knew much about comparable American leaders.

In Scotland Harris had belonged to the Socialist Labor Party,
although he never joined in Seattle. While very critical of the
reformism of the Socialist Party, as well as of the syndicalist
attitude of the IWW, he expounded the program of De Leonism* to me daily. He brought me literature to read, especially

*Daniel De Leon successively joined the Knights of Labor, Edward
Bellamy's nationalist movement and the Socialist Labor Party. He was
one of the founders of the Industrial Workers of the World, from

the galaxy of De Leon's pamphlets, from *What Means This Strike?* to *As to Politics.* He took me to meetings and got me to subscribe to the *Weekly People.*

At the same time, Harris worried about the Socialist Labor Party because of its refusal to get into the midst of the struggles, although ever ready to stand on the sidelines and criticize. He kept saying this was the difference between the party in Britain and the United States. When, some years later, the local trade unions decided to run their own slate of candidates for city council, my friend told me he voted for one Socialist Labor candidate, but cast all the rest of his votes for trade union candidates, even though he knew this was against the party's policy.

While his instinct was undoubtedly correct, he still felt that the Socialist Labor Party, with its socialist program combining political and economic action, was superior to the Socialist Party and the IWW. By December 1918, he had succeeded in convincing me of this, and I joined the Socialist Labor Party.

I have always thought of Harris as an example of a patient propagandist (in later years I found that such men were also legion within the Communist Party). To influence and develop one's shopmate was the important thing.

Now every struggle began to have a definite political significance. The shipyard workers — myself included — participated in two half-day sympathy strikes to free Tom Mooney.* Both of these were part of a national effort. The first, in November 1918, resulted in his death sentence being changed to life imprisonment. The second, in July 1919, was participated in by nearly one million workers nationally who demanded Mooney's release or a new trial.

Another manifestation of the political development of the Seattle labor movement was the refusal of the AFL Longshoremen to load the *S.S. Delight* with munitions, which were being

---

which he was expelled. A translator of Karl Marx, he was a vigorous agitator and polemical writer. As the leader of the Socialist Labor Party and editor of its paper, the *Daily People*, his influence was considerable despite his doctrinnaire mistakes.

*The frame-up of Tom Mooney as an alleged participant in the bomb killings in the 1916 San Francisco Preparedness Day Parade drew international attention. His unconditional pardon by Governor Culbert L. Olson of California in 1939 was a triumph for those who fough long and stubbornly for his vindication. Communist parties in all coun tries played a major role in the compaign for his freedom.

shipped to Vladivostok, the Russian seaport then held by the Japanese. These munitions were intended for one of the White Guard generals backed by American, British, French and Japanese imperialists in their efforts to destroy the Russian Revolution. The night this action of the longshoremen became known, a spontaneous gathering at the Longshoremen's Hall overflowed into the streets.

Public debates were very popular in Seattle working-class circles. Every Sunday in 1918 and 1919, weather permitting, a big open-air meeting attracted as many as 10,000 people in a large empty area at Fourth Avenue and Virginia Street. The main speakers were often nationally prominent, sometimes coming from distant cities. The meetings were held under the auspices of a loosely organized united-front body called the Workers, Soldiers and Sailors Council. The influence of the Russian Revolution may be seen in the name. It was composed mainly of left trade unions, Socialist Party branches, some IWW members and other left individuals. The Council had its own weekly paper, called *The Forge*, edited by Walker C. Smith.

In addition to these open-air meetings, hardly a week went by without a meeting at either the Labor Temple or the Longshoremen's Hall. At such meetings I heard John Reed, William Z. Foster, Louise Bryant, James P. Thompson, Elizabeth Gurley Flynn, "Little Giant" Mills, Raymond Robins, Ralph Chaplin, George Vanderveer, James Fisher, James Kennedy and many others. I remember well the big reception for Hulet Wells, a ocal Socialist and trade-union leader, when he returned from rving a prison sentence at Leavenworth as a conscientious ob-
tor.

These meetings were a great education for me. I was still ng and new to the Socialist Labor Party, so had not de-ed their dogmatic attitude and closed mind to new de-nents and challenging ideas.

Seattle general strike—the first of its kind in a large n city—started on February 6, 1919. When the workers le their demands for a wage increase, the war was still he trade union leaders had agreed to arbitration. In the answer came, in what was known as the Macy th the armistice signed, the employers were pre-their postwar crackdown. We shipyard workers ll-out strike to force revision of this award. And on ?,000 shipyard workers struck solid.

The atmosphere was tense. Not a wheel turned in any of the yards. Each gate was picketed. There was no tendency toward strikebreaking among the workers. While work was still plentiful, there was a certain apprehension as to what the peace would bring. To add to the tension, a big open-air meeting, where the impending shipyard strike was the main subject, was attacked by the police, under orders from Mayor Ole Hanson. They brutally beat everyone they could lay hands on.

The strikers appealed to the Seattle Central Labor Council for help. After much discussion it was decided, over the opposition of the right wing, to submit the question of a general strike to a referendum vote of tthe affiliated unions. One hundred and ten unions voted for the strike.

The general strike began on February 6. Not a single industry operated, not a streetcar moved. All city institutions were closed down. The only workers who refused to join the strike were the typographical employees on the newspapers. A central strike committee was in operation. Pledges of support came in, including many from non-union workers. The central strike committee decided on exemptions for hospital facilities, home-lighting and milk deliveries for babies. They opened 21 feeding centers that were run by the Restaurant Workers Union. The strikers had their own unarmed labor guard of 300 ex-servicemen patrol the streets; they were identified by special armbands.

A terrific wail went up from the employers and the press. Mayor Hanson, an ignorant demagogue, shrieked "revolution" and claimed the instigators were the "Russian Bolsheviki." Hanson was the darling of the anti-labor Seattle *Times*, and he gained national applause from industrialists. The mayor's pleas for state and federal troops were refused, but he deputized 2,500 armed men.

Hanson then issued an ultimatum that the city would be placed under martial law if the strike was not called off by February 8. But this did not move the workers. The strike was equally solid on February 8, and Hanson did not dare enforce his threat.

Despite all efforts at provocation and intimidation, the self-discipline of the strikers, helped by the labor guard, was wonderful. The only act of violence occurred when a worker was assaulted by a policeman for refusing to read a copy of the Seattle *Star* which carried the mayor's proclamation in screaming headlines on its front page.

The federal government and the national American Federation of Labor leaders were panic-stricken. The former issued
appeals and rushed in special government mediators, while the
latter threatened and began pressuring local union officials.

After five days, during which the strike was solid, the Central Labor Council called off the general strike, following
a bitter debate. After having thus betrayed us, some trade-
union leaders claimed that the strike achieved its objectives
as a demonstration of solidarity with the shipyard workers, who
were then left to struggle alone with the employers and the
federal government. The issue of the Macy Award was still un-
resolved. After another month's struggle, the strike was called
off and we faced defeat. Our demands were not granted, and
the employers even tried to withdraw some previous union
gains.

A big anti-union drive was launched, and a well-financed,
open-shop employers' outfit, called the Associated Industries,
was established. The United States government began arresting
editorial staff members of the *Union Record*, including Anna
Louise Strong, charging them with sedition. The police raided
and closed the IWW and Socialist halls. Indictments were issued charging 31 IWW members with criminal anarchy, but no
one was ever convicted. Like every lost battle, this one created
temporary discouragement. But it didn't last long in the atmosphere of Seattle.

The labor movement, except for those influenced by the
IWW, decided to fight back on the electoral front. In the autumn
of 1919 and the spring of 1920, labor candidates representing
the "triple alliance"—the AFL, the Railway Unions and the
Farmers' Grange—ran in elections. While getting a substantial
minority of votes, none were elected.

I participated in the strike, but since I was still only 16 and had
just become politically conscious, I was content to report each
day and to argue in support of the strike. I remember daily
walking into the city, a distance of six miles, to keep in touch
with all developments. I was able to get the strike committee's
daily printed bulletin and the Socialist *Call*, a weekly paper
printed daily during the strike.

In 1919 the Central Labor Council planned a demonstration
to free political prisoners. President Wilson was making a national tour to enlist support for affiliation to the League of

Nations. The Council decided that while it would participate in the official welcome to greet the President, each member of Labor's delegation would wear a large ribbon from shoulder to waist, with the inscription "Free Tom Mooney and All Political Prisoners."

How proud we all felt as they marched down Second Avenue behind Wilson's car. Later, at the big public meeting, the labor delegation — mostly right-wingers — also marched with these sashes on. News of this action rang throughout the nation, but there was no word of it in the local press.

During this period I was a member of the Socialist Labor Party, which I joined in August 1918. Unlike the IWW and the Socialists, it advocated a revolutionary road to socialism and not just reforms; it pointed out the need for combining political and industrial action; it advocated industrial unionism; it declared itself unequivocally as a Marxist party; it was against the war as an imperialist war; and it emphasized the importance of theory and the need for study.

At that time I didn't know the background of the Socialist Labor Party. I still had to learn that the adherent of revolutionary socialism can and must fight with his fellow-workers for immediate demands, without sacrificing his socialist principles. Neither did I understand that theory is only meaningful if it is a guide to action, and that this necessitates being active among the workers at their own level of political development and in the organizations to which they belong. I must say that the Socialist Labor Party's position on this question always bothered me, and it was on that issue that I finally broke with it in 1922.

Historically the party was the first national Marxist political party in the United States. Organized in Philadelphia in July 1876 as the Workingmen's Party of American, a year later it changed its name to Socialist Labor Party. It is best known for its activity during the period of Daniel De Leon's influence and leadership, starting in 1890.

While many aspects of the party's program and policy were correct, it never understood the tactic of combining revolutionary policy with the struggle for the immediate demands of the workers. While correctly estimating the greater effectiveness of industrial unions, it adopted a policy of hostility and withdrawal from the craft unions, thus isolating itself.

For De Leon and his party there was no transition between capitalism and socialism, no role for the working class or the revolutionary party after the successful revolution. While propagating many basic Marxist concepts and relentlessly fighting right opportunism, De Leon and his followers were not creative Marxists but dogmatists and sectarians.

It was only when the Russian Revolution resolved a number of these vital questions, when the Marxist writings of Lenin finally reached the United States and the Communist Party was formed, that the direct and indirect ideological influence of De Leon was finally broken.

Before my break with the party, I and a couple of young men in their mid-20's together with 10 or 12 of the teen-age children of some of the married members, took the initiative and organized a youth group.

We called it the Junior Socialist Labor League and issued our own cards, adopted by-laws and paid dues. I was elected secretary. It was a breath of fresh air to all of us, allowing a development of social life and relations among young people within the serious political and educational purposes of the organization.

3

I Make My Choice

After the Vancouver shipyard closed down, I returned to Seattle and saw for the first time what happens to a war-boom city when the bubble bursts. I tramped the streets and scanned the want ads looking for a job.

After many disappointments, I finally landed a job in a neighborhood cleaning and pressing store. It was called the Balloon Cleaners and Dyers; its slogan was "We Dye to Live." Operating a Hoffman steam press was completely new to me. It was a typical family business; husband and wife both worked (and fought) all day. They employed me as the presser, although the boss did the fancy jobs. The dry cleaning was done by a wholesale company, but pressing, spotting and repairing were done in the store. For 54 hours every week I pressed men's and women's suits, coats, dresses and skirts. My starting pay was $18 which increased to $21 before I left.

Since this new job was in the university district, we moved there to a two-room-and-kitchen house located on the grounds of a larger house. Later we moved to a few rooms above a shop, just blocks from the university campus. During this time my mother held two successive jobs in the neighborhood, first repairing clothes in a tailor shop, and later working in a boardinghouse.

At about this time, along with many other progressive youths, I became infatuated with health fads. In addition to buying a pair of spring exercisers and following Bernarr McFadden's instructions daily for about a year, I also became a vegetarian. I would only eat bread made of a special whole meal flour, which my poor mother had to bake. This phase lasted roughly a year, and I don't think it had any negative consequences.

In the course of my activities in the Socialist Labor Party and the Junior Socialist Labor League, I was subject to many influences, social and individual. Attending so many meetings to sell literature exposed me to every ideological current and to a variety of reading matter—although regularly I read only the daily Seattle *Union Record* and two weeklies—*Soviet Russia* and *The Masses*—aside from the SLP *Weekly People*.

Many of our family friends with trade union backgrounds were rejecting Socialist Labor policies and arguing with me about them. I couldn't satisfactorily explain to myself the growing hostility of the party to the Russian Revolution. Nor did I like the way they stood aloof and merely criticized local mass activities and other workers' organizations.

Gradually, a few key theoretical questions began to disturb me. Without knowing it as yet, I was grappling with problems that Lenin had already dealt with: the role of the state, the majority power of the working class after overthrowing capitalism, the question of allies, the transformation of the state, and the decisive role of the party of the working class.

About this time a young auto worker belonging to the Socialist Labor Party in Detroit visited Seattle and I found I was not alone in my questionings. When he returned to Detroit, we continued correspondence, disagreeing quite sharply at times. Then he began to send me pamphlets, some published by the Socialist Labor Party of Great Britain and some by the Marxian Educational Society in Detroit.

The Society published such classics by Lenin as *Proletarian Revolution, State and Revolution, "Left Wing" Communism* and *The Great Initiative.* Also *The Dictatorship of the Proletariat,* by L. B. Kamenev; *ABC of Communism,* by N. Bukharin; *Militarism and Anti-Militarism* by Karl Liebknecht; and *The Mass Strike* and *The Political Party and the Trade Unions* by Rosa Luxemburg.

These I read avidly. The two that had the greatest impact were *State and Revolution,* which exposed with searchlight clarity all the errors and omissions in De Leon's theory, and *"Left-Wing" Communism,* which tore to shreds the sectarian ideas of the Socialist Laborites. I also realized that many of the proclamations by early Communists in the United States about armed insurrection, calling for the formation of Soviets, did not accord with Lenin's thinking.

There also came into my hands during these years a pamphlet by Lenin titled *A Letter to American Workers.* In a simple, patient way, Lenin took a series of issues that were being raised by all the propaganda media of capitalism and by socialist reformists and answered them, using American historical experience to buttress his arguments. The pamphlet concludes prophetically with these realistic and confident statements:

"We know that help from you will probably not come soon, comrade American workers, for the revolution is developing in different countries in different forms and at different tempos (and it cannot be otherwise). . . . We are banking on the inevitability of the world revolution, but this does not mean that we are such fools as to bank on the revolution inevitably coming on a *definite* and early date. . . . In short, we are invincible, because the world proletarian revolution is invincible."*

These pamphlets, with their challenging yet clear thinking, made a deep impression on me. My confidence in Socialist Labor and De Leonism was deeply shaken, but I still hesitated to break away, partly because Lenin had made a positive reference to De Leon's thinking. Furthermore, the United Communist Party stated in its program as late as June 1920 that: "Craft unionism has become the bulwark of capitalism in this

*Lenin's *Selected Works,* Volume 3, New York, 1967, pp. 27-8.—*Ed.*

country.... The Socialist Party policy of 'boring from within' the A. F. of L. is vicious in that it is only an indirect and hypocritical method of supporting an inherently reactionary labor organization. A Communist who belongs to the A. F. of L. should seize every opportunity to voice his hostility to this organization, not to reform it but to destroy it." This was not much different from De Leonism.

While Lenin's writings made a great impression on me, the confusion and left sectarianism and adventurism of the early American Communists still repelled me.

During these months many Marxist lectures and classes were being conducted in Seattle by "free lancers," people without any party affiliation. Prominent among them was James H. Fisher from Canada, who was an outstanding orator and had an ability to explain Marxian economics in graphic style. Another was James Kennedy, former Socialist Alderman from Chicago, more a classroom lecturer but also an able speaker. A free-lance preacher, the Rev. D. Whittaker, who had a Peoples Church, was also in town and gave his support to the Left in all its activities. Another pro-labor minister, with an old established church, was the Rev. Strong, the father of Anna Louise Strong.

In early 1922, representatives from various trade unions and left organizations, along with other interested individuals, attended a conference and organized the Seattle Labor College. I had succeeded in persuading the party branch to send me as a delegate, and was elected one of the college trustees who, with the officers, constituted the board of directors. We worked out a schedule of classes dealing with history, economics, political science and even drama. The executive board met weekly, sometimes at dinner, a new experience for me since I had never eaten in restaurants before. We decided that the executive would not be paid but that tutors were to receive a fee for each class.

This new activity on my part brought things to a head for me in the Socialist Labor Party. While the specific issue was the Labor College, there was a sharp discussion on party policy on attending unity conferences. I was ordered by the national secretary, Arnold Petersen, to sever all connections with the Labor College because only the party could represent or teach the workers. I refused and not long thereafter submitted my resignation from the party and from the post of state secretary to which I had been elected the previous year.

My differences with basic policy had been accumulating over the previous months. The central issue was the significance of the Russian Revolution. The lessons to be drawn from that historic event demanded the reorientation of all socialist forces as to policy, strategy and tactics and, above all, the role and purpose of a workers' revolutionary political party.

These issues — and the need for united action by the Left — determined me to make the break. No doubt, individuals played a role in influencing me, but only a secondary one. I was still in a quandary about the policy of the Communist movement in the United States. I therefore threw myself more energetically than ever into Labor College activity.

In a program of classes and lectures, the first main lecturer of the season was William Z. Foster, on "Outlook for American Labor." Classes covered such subjects as the History of the American Labor Movement, Social Theories of Karl Marx, Practical Problems of the Labor Movement, Social Psychology, Science, Geology and Modern Drama. There was also a library and a Junior Labor College for boys and girls between 6 and 14 years of age.

Now, for the first time, I visited trade union meetings, as a representative of the Labor College and was greatly impressed with the procedures. Usually two of us attended. We first presented our credentials to the doorkeeper, and if the meeting granted us permission to speak, we would be accompanied to the platform by the sergeant-at-arms. As we came in, all the members would stand until the president banged his gavel. I was the speaker, and after a ten-minute appeal for their support and their attendance at our classes, we were usually thanked — sometimes with flowery superlatives, sometimes gruffly — depending upon the political slant of the president. They told us our request would be acted upon after we left and we were again accompanied to the door.

During this Labor College activity I also came in contact for the first time with groups of intellectuals centered in the University of Washington. They had weekly gatherings at the home of a progressive lawyer by the name of Mark Litchman. This was a new world for me, where I heard discussions on philosophy, psychology and economics. Most of this went over my head, but occasionally they came down to earth and discussed the new aspects of socialist theory with which the Russian Revolution and life itself were confronting the workers' political movement. When this occurred, I would participate actively, with all the brashness characteristic of youth.

Meeting these intellectuals disclosed to me how removed most of them were from working-class life and problems. But it also showed me how ignorant I was on many general subjects, a consequence of my lack of formal education. I began to read such books as *Mind Over Matter, Dynamics of Mind, Ancient Lowly,* and books by Winwood Reade, Kilpatrick, Dewey and Beard. I also broadened out my reading to include plays by Shaw, Galsworthy and Barrie.

I became an ardent participant in many forums during these months. Already a stream of prominent European Social-Democrats were touring the country, combating the communist philosophy and the prestige of the Russian Revolution. I recall vividly my run-in with Henri De Mann of Belgium, one of the most prominent of the visitors. He gave a series of lectures in the Labor Temple. At question time I asked some questions that somewhat embarrassed him. Having him on the run, I argued unsuccessfully with the chairman for the right to have the floor to take issue with De Mann.

Some of my new university acquaintances considered my conduct to be in bad taste, although actually what they didn't like was my success in challenging this supporter of the imperialist war, wearing the halo of a "great socialist." I did, however, draw the lesson for myself that an effective working-class propagandist had to learn to combine aggressiveness with a certain finesse.

That autumn various hitchhikers from the East visited Seattle and contacted me. Frankly, some of them didn't make too good an impression, although they were all left-wingers. They tended to be very aggressive and loud. Some of their practices offended my standards of behavior.

About this time, the newly organized Workers Party (the legal expression of the Communist Party) sent as its organizer, Max Lerner (not to be confused with the Lerner of the New York *Post*). Two couples from the East also came to settle in Seattle.

Gradually we all became friends. The younger people joined in Labor College activity. With them I entered into a lively political and social atmosphere, which included folk music and rambles into the country. My friend in Detroit and I were still corresponding regularly, and he finally told me that he and some of his friends had decided to join the Workers Party. They were thereupon expelled from the Socialist Labor Party.

Max Lerner began to have regular discussions with me, especially concentrating on the questions I raised about the program and policies of the Communist Party. He gave me some of the literature of the underground Communists, in which a vigorous discussion was going on about working with the masses and fighting for immediate demands versus standing on the sidelines in political "purity." The latter policy tended to ignore existing American conditions and the level of development of the working class. Another discussion centered on whether the Communist Party should be illegal or whether it should aim to be a legal party with a Marxist revolutionary program.

In the July 1922 issue of *The Communist* there appeared a thesis which had been prepared for the second convention of the Communist Party. After declaring its adherence to the principles of the Communist International, it said in part:

"The major task of the revolutionary party in regard to the broad masses of workers is, therefore, not abstract propaganda and theoretical education, but participation in all the struggles of the workers as the most active force. The leadership of the masses . . . can be attained only by directly engaging in all their struggles. . . . In a country where political conditions permit the possibility of mass political organization of the working class, the revolutionary party cannot secure leadership without a powerful and finally dominant position among such mass political organizations of the workers. . . . In America it has become the most urgent immediate task of the Communists to secure a public, open, so-called 'legal' existence as an organization."

Despite some weaknesses and leftist confusion, this was a big step forward. My interest was aroused. However, I decided to await the decisions of the underground Communist convention. Meanwhile, I agreed to help the young people from the East to organize a Seattle branch of the Young Workers League of America.

In 1922 the underground Communist convention approved the line of the thesis that favored a legal Marxist party. It also endorsed the concept of a dictatorship of the proletariat.* With

*Probably no Marxist scientific term has been subject to more thorough falsification than "the dictatorship of the proletariat," which in simple

reference to trade union policy, the convention decided that "work in the trade unions must be increased tenfold. Every member must not only be a member of a trade union, but if possible become a leader. . . . The most important labor union work is within the AFL." It was also stressed that the main campaign of the party was "against the government rather than against the trade union bureaucracy and the yellow Socialists."

Shortly after the convention, the central committee announced that it was emerging from underground, and from then on would wage a steadfast struggle for the legality of a Marxist party. The desire for legal status is characteristic of parties everywhere. Reactionaries assert that Communists prefer a state of illegality and secrecy, and certainly the capitalist class does all it can to drive them underground. Accusing the victim of creating his own plight is one of those contradictions of logic in which the defenders of private profit often indulge.

Finding myself in substantial agreement with the convention decisions, I joined the still underground Communist Party in November or December of 1922 and shortly thereafter received my Workers Party card, signed by the local secretary, Mike Cassidy.

Joining the Communist Party was the most significant action of my life. It opened up new vistas of understanding, experience and activity that determined my life from that day forward.

terms means the role of the majority class, the workers, after state power has been secured. With the rise of Hitler and Mussolini, there was an increased effort to equate the dictatorship of the proletariat with the dictatorship exercised in fascist countries. Its real meaning is best grasped by reading Lenin.

4

Young Workers
Confront Gompers

The composition of the Seattle branch of the Young Workers
League accounted for its all-round activities. The members from
the East brought in imaginative proposals, especially on meetings and social affairs, while we local members emphasized contact with the labor movement, sale of press and literature, and
systematic education. Within three months I had been elected
local organizer.

Repeating Labor College practice, we visited and spoke before various unions, including the machinists, boilermakers,
blacksmiths and laundry workers. We sold literature at several
meetings of the striking railway shopmen and at the stadium on
Labor Day. The magazine *Young Worker* commented: "Seattle
members are appearing before union men and women and ad-
dressing them on the strike situation. The Seattle comrades are
after union men and women for members of the YWL. . . Other
Leagues would do well to follow this form of activity."

The League also took an active part in Russian Famine Relief
and Friends of the Soviet Union bazaars, tag days, picnics, medical aid and the like. Similarly, we helped in the relief activities
for the striking miners.

We held two successful mass meetings. The first, on International Youth Day, was addressed by three speakers, including
myself. Then there was a most successful meeting of 300 on
Liebknecht Day, which I chaired. These were the first Communist meetings at which I had spoken since my break with the Socialist Labor Party, and it created a stir in local circles.

Visiting national speakers from other organizations addressed
our local branch meetings. I remember J. B. S. Hardman of the
Amalgamated Clothing Workers, a fellow named Roberts from

Russian Famine Relief, and Winsted of the IWW. Then there were Professor Smith of the University of Washington, Kate Sadler of the Workers Party, and Harvey O'Connor.

The imaginativeness and experience of our comrades from the East found full expression in a midspring dance we organized. We took a big hall, and the local secretary, Mike Cassidy, and others moaned and groaned. The girls outdid themselves in decorating the hall, preparing refreshments and planning entertainment. We had never done anything like this before, but it was a great success. Over $100 profit was made. Our friends from the East were not satisfied with this, but we thought it a fortune.

At this time I got a new job. After a year as a clothes-presser, I finally got disgusted and quit. In a few weeks I found a job as a clerk in Mitchell's, a retail store on Third Avenue. It specialized in surveying and drafting instruments and supplies as well as in artists' paints and papers. The owner was an old rock-ribbed Republican who would have collapsed had he known he was employing a Communist.

In May 1923, the second convention of the Young Workers League was to be held in Chicago. After appropriate discussion, I was elected as delegate and also made proxy delegate from the Tacoma and Aberdeen branches. To travel and attend a national convention 2,000 miles away was the biggest event in my life up to then. I was elated and awed with the responsibility.

Now, so many years later, it is difficult to put into words the excitement of the weeks that followed. Decisions that might be taken for granted by sophisticated New Yorkers were amazing to us in the Far West. I made notes of all the issues the three branches I represented wanted to have raised.

Several weeks in advance I bought my return railroad ticket by daycoach on the Chicago, Milwaukee and St. Paul Railroad. And I bought a new hat which, when I reached Chicago, really marked me as a hayseed. I was making in reverse the railroad trip of nine years earlier. But now I was standing on my own feet and I felt important, though scared, as I traveled to a national convention.

Until that moment I had not given much thought to what was happening nationally. On local and international issues I was better informed. The United States was more powerful than ever before, as a result of World War I. It played a decisive role in writing the Versailles Treaty; it dominated the economic life of the defeated countries, especially Germany; it asserted its power in the Pacific and extended its influence in Latin America.

At home, the most ferocious offensive was launched against the wartime gains of the workers and the trade unions. Plans were devised to destroy or weaken the unions and to hold out against the workers' demands. The open shop drive and the establishment of company unions were in full swing.

Over four million workers engaged in strikes in 1919, the largest number in any year up to then. Between 1919 and 1922, some ten million workers went on strike. These actions were mainly defensive. The great majority were lost, and the new unions — steel, meat packing, lumber and maritime — were wiped out. Coal, railroad, printing and clothing experienced setbacks. The AFL dropped in membership from 4,160,348 in 1920 to 2,926,462 in 1923.

The effects of the ruling-class offensive were sharpened by the outbreak of one of the recurrent economic crises of capitalism. Over five million were unemployed.

Conditions of young workers, who were not organized at all, were very bad. In 1920, 22 million people were between 13 and 25 years of age and child labor was commonplace. There were at least two and a half million child-workers. The Secretary of Labor stated that one and a half million were between the ages of 10 and 15, and the number was increasing.

Under these conditions, their wages were slashed even more severely than those of the adults during this employers' offensive. The new Workers Party in 1922 decided to set up a national committee to organize the Young Workers League.

The Young Workers League convention was held on May 13 and 14 in a hall called Folkets Hus, belonging to the Scandinavian Workers Club of northwest Chicago. According to Harry Gannes, the national secretary, this second convention had to demonstrate that the League was national in character and was to "lay the basis for a league which can take into itself any young worker whether he happens to be a Communist at the moment or not."

Thirty-one delegates representing 2,000 members, came from 13 states. It differed from the earlier organizing convention in that its representation was really national, it attracted more industrial workers and it attempted to grapple with real problems confronting young people.

After getting organized and electing a permanent secretary, Bill Schneiderman of California, and a rota of chairmen that included me, the convention got under way. I remember sharp debates on three outstanding questions: the reorganization of factory branches (called shop nuclei), youth's economic demands, and the attitude of the YWL to the trade unions.

The convention formulated an approach to basing the League among the young industrial workers, raising youth demands, issuing material to youth in specific industries and trying to win the trade unions to fight for youth's interests. It adopted the slogan "every young worker an agitator on the job."

It was decided to establish industrial organizers at all committee levels, and the leadership was instructed to draft and send a letter to the AFL leadership "to inaugurate a campaign for the organizing of the young slaves of America." This was to result in an extraordinary confrontation with Samuel Gompers, the AFL president.

Before adjournment, a national committee of eight members and eight alternates was elected. The overwhelming majority, including myself, were young people who had never before been on a national committee.

The convention met all my expectations. I was especially pleased by the cut and thrust of the debates. And, above all, I was in the pleasant company of people who were all young— many of them industrial workers like myself.

To my surprise, after the convention it was decided in the executive committee that I should move to Chicago and take over the post of national industrial organizer. My first reaction was against leaving Seattle but the pressure of argument finally convinced me. It was further decided that on my way home I should stop at Milwaukee, Minneapolis, St. Paul, Superior and Butte. In each of them I was to make a convention report and, if possible, address a public meeting and get subscriptions for the *Young Worker*.

In the Twin Cities I spoke at a big picnic of the Farmer-Labor Party, sharing the platform with United States Senator Magnus Johnson,* an example of the broad contacts the local League

---

*Johnson, a dirt farmer, had been the victor in one of the most surprising election upsets in the history of Minnesota. He defeated the entrenched Republican, Frank B. Kellogg, corporation lawyer, darling of the trusts, later Secretary of State and co-author of the Kellogg-Briand Pact.

had in those days. In Butte, my job was to try to convince the
local party to organize the Young Workers League. I was thrilled
to be taken by Bill Dunne, editor of the *Butte Miners Bulletin*, to
his office. The paper was under constant armed guard against
the terror of the local mine owners, and in Dunne's editorial
office three guns were slung on the wall in case of emergency.

I returned to my job in Seattle and gave a week's notice. To
the credit of my mother, she never raised an objection, although
I was an only child and her main support. She insisted, "If that
is what you want to do—but be sure it is—then I will never say
no." We agreed she would come to Chicago after I had a job
and had found a place for us to stay.

In Chicago, during the next 12 months I worked first in the
stockroom of the Marshall Field department store and then in
the big factory of J. Dietzgen Co., where I made triangular box-
wood rulers. I almost landed a job as a streetcar motorman, but
was a few months short of their 21-year minimum age requirement. I did my political work in the evening. As industrial organizer I had the main responsibility of implementing and developing the convention's new policies.

In 1924 my mother moved to Chicago, and we set up house at
the corner of Clark Street and Fullerton Avenue. In the same
building lived Walt Carmen, a popular Communist journalist
of those days. One of his close friends and frequent visitors was
the late Fred Ellis, the well-known cartoonist. I became well acquainted with Fred, who was one of the warmest-hearted comrades you could know, without any of the supposed egocentri-
cities of the artist.

Our national executive committee on June 1 sent an *Open
Letter to the American Federation of Labor*. It described the conditions of youth and child labor and further stated:

"The League turns to the organized labor movement to find
the means to remedy the conditions that now exist. Our organization cannot carry on the struggle alone and isolated from the
unions. Moreover, we emphatically reject the idea of special
youth organizations in the economic field.

". . . The young workers want to join the unions. So far, however, they have been prevented from joining them by barriers
such as age limits, etc. . . . We deem it necessary that all barriers
be abolished and that the gates be thrown open to all above the
age of 15 to join the unions with full rights."

In what now seems a rather arrogant tone, the *Open Letter* went on to say, "We call upon you to examine our demands and to let us know at an early date what decision your committee has arrived at."

While being very sceptical of receiving a reply, we chose a delegation, on which I was included. To our amazement, Gompers said that he would meet the delegation the next day at the Morrison Hotel.

Samuel Gompers was born in England of Jewish parents. He came to America, became a leader of the Cigar Makers Union, and in 1886 was elected the first president of the Federation, a post he held until his death in 1924.

Gompers symbolized not only craft unionism but also the heavy hand of class collaboration which became characteristic of his successors, William Green and George Meany. Theirs was and is the game of shameful compromise with the employers. Betrayal, unnecessary retreat, denial of rank-and-file democracy—these are the hallmarks of leaders whose attachment is primarily to the propertied class.

Unfortunately, when Gompers' reply came, I was already on my way to the West Coast and had to be replaced on the delegation. But the story of that confrontation was made known to me in all its details.

Present besides Gompers were members of the executive board of the Cigar Makers Union, whose executive sessions Gompers was attending, and John Fitzpatrick and Ed Nockels, president and secretary, respectively, of the Chicago Federation of Labor.

After some preliminary conference business, Gompers began to question the delegation about the League and its political objectives. It would appear that this usually astute right-wing trade union leader had not realized, when he acknowledged our letter, who we were and the nature of our program.

Prior to the meeting, however, someone enlightened him. Instead of reading and discussing the specific proposals, he had the League constitution read to him. He almost exploded at the references to the dictatorship of the proletariat and the establishment of soviets and communism.

His attitude became hostile to everything we stood for. Instead of discussing young workers and how to organize them, he launched into a recitation of all the Federation's activities against child labor. With a flourish, he demanded to know: "If you are against the principle of child labor, why do you want the international unions to lower the barriers against the admission of these youthful workers into their ranks? Is it not enough that the A.F. of L. is doing all it can, has been doing all you propose, for the last decades? It is because the unions do not believe in having children employed in industry, that they have clauses against their admission. . . . While the organization of the young workers is important, it is secondary in relation to the necessity of organizing [the remaining] 22 million unorganized."

Finally, the League letter was read to the meeting. It is such an important document that I incorporate it in full:

Mr. Samuel Gompers, President, A.F. of L.
Dear Sir and Brother:
With more than 5,000,000 young workers up to the age of 20 years employed in American industries, their importance to the trade-union movement is plain. They are, however, up to now, largely unorganized. Heretofore, the employers have been able to use them for their ends. We believe that they *can* be organized by the American Federation of Labor. Their enthusiasm, energy, and idealism can be made a tremendous factor as a source of strength to the organized labor movement. Separate young workers' unions within the A.F. of L. are unnecessary and out of the question. Still, a certain specialization in methods to reach the young workers, adapted to their psychology, is necessary. Therefore, we make the following proposals:
That there be created in the American Federation of Labor a special young workers' bureau or secretariat for the purpose of stimulating the trade-union education and organization of young workers, this bureau to have, among others, the following functions:
1. To point out the importance of the young workers in industry and to encourage all branches of the trade-union movement to carry on a vigorous campaign to organize them.
2. To compile and publish statistics dealing especially with child labor and other features of industry, particularly relating to the young.
3. To issue a regular news service to the labor press, and to induce the various labor papers to develop special departments devoted to the problems of young workers.
4. To issue organizational and educational pamphlets especially written to appeal to youthful workers, and pointing out the philosophy, the achievements and the goals of the labor movement.
5. To carry on a special campaign among adult unionists showing them the dangerous "open shop" tendencies their children are exposed to, and providing them the means wherewith to educate their young to the necessity of labor organization.
Hoping that this suggestion, which we believe meets a great need in the labor movement, will meet your approval and support, we remain,
Fraternally yours,
The Young Workers League of America,
Martin Abern, Secretary

The crafty Mr. Gompers, when the letter had been read, immediately asked, "You speak of the goal of the trade union movement. You mean, do you not, that the goal is to be that mentioned in the Young Workers League constitution we read before?" Abern walked right into the trap and answered, "Yes."

Gompers was off again, conveniently neglecting the issues that concerned youth. When the conference was coming to an end, the delegation asked whether the proposals would receive further attention. Gompers responded indignantly, "Of course. That is why this conference was called. It will be given the closest consideration by the executive of the Federation." But, added Gompers, "I can give no promise as to the results."

The League issued a statement, which said: "The conference with Mr. Gompers is not our final goal. We want to bring this important question before the rank and file of organized labor in this country."

The fact that Gompers had met us provided a favorable atmosphere to develop activity on this vital issue. Inside the League itself much more had to be done. The first industrial registration of the League, although far from complete, indicated that while 60 per cent of the members were industrial workers, only 22 per cent were members of trade unions. Exceptions were Detroit, with over 90 per cent in the trade unions, and Chicago, with 40 per cent.

In an article in December 1923, headed "Breaking into the Industries," which discussed the organizing of the first two factory branches (a Chicago clothing factory and a Pennsylvania mine), I commented: "Many places we find that our members are eligible to union membership but through sheer neglect do not join. What right have they to kick that Gompers takes no progressive action? What comeback have they to the union man, who knows we are demanding the AFL organize the youth, when he asks if they are union members? None."

So a big ideological campaign was started among the members to join the trade unions. We had to overcome the problem of high initiation fees and even hostility in the craft unions to allowing youth to join. We also had to overcome sectarian ideas about "having nothing to do with these labor fakers." Above all our aim was to show that trade union organization of youth was in the mutual interests of young and old workers.

The monthly magazine *Young Worker* had several pages in each issue devoted to letters from League and non-League members in factories and mines, under the heading "On the Job."

This correspondence gave an insight into the conditions of young workers and reflected the determined efforts of the new League to sink its roots in industry.

In five issues of the magazine a total of 34 letters appeared, coming from steel mills, mine pits, department stores, auto, needle, can, toy and candy factories, silk mills, hotels, hospitals, Western Union and telephone companies—a cross section of employment.

From the Missouri Can Co. in Kansas City, a letter said that 70 per cent of those employed were between 14 and 21 years old. In the operating room, based on piecework, they made $10 to $11 a week. The machines were unprotected and injuries were common.

From the Bethlehem Steel mills in Pennsylvania, the correspondent, a worker in the Merchant mills, where rods were made, said 65 per cent were about 15 years of age and worked 60 to 72 hours a week. Even in the open hearths, young workers were employed as furnace-door pullers. While making "good wages" they had to work a 12-hour day and 24 hours on Sundays.

From the Studebaker auto plant in South Bend, Indiana, came a story of how a member of the League got fired while trying to organize a factory branch and fighting against conditions that included a 12-hour day, from 6 A.M. to 6 P.M. Next to it was a letter from a young miner, a trapper boy, at a coal mine in West Virginia. Most of the boys were 16 and 17. While there was an eight-hour day, they "worked like horses," and got $15 to $16 a week.

A girl working for the Chicago Western Union told how they were given roller skates on the job. They worked six days a week and every third Sunday. In a toy factory in Chicago, most were 14 years of age but claimed to be 15 or 16. The letter cited three accidents in the course of three weeks: a 14-year-old boy lost a hand, a girl two fingers, and the writer of the letter also had an accident.

After waiting a month, we asked Sam Gompers what action had been taken. No answer was received then or later to our proposals. But we were not waiting. We helped organize 800 plumber's helpers in New York City. When they were refused admission into the Plumbers Union, they formed the United Plumbers Helpers and Assistants Union.

Our biggest breakthrough came in November 1923, when the Michigan Federation of Labor adopted a resolution which described the entry of youth into industry (although still characterizing them as "a type of youth that is influenced by the propaganda of the employing class") and concluded by resolving that "the Michigan Federation of Labor calls upon the A. F. of L. to institute a campaign to organize and educate the American youth and establish the necessary machinery to insistently carry on this task."

The same type of activity was being conducted elsewhere. A resolution adopted by the Butte (Silver Bow) Federation of Labor to the 43rd AFL national convention in 1923 was much more comprehensive than the Michigan resolution. After describing the plight of youth in industry it said, "These young workers can easily be organized and their enthusiasm, energy and idealism can be made a tremendous factor as a source of strength to the organized labor movement." It went on to urge the establishment of "a special young workers bureau or secretariat" for initiating trade union organizing work.

Unfortunately, this proposal never even came before the convention, since Gompers, John L. Lewis, William Green and Philip Murray embarked on a red-baiting jamboree and unseated Butte's delegate, William F. Dunne, solely for being a Communist.

Following this action of the Michigan Federation of Labor, I wrote: "Our duty now is to follow up this opening wedge and plan to have every union and state labor body take up the slogan of organizing the youth. . . . But we must also show that we have concrete proposals to offer and not merely empty criticism. Our proposal to Gompers . . . still stands good today."

As we extended this campaign throughout the country, we tried to develop independent League activities to arouse the industrial youth to action and union membership.

We decided to concentrate on two big monopolies who employed young people primarily and had many outlets throughout the country. These were the National Biscuit Co. and Montgomery Ward. For each a 16-page pamphlet was written based on their employees' experiences. We held factory gate meetings, sold pamphlets and the *Young Worker* before Nabisco factories in Chicago, New York, Philadelphia, Pittsburgh, Minneapolis and Detroit.

The pamphlets were eagerly received and read at the plants. But the young workers lacked the initiative and experience to organize a trade union against such formidable obstacles as the hostility of the companies and the indifference of the AFL leaders. The League did not think it could substitute for the trade unions and, aside from popularizing the League and enlisting some members, years still had to elapse before union organization was to be achieved. But such League activities had an impact on the lower ranks of union leadership.

There was a steady growth in League membership. At the beginning of 1924 the *Young Worker* became a fortnightly tabloid newspaper and two years later a weekly. The children's section developed and grew, and it issued its own paper, edited by Nat Kaplan.

Nevertheless, our propaganda suffered from the combined effects of various influences that had been brought to bear on us. We tended to lecture from above, to deal in wordy generalities and, too often, to fall back on clichés. As long as the *Young Worker* remained a magazine, it seemed to suffer from all these tendencies.

Now, by virtue of my becoming a delegate to the party from the League, I was to come up against that malady which has caused so much damage in the Marxist movement — factionalism. The arenas of contention were the third and fourth conventions of the Communist Party, both held in Chicago, in 1923 and 1925. The debilitating struggle was to continue until 1930. From the beginning, it had serious effects on the League and on me.

The factional fight resulted in the virtual ignoring of the League and the youth movement. Even when the League was on the agenda, it was subordinated to the major dispute and hence dealt with ineffectually. In 1924 I was named as representative of the League to the central committee of the party. A far more momentous political struggle lay ahead.

5

Journeys to Moscow

In January 1924, I was selected by the national executive committee as one of two delegates to the Fourth Congress of the Young Communist International to be held in Moscow. This was a far greater event in my life than leaving Seattle for Chicago — I was going to see the first socialist country!

Stopping off in New York, I had a close view of the bitter factional fight raging between the groups, one headed by C. E. Ruthenberg and Jay Lovestone, and the other by William Z. Foster, Earl Browder and Alex Bittleman. That dispute had entered into the League and was having the same divisive and paralyzing effect as it had within the party.

The New York leadership of the League was in opposition to its national executive committee whose position I upheld. In three days of membership meetings I failed to win majority support four times, an experience that unfortunately only embittered me against New York and left me with the determination to be a better factionalist than my opponents. But for the moment the home-front quarrels were forgotten; ahead of me lay Moscow.

The first stop was Berlin, where the German party was under heavy attack from the authorities. We were to make contact with friends through cover addresses, but it was ten long days before we could proceed. During that time we were put up in a comrade's house in the workers' section of Berlin, and were obliged to stay under cover. I found this very difficult because I had no real experience of even semi-legal life; my scant patience was ill-suited to confinement and I wanted to see Berlin. Only ten years later, a frightful terror was to be unleashed against the German working class in which thousands upon thousands perished at the hands of the Nazis.

Even the tedious ten days passed. We were now on our way eastward by train to Riga, where we stayed overnight. We changed trains and traveled to the Russian border, where another change was necessary because of the wider rail gauge on the Russian railroad system. When we passed under an arch with a big hammer and sickle above and a sign, "Workers of the World, Unite," we knew we were standing on socialist soil. I was overcome with emotion and tears came to my eyes. In the years to follow I made ten more trips to the Soviet Union, and every time I crossed the frontier, there was a special feeling.

This does not mean, as so many foes of socialism interpret such reactions, that non-Russians like myself think of the Soviet Union as our homeland. We are Americans, British, French, Cuban or Indian, as the case may be. Our loyalty is to our particular nation or people, but the emotional pull of the Soviet Union is there because we know the historic role it played in opening up a whole new epoch for mankind.

I can well imagine similar emotions on the part of oppressed Europeans arriving in the United States after the American revolution, which also raised a banner of freedom and hope to humanity, until it was lowered and soiled with the onset of imperialism.

Prior to the opening of the Young Communist International Congress, the Fifth Congress of the Communist International was to take place (from June 17 to July 8, 1924). I was included in the Workers Party delegation as an observer. Miracles seemed to be endless. Only a year before I was still in Seattle; now, at 21, I was attending the Communist International Congress in the Kremlin Palace. I heard reports and debates on such questions as the united front, the draft program of the Communist International, the economic situation in Soviet Russia with particular attention to the N.E.P. (the new economic policy outlined by Lenin before his death), and the national and colonial question. It was a heady experience for one of my years.

People who had been only remote names to me became living, dynamic individuals. Permanent chairman was Kolarov of Bulgaria. Making reports were Zinoviev, Varga, Bukharin, Thalheimer, Rykov, Manuilsky and others. Present as delegates and actively participating were Stalin, Trotsky and Radek, from the Soviet Union; Ruth Fischer, Brandler, Thaelman and Clara Zetkin, from Germany; Kuusinen, from Finland; Smeral, from

Czechoslovakia; Semard, from France; Ercoli (Togliatti) and Bordiga, from Italy; Katayama, from Japan; Larkin, from Ireland; Buck, from Canada; McManus and Stewart, from Britain and many others.

The debates were sharp but there was a feeling that we all "belonged." While Thalheimer, Bordiga, Zetkin, Smeral and Radek were criticized unmercifully, nevertheless all except Radek were elected to the executive committee. The one unforgivable thing was to violate the majority decision after free debate during which everyone presented and fought for his viewpoint.

Following the Comintern Congress, the Fourth Congress of the Young Communist International took place. The main topics on the agenda were concerned with the program and work of the Young Communist Leagues throughout the world, with strong emphasis on antimilitarist activity. When the executive was elected, I was chosen from the United States. This meant that in the course of the next four years I was to stay in Moscow for nearly a year, participating in the work of the executive committee and attending the Fifth Congress of the Young Communist International.

At home, the work of the Young Workers League expanded and its membership grew. But the intrusion of the party's factional quarrel—now increasing in intensity—was a setback to wider advances. In September 1924, I was elected national secretary, but after the Fourth Convention of the party in August 1925, I was removed.

This came about when the adherents of Ruthenberg and Lovestone were arbitrarily given a majority of one on the party's central committee, despite the fact that they were supported by a minority of delegates at the convention. The new majority of the party central committee reorganized the national committee of the Young Workers League on a 50-50 basis, with the party representative having the deciding vote. In this manner, a practice later made impossible by changes in the party constitution, I was removed as national secretary and returned to my old post as industrial organizer.

In the light of events that unfolded later, an incident in these inner struggles is worth recalling. In the midst of a League membership meeting in New York, some of Lovestone's followers were provocatively attacking Bill Foster (then a national organizer of the steelworkers for the AFL) because he had sold war bonds during World War I. I snapped out angrily, "At least he wasn't a stool pigeon like Jay Lovestone!" Pandemonium broke loose, and later someone preferred charges against me. The background of my outburst was a belief shared by many in the Foster faction that Lovestone was unreliable, especially since in his youth he had been a truant officer. Various suspicious events had been attributed to him, but no definite evidence was forthcoming.

In this situation I became a convenient scapegoat for an attack on the entire Foster group. The end result was that I was censured by a majority (of one) vote of the executive committee, with a warning that if this unsustained charge was repeated, disciplinary action would be much sharper next time.

Lovestone's subsequent nefarious career* proved him to be a lackey of imperialism, but I learned the valuable lesson that it is highly irresponsible to make charges without proof. This was the only disciplinary action ever taken against me in my years of party membership. In later years, some of my comrades would comment on my cautiousness and deliberation, but I had learned to think twice to avoid making rash judgments or unwittingly becoming a mouthpiece for others.

---

*Lovestone, the national secretary of the Communist party, was expelled in 1929 for both factionalism and a political line which held—on the eve of the depression—that the United States was immune from the impending world-wide economic catastrophe. For a time he established a splinter party; then he founded the Independent Labor League of America. He had strong ties with David Dubinsky and the International Ladies Garment Workers and later, as the CIO emerged, with Homer Martin, the president of the United Auto Workers. With the exposure of Martin as an agent for the Ford Motor Co., Lovestone's links with the militants in the labor movement were so damaged that he gave up any pretense of maintaining a left position.

Turning to bitter attacks on Marxism, Lovestone endeared himself to William Green, president of the AFL, George Meany, then secretary-treasurer, and Dubinsky. Working through a number of government agencies, Lovestone became a favored labor man of federal authorities in the cold-war era. With two million dollars annually at his disposal from the AFL, Lovestone's activities include undermining unions abroad, especially in the dependent countries, and complement CIA activities which do not stop at murder, bribery and the overthrow of democratically elected governments. Of late (far too late) Walter and Victor Reuther of the United Automobile Workers have complained of Lovestone's arranging to have CIA agents given the

During those early years in Chicago, my mother saw me only when I came home to sleep. She never complained, but would always wait up to make sure I had eaten a substantial meal before going to bed. My time was occupied with Young Communist League work, meetings, speaking and organizing trips, as well as traveling abroad.

I had also fallen in love. When I finally told my mother in 1926 that I was going to get married, she expressed her happiness. We agreed that it was best for young married couples to live on their own, and she prepared to return to Seattle.

My marriage to Lenore Sarnay, an active Young Communist Leaguer, who had emigrated from Poland to live with relatives in Chicago, took place in the autumn of 1926. We set up house and, with help from her aunt and cousin and from comrades, we furnished our basement flat on North Halsted Street. She continued working as a bookkeeper, while attending night school and pursuing her political activities.

My mother was happier in Seattle, although, when I think of it, hers was a lonely and difficult life from beginning to end. Early in her married life she was denied the companionship and love of my father. Her sole interest became her son, who, like all young people, was largely concerned with his own life. She was never in the party, claiming that politics were not for her, but was friendly to its aims and to all my comrades.

As she grew older and lonelier, she decided to spend her last days in the old country. Her pluck was that of her class, and she had always showed remarkable initiative and resourcefulness in meeting great difficulties. Small and stocky, meticulous and conscientious about the household and our appearance, she would rather go without than owe anyone a penny.

Life in the United States never diminished her broad Scots accent. On her return to Scotland, she was employed at odd jobs, and after World War II she was on National Assistance, unable to qualify for an old-age pension because of her absence from the country too long. She retired at Eaglesham, where her mother had lived, occupying what is called a "single-end," one room with a toilet on the landing and of course no bath. I was not to see her until 1955, after my deportation.

cover of union credentials in an illegitimate operation in Panama. But the executive council and other officials have rejected this complaint and thus share the responsibility for this shameful page in American labor history.

During these years, comrades who were to become well-
known party leaders joined our ranks. Among them was Gil
Green, who became secretary of the Young Communist League
and was one of those sentenced to jail under the Smith Act.
On a trip to Wisconsin, to teach at a school sponsored by the
Finnish Workers Federation, I met a young teenager from the
Minnesota Iron Range — Arvo Hallberg, better known as Gus
Hall, later the general secretary of the Communist party and
another of the Smith Act victims.

Under the Lovestone majority the party and league offices
and the *Daily Worker* were moved to New York. As the factional
fight continued, I was moved out of the national office and made
organizer for the New York district. But I was still an elected
member of the executive committee of the Young Communist
International, and efforts by the Lovestone grouping in both
the party and the league to remove me failed. It was agreed that
since the Fifth Congress of the Young Communist International
would be held at the end of 1928, I should be present in Moscow
to help prepare for it.

In early 1928 my wife and I left for the Soviet Union and spent
nine months there, during which I attended the historic Sixth
Congress of the Comintern as a full-fledged delegate from the
executive committee of the Young Communist International.

These trips to the Soviet Union and my long stay there in 1928
were of great educational value. My party education and development never included full-time schools with an opportunity
for sustained class and home study. It had been comprised of
self-education and reading while at work, participating in meetings and finding answers to problems and questions in the course
of participating in struggles.

I recall preparing draft reports on the problems of youth of
Latin America, on the leagues in Australia, Canada and Britain. I visited a congress of Chinese youth held in Siberia. During these months in 1928 in Moscow, I also made an effort to
learn German, the official language of the Young Communist
International. I met with only limited success, as too many things
were happening and Russian was being spoken all around me.

In the years 1924-27 a system of "patronage" was set up between specific districts of the league of the Soviet Union and
leagues in other countries. The American league held patronage
over the Kostroma district, and I spent nearly a week there.

We spoke at textile factories and at large meetings and affairs organized by the local Komsomol.

Another never-to-be-forgotten visit was to the Red Army quarters in that region. We spoke to large gatherings of young Red Army soldiers, telling them about the United States. The general in command suggested we go horseback riding. I had never been on a horse, but was too shy to say so. They brought up a couple of great big horses—the saddle came up to my head—and helped me mount. The general and his colleagues started off slowly, but quickly broke into a gallop. The wise horse I was on undoubtedly knew he had a novice riding him and disregarded me completely. Off he went in a great gallop to keep up with the general's horse. I just leaned forward, threw my arms around his neck, and yelled while holding on for dear life. Finally a soldier rode alongside and stopped the horse. That was my first and last attempt at horseback riding. Not only had I been scared stiff, but I could hardly walk for a few days.

On that trip, we had an interpreter and translator named Dave Metropolitan. I swore he made up his own speeches, irrespective of what we said. Fortunately, he was born in the United States and knew conditions there, so the translation must have had some relationship to the facts. When we left, we were loaded with presents for the league at home and given a grand send-off.

On one of my trips to the Soviet Union there was a shortage of rooms for international visitors at the Lux Hotel where we always stayed. I was put up with Bill Haywood for three weeks. I heard invaluable stories from him and from Jim Larkin, who would come and visit with Bill after the sessions, and I learned a lesson which I never forgot.

While Bill had the best of everything that the Russian comrades could give him as a respected old-time revolutionary of the United States, he was like a fish out of water. Age and ill-health were affecting him; his greatest privation was separation from his native land and its workers, with their struggles and problems. Even the most experienced leader in political exile faces the danger of isolation, frustration and despair, with a consequent turning inward. This was multiplied a hundredfold in the case of Haywood, who had always been in the thick of the class struggle, had little theoretical grounding and who at an advanced age had settled in another country, even though it was a socialist country.

I drew the conclusion, even in those youthful years, that we should not isolate ourselves from the class struggle of the country or countries in which we have roots. If political exile is unavoidable, it should, if at all possible, be only a stopover for a return to one's own country. And even during such enforced exile, there should be close contact with, and participation in, some aspect of the struggles at home.

The Sixth Congress of the Comintern was held from July 18 to September 1, 1928, in the Hall of Columns in the House of Trade Unions. The validity of the decisions reached there have stood the test of history well. Central to the accepted analysis of what lay ahead in the next years was the conclusion that the contradictions of capitalist stabilization would lead to the severe intensification of its general crisis. The need to prepare all Communist parties for leadership in impending class battles was quickly confirmed by the economic crisis in the United States, beginning in 1929. This became the most severe and prolonged world crisis in the history of capitalism.

The Congress also called for a struggle against the Trotskyites, with whom a final break had occurred, and adopted a number of lengthy documents, among which was a perceptive examination of the revolutionary movement in the colonial countries.

The Trotskyite question was to have its reverberations on the American movement. It became clear to those of us present at the Congress that one of our delegates, James Cannon, was moving fast in the direction of an ultra-leftist position.

Cannon had been associated with the Foster group of which I was a part. Now he came under sharp attack from those with whom he had worked. Upon his return to the States from the Sixth Congress, Cannon openly espoused and defended Trotsky's position. He was expelled from the party by a united vote from both factions and began his course down that trail taken by splinter groups who in the end lose all influence with the working class.

Cannon was not alone. A few individuals with whom I had a working association since entering the league in 1922 joined him. This led me to face up to the principle that the defense of the party and its policies has to override personal associations.

The Fifth Young Communist International Congress, held in Moscow immediately after the Sixth Comintern Congress, emphasized the special responsibilities falling upon youth with the increase in the war danger. We sought to create special forms of youth organization in areas where the trade unions had ignored young workers. Long sessions were held with the American delegation, the majority of whom were active supporters of the Lovestone group. It was decided that "the most important task confronting the party is to put an end to the factional strife" and that an open letter would be sent to the league members in the United States.

I returned to the United States with the understanding that I would leave the league at the coming convention. I went to Canada to visit its league, as the representative of the Young Communist International. There I helped to mobilize the league to fight against the supporters of Trotsky, on the one hand, and the right-opportunist general secretary, McDonald, on the other. The latter was replaced as party leader by Tim Buck. a close friend of mine over the years.

The Fifth Convention of the American Young Communist League, in April 1929, took place against a background of the sharpened economic struggles of the workers in many industries. There had been a growth in the number and importance of youth in industry. Militarization of the youth through the Citizens Military Training Corp and the ROTC in the schools was in full swing. A more conscious effort than ever before was being made to win the youth for capitalist ideology.

In very self-critical language the resolutions before the convention said that "the Young Communist League still remains a small organization, largely isolated from the masses of the young workers," despite some good activities. They were similarly critical in their analysis of each aspect of the work. They pointed out how unsatisfactorily the center had functioned, that in 1928 practically no industrial department existed, that the working-class composition had declined from 51 per cent at the Fourth Convention to 44 per cent at the Fifth, that factionalism had "kept unfit comrades in certain posts" and had "prevented the development of American working-class elements."

Prior to this convention, the Young Communist International had addressed an Open Letter to the entire league membership, in which it said, "There is a direct correlation between factional struggle and the weakness of the League. Therefore one of the chief means of overcoming factional strife is development of the League's activity." This became the rallying theme of the convention, since it was feared that the identity of the league as a separate youth organization was being destroyed.

The Open Letter dealt with the factional situation in the toughest language possible. While saying that "both groups carried on an unprincipled factional struggle," the letter became specific, saying that the efforts to overcome the factional struggle "were chiefly frustrated by the joint resistance of the executive committee majority of the League and the political committee of the Party" and that this "was the chief cause of the intensification of the factional fight and consequently resulted in a tremendous setback to the entire League." This of course did not mean that we of the minority were blameless.

The convention elected a considerable number of new forces to the leadership. Many of the old-timers, including myself, were released from the league for party work. Against my wishes, John Harvey was slated to be the new national secretary. We had recruited him in Chicago in 1924 or 1925, but he was not of working-class origin. In a few short years he was succeeded by Gil Green, one of the ablest of the league's national leaders.

My seven-year association with the league came to an end with this Fifth Convention. I see those seven years as an important period in my development as a Communist. Looking back, one can see how the very promising beginning of the league had been severely threatened by the factional struggle in the party. No wonder the Fifth Convention resolution said, "The last factional struggle has so exhausted the League that a certain demoralization is already observable which must be energetically and speedily combated."

Even with all the handicaps arising from factionalism, the activity, development and growth of the league proved the urgent need for a Communist youth organization. Aside from its role in influencing and giving leadership to sections of young workers and students on urgent issues of the day—and this was a unique and new feature for the labor and socialist movement—the league also contributed Marxist ideas to a cadre of young workers who made important contributions to the party leadership at all levels in later years.

6

A United Party is Created

As the party began to shed sectarianism and leftist phrasemaking, its program came to be based more solidly on conditions in the nation. We drew upon the positive aspects of American traditions, explained the rise of imperialism, exposed the class character of the state and indicated the international character of the working-class struggle.

More and more we recognized the need of the party to forge firm ties with workers, farmers and Negro people. While stressing socialist goals, we were concerned with intermediate steps such as the formation of a labor party. The program bore fruit as we reached out into wider circles who were interested in a labor or independent party movement.

The Trade Union Educational League,* led by Foster and Jack Johnstone, did an increasingly effective job from 1922 on in developing vigorous movements around the slogans "Amalgamation or Annihilation," "For a Labor Party" and "Recognize Soviet Russia"; and also in helping the workers organize progressive election challenges to the entrenched right-wing bureaucracy in the miners, carpenters, machinists, railway and needle-trades unions.

This was the first break from party isolation, which C. E. Ruthenberg had characterized as "wandering along many by-paths."

*Organized in Chicago, November 1920, by William Z. Foster and others who had been active in the great national steel strike of 1919 that was betrayed by Gompers. These leaders wanted a means of organizing the militant minority in the trade unions to fight the Gompers class-collaboration policies. At the beginning, the Trade Union Educational League still had syndicalist tendencies. It established groups of progressives in the various unions and industries, and its official organ, *The Labor Herald,* was a campaigning force that drew wide support from left and progressive people.

One of the enormously important achievements was the establishment of the *Daily Worker* in 1924. Undertaking to reach workers who were surrounded by a sea of capitalist newspapers was a project of major significance and difficulty. The birth of the *Daily Worker* was made possible only after achieving the herculean task of raising $100,000. The response was magnificent. Language federations were generous; over 100 trade union locals and committees donated money or purchased shares; the noted writer, Upton Sinclair, called upon workers to help in the drive. On the night of January 12, on Washington Boulevard in Chicago, the presses rumbled. The first issue came out, to the accompaniment of shouts and cheers. It attacked the Dawes plan for rebuilding the military power of Germany and had a powerful and timely cartoon by Bob Minor.

Reflecting the immigrant character of the American working class, the structure of the early Communist movement was taken over in its entirety from the Socialist party. While one party in name, in effect there were 19 parties — 18 of them language federations and one composed of the English-speaking branches. The total membership in 1924 was 17,377.

In addition to their attachment to a national language federation with its own national committee and officers, each of the hundreds of language branches was also attached to, and received guidance and direction from, the 13 districts into which the party was divided. The reasons for the subsequent confusion and lack of united action in retrospect seem very clear, in view of the tendency toward separatism and concern with narrow group interests. To replace this archaic structure was a difficult process.

The members of English-speaking branches constituted only 11 per cent of the total membership, and about half of these were Jewish comrades who preferred to speak English. A substantial proportion of the others were to be found in four areas — Seattle, Chicago, Ohio and California. A considerable change in composition had already occurred since the formation of the party in 1919, when the English-speaking branches accounted for only seven per cent of the total.

The Palmer anti-Red raids in 1919 which imprisoned and deported hundreds of foreign-born workers, as well as the return to Soviet Russia of thousands of Slavic workers, were responsible for the membership decline of some of the federations.

For instance, the Russian federation, which accounted for 7,000 members in 1919, had declined to 941; the Lithuanians, from 4,400 to 941; the Ukrainians, from 4,000 to 781 and the Latvians from 1,200 to 443.

Indicative of the old-fashioned and non-Communist approach to membership and party organization was the provision in the party constitution as late as 1925, which stated, "Husband and wife belonging to the same branch may purchase dual stamps, which shall be sold at the same price as the regular stamps."

While it is true that in those days far fewer wives worked in industry, the concept of dual dues stamps belittled the individual role of the woman comrade and made her a sort of appendage to her husband. This was clearly a reflection of the present origin of many of the members of the language federations.

The Fourth Convention of the party in Chicago in 1925 became known as the "Bolshevization convention." This was a time when the terminology of the Communist International was borrowed freely. The convention decided that within a period of six months there was to be complete reorganization. All members were to be placed in factory or local branches; the language branches were to be converted into language clubs open for general membership. National language bureaus and the language press were to be supervised by the party leadership.

The reformation of the party, a vital necessity, was put into motion as the factional struggle reached a more serious stage. Each side wished to prove that it knew best how to achieve the goals set by the convention. Lovestone, in particular, as organization secretary, saw in the reorganization an opportunity to make factional advances, and in his efforts in this direction he denigrated the party by speaking of it as "sick" and in need of ridding itself of "social-democratic elements."

In the long run, the new structure of a united party based on democratic centralism, with an orientation to the factories and industries, was beneficial. The greater part of the members of the old party language federations became members of the new language workers clubs, although many allowed their party membership to lapse. The workers clubs grew and developed; later they voted to constitute, with other groups, a large sickness-and-death benefit society, the International Workers Order.

While these were the outstanding aspects of the Fourth National Convention, it also covered such important issues as the Farmer-Labor Party, the united front policy, our first participation in a presidential election, and an unprecedented analysis of the Negro question with the subsequent adoption of a resolution to champion Negro rights.

By 1926 the party was issuing a printed organization bulletin, the forerunner of the *Party Organizer* of later years. In *Bulletin No. 1*, under the signature of Secretary C. E. Ruthenburg, a sharply worded resolution appeared on the financial responsibility of party units as well as a wage standard statement. It made reference to "the irresponsibility and lack of strict accountability in regard to financial matters which exist in the party."

One of the results of earlier financial looseness had been that at the end of that current year $6,000 in unpaid wages was owed to the comrades employed by the national office and another $9,000 to those on the *Daily Worker*. A set of strict rules was then inaugurated, which Ruthenberg rigidly enforced till his death.

The proposed weekly wage rates for party workers of $30 to $40, depending on family status, bring back thoughts of the $5 we used to receive in Ohio as late as 1933, and how in 1938, when our first son, Bob, was born, it was voted that I must be raised to $15 a week.

A strict approach to finances was characteristic of "C.E.," as Ruthenberg was known to all of us. When I became Young Communist League national secretary, he called me into his office and gave me a talk on the sacredness of accounting and caring for party and league funds. And my years of experience have borne out the wisdom of his counsel. Nothing can undermine the party or an official of the party quicker than the careless handling of workers' funds. Every single penny must be recorded and accounted for.

Ruthenberg's death on March 2, 1927, at the age of 45, was a severe blow to everyone. He died of peritonitis, which the doctors said need not have been fatal if it had been given immediate attention.

Born in Cleveland, of German-American parents, his early ambition was to train for the ministry. He went to work at 16 in a picture-frame factory. Then for eight years he worked for a book publishing company as salesman, bookkeeper and head of the sales department. For the next seven years he worked first in the sales department of a roofing material firm and then as purchasing agent for ladies' garments.

He joined the Socialist Party in 1909 at 27, and ran for public office many times. He became full-time secretary of the Socialist Party in Cleveland in 1917. During that year he received 27,000 votes out of a total of 100,000 when he ran for major.

At the historic 1917 Socialist convention in St. Louis, C.E. was the chief spokesman of the developing left wing. As secretary of the subcommittee which presented the anti-war resolution, Ruthenberg was mainly responsible for its sharp formulations. It branded "the declaration of war by our government as a crime against the people of the United States," declared the party's "unalterable opposition to war" and warned the workers "against the snare and delusion of so-called defensive warfare." In 1919, he was acknowledged to be the foremost leader of the left wing in the Socialist Party, which split to organize two Communist parties. It has always been a puzzle to me how Ruthenberg, who idealized everything American, found himself the spokesman for groups composed primarily of the language federations when they were in opposition to groups made up mostly of native Americans.

Ruthenberg, a colleague of Debs, was called "the most arrested man in America." He had been arrested more times for "overthrowing the government of the United States" than any man in history and he spent a number of years in prison.

When the two original Communist parties united, Ruthenberg was elected general secretary and, thoughout the later factional fights, maintained that position with the unanimous support of the party, just as Foster did later as chairman. A keen student of Marx and Lenin, Ruthenberg combined the fight for political principle with an inexhaustible zeal for organizational detail. His integrity did much to check the unscrupulous Lovestone and his associate, John Pepper.

On the personal level, C.E. was a difficult man. He always appeared somewhat aloof and stern. Once, in our arrogance, we younger fellows plotted to break down this aloofness. We agreed that one of us would go in to consult him and address him as "Charlie." When this happened, Ruthenberg stood up and said, "Comrade, the name is Ruthenberg. To my friends it is C.E. Please make your choice." That took care of us.

His death was a blow to the party and to each of us personally. His body lay in state in the Chicago Carmen's Auditorium, and the funeral meeting was also held there. I had the honor to be one of those who stood guard over the body during that tremendous outpouring of people.

The passing of Ruthenberg left Lovestone and John Pepper in the drivers' seats. Lovestone had himself elected executive secretary. The factional fight grew more bitter just at the moment when the need for unity was greatest. In the next two years, along with the postwar boom, there was a widespread net of schemes for class collaboration, identified by the names of their sponsors (the Baltimore & Ohio plan, Tugwell, Carver, Gillette, etc.) and advanced with such titles as the "new wage policy" and the "higher strategy of labor." This sort of demagogy went so far as to claim that the "new capitalism" was turning into socialism and that Henry Ford had superseded Karl Marx.

The AFL leadership, now headed by William Green, swallowed this, hook, line and sinker. Instead of challenging and fighting the sweep of company unionism, the AFL leadership sank so low as to declare, "there is nothing that the company union can do within the single company that the trade unions cannot develop the machinery for doing and accomplishing more effectively."

In this situation, the Workers (Communist) Party, despite the paralyzing effect of an intensified factionalism, made heroic efforts to arouse and give leadership to the workers in challenging the onslaught of the capitalist offensive which was aided and abetted by the AFL leadership.

The names of Passaic, New Bedford, Fall River and Gastonia in the textile industry are each worthy of a book. This is also true of the needle trades and the furriers in New York, Chicago and Philadelphia. In coal mining, where the United Mine Workers of America were chopped to pieces by the coal operators, it was the Left and the Communists who tried to organize in West Virginia, Kentucky and other mine fields. In 1928 it was the combination of progressive and Communist forces in the "Save the Union" movement that led the year-long Penn-Ohio strike. The strikers were unable to win against the opposition of both the operators and John L. Lewis. In these struggles, Lewis ruthlessly expelled Pat Toohey, Dan Slinger, Freeman Thompson, Tony Minerich, Frank Borich and hundreds of others. While the Communists made valiant efforts to turn the tide, the capitulating AFL showed a loss of membership and in 1929 had fallen below the three million figure.

The threatened destruction of the Communist Party of the United States by factionalism — unless a halt was called, such a result was inevitable — became the concern of Communist parties throughout the world. Here, at the center of capitalism, where imperialism and aggression exerted such a powerful control, the party of the working class was unable to move at anything like its full capacity.

In the face of warnings like these from experienced comrades, the party went into its Sixth Convention, the outcome of which was a stalemate. Out of the impasse came the decision to send a delegation to Moscow to meet with leaders of other fraternal parties. Discussions went on for a month, during which sound remedies were proposed to cure the political disease. These were later incorporated into a statement called "Address to the American Party." The factionalism of both groups was severely criticized and expulsion was recommended for those who failed to cease their activities.

With the gravest economic crisis in America only six months away, the convention was not deceived by the facade of American prosperity. "United States capitalism is now exhibiting the effects of the inexorable laws of capitalist development. . . . The general crisis of capitalism is growing more rapidly than it may seem at first glance. The crisis will also shake the foundation of the power of United States imperialism."

Castigating the concept of "American exceptionalism," the Address states: "The ideological lever of right errors in the American Communist party was the so-called theory of 'exceptionalism,' which found its clearest exponents in the persons of Comrades Pepper and Lovestone, whose conception was as follows: a crisis of capitalism, but not of American capitalism; a swing of the masses to the left, but not in America; the necessity of accentuating the struggle against reformism, but not in the United States; a necessity for struggling against the right danger, but not in the American Communist Party."

The answer by Lovestone and his followers was to attempt to withdraw the American Communist Party from its fraternal relationships with other parties throughout the world. The answer of the American Communists to Lovestone was to expel him and some 200 others, most of whom wound up, like Lovestone, supporters of American imperialism.

In 1929, the year of the great stock market crash, I was assigned to assist Bill Foster in the arrangements for the Trade Union Unity League convention. The TUUL was an outgrowth of the Trade Union Educational League, which had placed its main stress upon work within the existing conservative unions.

The new League was to continue this activity, but its main efforts were to be directed toward organizing the unorganized into industrial unions. The League did lay some groundwork for the CIO. But in the new industrial unions the league made the mistake of narrowing its approach to the workers by using such phrases as "the dictatorship of the proletariat" in its program. It also neglected work in AFL unions.

My task at the convention was a relatively small one — to help Foster circularize all organizations who might send delegates. I also had to make all the arrangements in Cleveland. We secured the South Slav Auditorium for the convention. But a much more difficult job was to secure places for an expected 700 delegates to sleep. After lining up all the spare beds in the houses of party members, readers of the *Daily Worker* and other friends, I started on a new tack. Since it was out of the question that the league or the delegates could pay for hotel accommodations, I made the rounds of the best of the flophouses and contracted for 300 beds at 20 and 25 cents for the night of August 31.

Since the same financial strictures prevented per diem allowances for food, I organized within the South Slav Auditorium itself a makeshift restaurant to feed the majority of the delegates. The South Slav and Finnish women did yeoman work in feeding the delegates with soup, stew and coffee. While I heard many complaints about the flophouse accommodations, there was only praise for the food.

When the day arrived, 690 delegates came from 18 states. Of these, 322 were from the three newly organized industrial unions (coal mining, textile and needle trades), 159 were from left-wing groups in AFL unions, 107 from groups in unorganized industries like steel, auto, rubber, maritime and electrical appliances, and 18 from AFL locals.

After this I was selected as assistant to the newly elected national organization secretary of the party, Henry Puro. This was part of the extensive reorganization that took place after the expulsion of Lovestone and his followers. Until then, all of Puro's experience had been with the Finnish Federation, where he was national secretary, prior to which he had been editor of one of the Finnish language dailies.

We all turned our efforts to setting the new leadership on the course of developing the mass work of the party. It had to be· made clear that all those who had broken away from their previous association with the Lovestone leadership would be given responsible work and. leadership posts. For instance, Jack Stachel, who had been the national organization secretary, was elected district secretary in Michigan.

The initial difficulty of learning to work unitedly at all levels, when for years the factions had been denouncing each other in public and private, was overcome quickly, expedited by two contributing facts: first, the intriguers had been expelled; and second, we rallied to fight back against the terrible consequences of the economic catastrophe. Within a few months a camaraderie was established that brought joy to everyone.

Lovestone and Benjamin Gitlow—the latter destined to become a fifth-rate informer—issued material still defending their policy and proclaiming that the party was in crisis. But the party was now prepared to provide leadership for the working class and, under the impact of the great economic crisis of the 30s, the illusion of American exceptionalism exploded, in the face of a cataclysm in which $160 billion in stock-market values were wiped out, production declined by nearly 50 per cent, over 5,000 banks failed, wages were drastically cut and millions lost their jobs.

It must be remembered that no such things as unemployment insurance benefits or social security existed in those days. President Hoover gained notoriety for his repeated announcement of "prosperity just around the corner." A committee of notables appointed by Hoover had the audacity to recommend apple-selling to the unemployed. With the growth of unemployment, evictions became common and Hoovervilles (huts of corrugated iron or shanties of old lumber) grew up everywhere.

The Communist Party threw the energies of its members into the struggle. Evictions became the scene of daily battles with the police. In every city, police violence was the order of the day. In New York, in January 1930, Mayor Walker's police killed a bakery worker, Steve Katovis. Fifty thousand workers filled the streets of New York at the funeral in a great protest. But this was only the first of many casualties that followed in the next three years.

The party decided that three measures were necessary to unify and raise these many struggles to a new level: a nationwide demonstration of the unemployed on March 6; a national organization of the unemployed (scheduled for July 4, 1930, in Chicago); a nationwide campaign for unemployment insurance.

The latter was initiated by an AFL Committee for Unemployment Insurance and Relief, headed by Louis Weinstock of the Painters Union. The focal point of the campaign in its first year was H.R. 2827, a bill introduced by Farmer-Labor Congressman Ernest Lundeen of Minnesota.

The unemployed demonstrations on March 6, 1930, held under Trade Union Unity League auspices throughout the country, shook both government and corporations and gave new courage to the workers. The three most popular slogans were "Work or Wages," "Don't Starve — Fight!" and "Negro and White — Unite and Fight."

The mass turnout on March 6 went beyond our fondest hopes. One-and-a-quarter million workers demonstrated on the streets of America that day — 110,000 in New York City, 100,000 in Detroit, 50,000 each in Chicago and Pittsburgh, 40,000 in Milwaukee, 30,000 in Philadelphia and 25,000 in Cleveland.

With this kind of response, the unemployed millions became a political force and unemployment relief and insurance became dynamic political issues. And all this had been under Communist leadership. Overnight the party felt a strength it never previously experienced.

But the ruling class was not going to give in so easily. They combined promises of a quick "return to normalcy," and some immediate local relief with threats of police action against demonstrations. The top AFL leaders, especially Green and Woll, helped them by denouncing the idea of unemployment insurance as "foreign propaganda" from Moscow. Pitched battles with the police took place at many of the demonstrations. In New York, Mayor Walker refused a permit for the demonstrators to march from Union Square to City Hall to present their demands. Twenty-five thousand policemen and firemen fought the demonstrators. The worst were the mounted cops, who bashed heads right and left from their advantageous position.

In the New York demonstration, the delegation which had been elected to see the Mayor — Foster, general secretary of the League; Robert Minor, editor of the *Daily Worker*; Israel Amter, New York district organizer of the party; and two unemployed workers, Harry Raymond and Joseph Lester — were arrested and later sent to the local prison on Ryker's Island with three-year sentences.

On March 6, the leading forces in the national office were divided between those who were to participate actively in the demonstration and those who would be held in reserve to cover developments. My lot was to be among the latter. Being strictly forbidden to go near Union Square, half a dozen of us spent hours in an office building listening to the news on the radio.

This historic day marked the beginning of years of mass activity and struggles by the unemployed, which resulted in the present system of Unemployment Insurance and Social Security. It was the Communists who initiated and carried on the fight for these important reforms, while many others, like William Green, were still opposing and denouncing them.

That same year, I had the privilege of representing the party leadership at the first two district conventions in the South, in Charlotte, North Carolina, and Birmingham, Alabama.

Up to now the party had been active, in an unplanned way, in the textile workers' strikes in Gastonia and other towns in the Carolinas and Tennessee, participating in activities among the unemployed and the early stages of the Sharecroppers Union movement. The first Communist public meetings were held in the South during the 1928 presidential elections by our candidates William Foster and James Ford, but we were very much dissatisfied with the slow progress of party building.

A very important resolution on "Our Party in the South," adopted in March 1930, declared there was a tendency "to underestimate in practice the basic importance of work in the South" and said "the importance of the role of our Party in organizing and leading mass struggles is of far greater importance than ever before." It went on to say that this underestimation was evidenced by the fact that the entire South was still considered a party district with only one organizer, and that there was as yet no party paper for the area. Against the background of bold perspectives for mass work, the proposals included the creation of two districts with full-time organizers, a regional organizer, a weekly newspaper, a director for work among the Negro people, and a six-week full-time training school.

The convention in Charlotte, an underground gathering, was in an old ramshackle hall; the delegates, Negro and white, were full of enthusiasm. The former were primarily from the tobacco industry while the latter came from textile mills, where few Negro workers were employed. The great majority were new to the party. In accord with their custom, the convention opened with prayer, the first and only Communist convention I ever attended where that took place. The delegates were not acquainted with the early days of the party or the more recent factional battles. The big problems were the economic struggles and demands in textile and tobacco, the struggle for Negro rights and self-determination and the battle against unemployment and terror.

From Charlotte I traveled to Birmingham. While the Negroes were subjected to the same segregation and discrimination typical of the entire South, I remember my impressions of Birmingham were different than those of Charlotte. Here I felt greater maturity, experience and, above all, potential power, Since the Birmingham police were more alert, arrangements for a convention of Negro and white delegates were particularly tricky. Most of the delegates came from Alabama, with a few from Tennessee and Georgia. We met for two days, each day in a different house. The local comrades, Negro and white, had had preliminary discussions of how best to carry it through. Comrade Hosie, a splendid local Negro comrade with deep roots in and around Birmingham, maintained emphatically that if we were to hold the convention, everyone must conform externally to all the mores of the South.

This meant that Negroes and whites must never walk together on the streets and that Negroes must always go to the back door to enter. Hosie was particularly worried about getting the white comrades to agree to this, since he knew we all hated these humiliating discriminations. Certain delegates were brought in the evening before the convention to avoid attracting the neighbors' attention. Once inside, voices had to be kept low and the radio was played loudly in an adjacent room. Under these circumstances, about 15 persons carried through the first district convention of the party and helped lay the foundation upon which much of the latter-day history of Birmingham has grown.

It was in 1930, either just before or immediately after the Seventh Party Convention in June, that I first met Eugene Dennis, who later became the general secretary of the party. Gene was only 25 then. Born in Seattle, he joined the party there in 1926 and moved to California in 1928. He was arrested in the March 6 unemployed demonstration in Los Angeles. About that time the Trade Union Unity League organized and led several strikes in Imperial Valley, involving 7,000 agricultural workers.

To try to break the strikes, warrants were issued for many of the leaders, among them Gene Dennis, who evaded arrest. Many of the others — I remember Jim Keller and Frank Spector among them — were later sent to prison for several years. When it became impossible to do useful work in Imperial Valley under such circumstances, the party in California sent Gene to New York City.

One day in the national office I was introduced to the young, husky, broad-shouldered man. I was to arrange a place for him to stay. Since he had to be kept under cover, the organization department was given the job of "re-christening" him. Comrade Puro left it to me, and I remember joking about it. Finally I took a phone book, closed my eyes, and opening it blindly, put my finger on a name. It turned out to be "Ryan." A good Irish name, to which I then added "Tim" and he left as Tim Ryan. His oldest son, now resident in the Soviet Union, is known to this day as "Tim." In the following years Gene Dennis, alias Tim Ryan, worked with the national liberation movements in China, the Philippines and South Africa. Thus started a long and close political and personal association between Gene and myself.

Recruiting was on the rise, now that we were increasing our participation in struggle. The party had declined to 9,642 in 1929 from 16,325 in 1925. At the Seventh Convention in 1930 we reported 6,167 new members, 85 per cent of whom were industrial workers and 15 per cent Negroes. At this convention I was elected to the central committee, a post I held without interruption until the time of my deportation in 1955. I was later assigned to Chicago as district organization secretary.

Following the convention, the central committee chose a secretariat, consisting of Earl Browder, administrative secretary; William Z. Foster, trade union secretary; and Will Weinstone, organization secretary.

During the years in New York City covered in this chapter, my personal life continued to be merged almost completely with Young Communist League and party life and activities. New York City has many amenities — fast transport, good restaurants and much cultural life, but it is not America. It lacks the roar of industry and the simple warmth and friendliness of the industrial workers of Chicago, Cleveland or Detroit. Neither does it have the natural beauty and the slower pace of life in Seattle, San Franciso, Minneapolis or Denver. It is just a few jam-packed islands where the people rush about pell-mell in a gigantic rat race.

Our spare time in New York was spent mainly with comrades with whom we were particularly friendly. Few meals were eaten at home, and spending time at theaters, concerts or museums (or even having children) was frowned upon as "hindering the work."

In 1930 my marriage to Lenore came to an end. During the subsequent years she has remained friendly with our entire family. After our marriage broke up, she worked for a while as a full-time party organizer in New England. Subsequently she remarried and settled in the Soviet Union, where she still lives with her grown daughter.

7

Chicago: Struggles
of the Unemployed

The city of Chicago, the prime example of the rapid and ruthless growth of industrial America, has been described by many writers: Theodore Dreiser, Upton Sinclair, Carl Sandberg, Nelson Algren and others. Lawlessness, tolerated by government on behalf of the wealthy, made the name of the city a byword for gangsterism. (Al Capone, prince of the city's rackets, in the years when his influence was declining, attempted to restore his standing with a diatribe against communism, in *Liberty* magazine.)

Chicago's factories spilled their dirt and soot over miles of flat land inhabited by their workers. The stockyards and railroads added their stench, and the polluted river cut through its center. The South Side housed the nation's second largest concentration of urban Negroes; near the stockyards was virtually a Polish city. Here the first strike for the eight-hour day took place; here the Haymarket martyrs met their death; here was the founding place of the Social Democratic Party, led by Eugene Debs, the Industrial Workers of the World and the Communist Party. It was the city of John Peter Altgeld, of Clarence Darrow and of the Republican convention that nominated Abraham Lincoln.

Nowhere was police terror so bad as in Chicago during those years. Corrupt to the core and in alliance with the gangsters, the police arrested hundreds of workers at meetings, demonstrations and strikes and beat them into insensibility in the local police stations. It was the infamous Red Squad, headed by Lieutenant Mike Mills and Sergeant Murphy, who raided party offices, broke up the furniture and brutally beat every Communist they could lay hand on. In 1930, the Communist candidate for congress, Lee Mason, a Negro worker, was murdered by the police.

It was in this atmosphere that I began my new assignment. While the party district office was in Chicago, the area covered at that time included all of Illinois and Indiana, plus the lower half of Wisconsin, the city of St. Louis and the area around Davenport, Iowa.

Among the unemployed our central demand was for the Unemployment Insurance Bill. While we were getting a tremendous popular response, we still hadn't built a solid enough foundation among the unemployed in their daily fight against evictions, in their demands for relief, for free water, and for gas and electricity, when these were shut off.

We had just developed a program which asserted the right of the Negro people to self-determination in the Southern states and expressed our resolution to intensify our efforts in the struggle for their full political, economic and social equality, with emphasis on the fight against lynching and discrimination. These were the issues around which we hoped to develop the broadest mass struggle of the Negro people in unity with the white workers.

This was a new approach, since Socialists in the past had for
the most part ignored the plight of the Negro. Even Eugene
Debs was weak on this question. It is doubtful whether he could
have attracted such large audiences in his presidential campaigns in the South had he declared for the right of the Negro to
vote and enjoy equality.

The wisdom of our conviction on this issue would be confirmed in the months and years to come, as America entered
the deepest crisis of its history. The Chicago district, like so
many others, was the scene of tremendous struggles, in which
Communists displayed high courage and leadership, won support and grew in membership and influence.

At that time we had a membership and leadership in Chicago
whose active core was a combination of foreign-born comrades
and younger people like myself who had been in the Young
Communist League. Bill Gebert and I worked out a rough division of labor whereby he, in addition to his general political
responsibility as secretary, gave attention to industrial work and
to Southern Illinois, Wisconsin and St. Louis; while I, in addition
to party organization and recruiting, devoted myself to activity
among the unemployed and the Negro people, and to work in
the Chicago, Indiana and Rockford area.

The daily struggles in those first days of the deepening crisis
centered around two issues: the demand for a system of unemployment relief and the prevention of evictions. The local headquarters of the Unemployed Councils were real nerve centers of
events affecting the jobless in the neighborhoods. After a while,
some of them functioned with military precision in outwitting
the bailiffs and police.

In August 1931, the police shot into a crowd on the South Side
that was trying to stop the eviction of a 70-year-old widow, Mrs.
Diana Gross. Three Negro workers, Abe Gray, John O'Neil and
Frank Armstrong, were killed. This aroused the community
to seething anger, and brought about a remarkable demonstration of Negro-white unity. From then on, the Unemployed
Councils gained strength, and tens of thousands of workers
in all parts of Chicago were involved in their common struggles.

During that summer a state hunger march to the capital was
organized, with the official support of the party. As it approached Springfield, the state troopers blocked all the high-
ways and the governor threatened to call out the National

Guard. The main body of marchers from Chicago, where our party influence was greatest, were corralled into a camp for the night with troopers and police surrounding them.

A committee of which I was a member had been established for the march. Anticipating the moves of the troopers, I had separated from my group in order to be mobile, but now the problem was how to have a committee meeting while still retaining freedom of action.

Runners established contact with me and led me back through bushes and trees, after dark, into the "corral." We had our meeting and worked out a strategy that was successful the next day. In negotiation with the state troopers, who were in touch with the governor and the speaker of the state legislature, it was agreed that if all the hunger marchers were allowed to gather in a meeting outside the state capitol, small delegations would be sent in to speak to the legislature and see the governor. After a last check-up, the committee adjourned and I was taken back through the woods, successfully evading the troopers.

In Chicago a real offensive had been started against the unemployed. Another worker had just been murdered; proposals were being made that all foreign-born unemployed (about 20 per cent of the Chicago total) should be deported; and the police force had been increased to deal with the growing crisis.

There was great discontent among Chicago's unemployed and their families. The action that precipitated a great new movement was a 50 per cent cut in relief payments to 160,000 family men on October 1, without even a day's notice. The party and those Unemployed Council leaders who were close to the event immediately organized the discontent into the biggest united-front demonstration ever held, under the joint auspices of the Unemployed Councils, the Workers Committee on Unemployment (under Socialist leadership) and the Workers League (led by remnants of the Proletarian Party). The main demands were withdrawal of the relief cut, an end to all evictions and cash relief. To achieve these demands we projected a march through the Loop and into Grant Park, and opened negotiations with the authorities at city hall. Mayor Anton Cermak emphatically refused our request for a permit.

Our judgment was that the existing conditions warranted our defying Cermak with some hope of success. The unemployed had never been so aroused. Despite the hesitations and sabotage of Socialist leaders like Karl Borders, the Workers Committee branches were enthusiastic for the march. Franklin D. Roosevelt was the Democratic candidate in the November presidential elections, against the infamous Herbert Hoover, and the local Democratic administration would hardly risk a bloodbath on the eve of the elections.

The joint committee announced that the hunger march would take place, as scheduled, without a permit. Its purposes were outlined and responsibility for any trouble was placed on Mayor Cermak and his police. It was also announced that two delegations of 35 each would drop out as the march passed the City-County Building to meet the Mayor and the Cook County leaders.

The newspapers predicted a bloodly battle and told of the police preparations. It was with elation that we saw the massive response, estimated at close to 50,000, that formed up into the hunger march. Headed by a phalanx of 45 men and women — 15 from each of the sponsoring organizations — we marched through the crowded Loop, stopping all traffic for over an hour.

Among our own group were Claude Lightfoot, Joe Weber, Leonides McDonald, Nick Blattnor, Brown Squire, W. Lamson and myself. While there was great enthusiasm in the ranks of the marchers, among the leaders, especially the Communists who had taken the initiative and bore the chief responsibility, there was great tension. Though our greatest hope for a peaceful demonstration lay in the large number who had responded, one never knew what the Chicago police were planning. We kept certain comrades out of the march in order to assure continuity of leadership, but those of us who were leading the march had little chance of any protection if the police did not back down.

At one point in the Loop we saw a solid wall of police blocking the road with all the top brass in evidence. We slowed down and a small group went forward to talk. The police said we were defying the law by marching in the Loop without a permit. The march leaders stood solidly on their right to peaceful demonstration and placed all responsibility for the consequences of trying to stop the march on the city administration. At a signal from Joe Weber, the leader of the Unemployed Councils, the leaders started forward, with thousands of marchers behind us. The wall of police fell back and joined others on the sidelines. As we passed them we were roundly cursed and threatened with what would happen the next time they had us at their mercy.

Needless to say, everyone was jubilant, although I will never forget the sweat running down my body under the pressure of responsibility. With perfect discipline, the marchers proceeded to Grant Park. I was a member of the delegation chosen to meet Mayor Cermak. He did not appear, but sent a representative. A lot of wrangling took place and we were given no satisfaction.

The next day, however, it was announced that the relief cut had been withdrawn—a great victory with far-reaching effects, arousing new enthusiasm and a consciousness of strength. This was reinforced by a second victory. Growing out of a state conference, a delegation was sent to the state legislature, and after our spokesmen had a heated exchange with the legislature, a $17-million relief appropriation was passed.

The Chicago hunger march had provided us with valuable lessons in united-front tactics. The Unemployed Councils, on the initiative of the Communists, now issued a call to all unemployed organizations, appealing for united action. The rank and file of these groups responded immediately, voting down their leadership in many instances. Yet they retained a loyalty to their own organizations. Then we achieved a joint conference of the Councils, the Workers Committee and the Workers League. The bonds that had united us were the march and the demand for the rescinding of the relief cut.

Karl Borders, Socialist leader of the Workers Committee, attempted to split the conference by disputing secondary points. But the Unemployed Council representatives stuck to the central issue, and when Borders tried to withdraw his delegates, they voted him down. The party was learning that through proper presentation of the issue and an alliance with the rank and file, a united front could be achieved without compromising principles. Our big weakness was the inadequacy of our efforts to involve the trade unions.

The electoral front became our next concern. In 1932 the national nominating convention of the Communist Party was held in Chicago. This brought together several hundred delegates from states where the party was mobilized for the all-out effort which finally got us on the ballot in 40 states. The main sessions were held in the Peoples Auditorium, and a public session was held in the Coliseum Annex, with 4,000 people. Here the nomination and acceptance speeches, and a certain amount of the ballyhoo that accompanies American political conventions, were to take place. The responsibility for organizing the convention rested in my hands.

The two major contestants were Herbert Hoover, on the Republican ticket, and Franklin D. Roosevelt, on the Democratic ticket. Roosevelt made the New Deal and "the forgotten man" key issues in his campaign.

Our program was radically different. We advocated unemployment and social insurance at the expense of the state and the employers. We protested Hoover's wage-cutting policies. Farmers were to be given emergency relief where needed and exemption from rents or debts. We demanded equal rights for Negroes and self-determination for the Black Belt. We opposed brutality on the part of the police and the suppression of workers' political rights. Nor did we forget our international obligations. We condemned imperialist aggression and spoke out in defense of the Soviet Union and the Chinese people.

Our candidates were Foster for President and James W. Ford for Vice-President. Jim Ford was a Negro and this aroused great public interest, especially among the Negro people.

Ford originally had been a steel worker in Birmingham, Alabama. His grandfather was lynched by the Ku Klux Klan. In the North he had been a postal worker after serving in the army during World War I. An experienced trade unionist, he was at that time one of two Negro members of the political committee of the party.

At the packed public meeting where Foster and Ford were nominated, I recall an episode concerning Bill Foster that only a few others may possibly have experienced. The session was planned so that everything would click on the minute. But with a lineup of speakers to make the nominating and seconding speeches that had to be politically and geographically balanced, and with a collection speech and the sale of literature as well, not everyone kept to time.

I was sitting on the platform holding the organizational reins of the meeting in my hands, so to speak. Next to me sat Foster. A superb organizer himself, he was, nevertheless, very nervous on the platform. I went through an hour and a half of torture. As each speaker made a point, Bill, in choice sailor's language, would say under his breath that another point of his speech had been cribbed. When the speaker went over his time, he insisted I stop him.

As the long list of speakers went on, Bill's tension mounted. It almost reached breaking point when the collection was taken. When finally a musical number was played by a band, a big event for us, he almost exploded and insisted they be stopped. At that point I told him we were running the session according to an agreed plan with the national office, and he told me that he had never in all his experience seen such a badly organized meeting.

However, after his acceptance speech and after they carried him around the hall shoulder-high and all the rest of the fanfare, he came back to me on the platform, all smiles, shook my hand and said quite casually, "One of the best organized meetings I've ever attended, Johnny."

In our district we decided not only to get the national ticket on the ballot in all five states, but to put up state and congressional candidates in four of them. This was a tremendous task. To get our ticket on the ballot, Illinois and Missouri each required 25,000 valid signature; Wisconsin required 10,000 (and an attempt was made to increase it to 24,000 by a new law); and Indiana, several thousand. To guarantee the valid minimum, we set as our objective in Illinois 50,000 signatures. Other states did the same. We got the presidential ticket on in all five states. In Illinois we also ran a full state ticket plus two candidates for congressmen-at-large, 12 for congressional districts and 11 in state senatorial contests.

We decided to hold a state nominating convention downstate where the party hardly existed. We invited other working-class organizations to help us nominate Communist candidates and to work out an election platform. Twelve hundred calls were sent and 350 delegates responded. The Chicago delegates left at three o'clock in the morning to make sure they would arrive on time. The convention was at the Workers Center in Decatur. The local branch secretary opened the convention with a short speech and committees were set up.

Normally the keynote speech should have been made by the district secretary, but since we were in territory where all the people were native-born, Bill Gebert insisted that his own imperfect English pronunciation ruled him out. I made the keynote speech and introduced the draft platform, while the organization of the campaign was presented by Andrew Newhoff. After the platform had been discussed and adopted, we nominated a full slate of candidates for state office.

In the early evening, Decatur saw its first Communist public meeting. It was held in the city park and we spoke from the bandstand. The main speakers were five of the candidates. While not more than a couple of hundred people attended, we considered it well worthwhile to break into new territory down-state.

Our party vote in these 1932 elections increased everywhere in the district except St. Louis. In Cook County we got 11,917 votes, which was 12 times that in 1928. In Lake County, Indiana, which included Gary, we got 646 votes; in East St. Louis, 508.

That was the worst year of the economic crisis. Starvation and misery were widespread; wages were steadily reduced till many employed people felt little better off than the unemployed. The answer to the resistance of the workers was increased terror and police action. A leader of the Chicago Unemployed Councils, Comrade Nels Kjar, was arrested, held in the Cook County jail for months and finally deported to Denmark. The party district secretary, Bill Gebert, and six others were arrested in the Southern Illinois coalfields, under the Criminal Syndicalist Act.

Indicative of the attitude of the ruling class was the insolent statement by Republican Governor Len Small that "there is no cure in charity, in handing out doles to idle men. That solves nothing, produces nothing, and breaks down the morale of the American men and women." Small's campaign slogan was "Back to Prosperity." Later, in his last term as governor, he was tried for stealing state funds.

The Illinois National Guard blatantly announced that year: "This winter, at its many conferences, the staff has been considering and settling plans for suppression of radical disorders" and, as to methods, its instructions read, "Never fire over the heads of the rioters. Blank cartridges should never be fired at a mob."

Toward the end of the election campaign, while Comrade Foster was on his way back from his tour to the Pacific Coast, we scheduled another big election meeting at the Coliseum Annex. We were determined to fill its over 4,000 seats, as we had done earlier in the year at the open session of the national nominating convention. But this time we had to do it without the help of the national office or the glamor of a convention.

After intensive work we felt we could expect a good meeting. Foster had deep roots in the labor movement in Chicago. He was known for his leadership of the steel organizing campaign and strike in 1919, and his earlier successful organization of the packing-house workers unions, as well as his long years of participation in the railwaymen's union and the Chicago Federation of Labor.

The night before the day of our big meeting, very late, we got a phone call from Rock Island, where Foster was scheduled to speak. He had been taken ill, but would travel into Chicago the next morning. I met him at the train and took him in a taxi to the Washington Hotel. It was all he could do to get into the room and he collapsed on the bed. We immediately got a doctor who informed us that he had had a heart attack. After meeting every night on a 9,000 mile trip, after a lifetime of hard work, nature had finally exacted a physical penalty.

Bill insisted he must make an appearance at the meeting. The doctor said this was madness and would mean death. We then brought in a leading heart specialist, who was known as a progressive. He not only confirmed everything that had been said, but insisted on hospitalization. Against this advice, Foster demanded to go home. He was taken to the train on a stretcher and then to his home, still resisting the hospital. It was five or six years before he made another public speech, and from then on his public speaking and, even more, his administrative activity was limited. But what was limited for him was more than an ordinary day's work for most others, and in later years he returned to the thick of the fight.

We got the *Daily Worker* editor, Clarence A. Hathaway, to fly into Chicago from New York to substitute for Foster at our big election rally. As chairman of that packed Coliseum Annex election rally, I had an experience I will never forget.

We had not made public Foster's last-minute illness. After the preliminary speeches and the collection were over, I announced Foster's illness and that we had a substitute speaker. It seemed to me, as I faced over 4,000 people in that big barnlike hall, that at least half of them rose from their seats, muttering to themselves, and formed solid lines to every exit. I could already picture the crowd dwindle to a few hundred bitterly disappointed people.

Dropping all further efforts to go on with explanations of Foster's illness and his message to the meeting, I introduced Hathaway. For the first few minutes he couldn't be heard, but finally order was reestablished. We had not lost half of the audience; it was nearer to one-fourth, but that was bad enough. Even a speaker as good as Hathaway was not acceptable to that crowd as a substitute for their own Bill Foster. There was also the fact that many of these workers who came to hear Foster still had certain doubts about the Communists. They thought we had fooled them, using Foster's name to get them there. It was several days and even longer before people generally learned, to their sorrow, that Foster was seriously stricken.

In 1933, the party in Chicago contested 26 of the 46 wards in the aldermanic elections on February 28. This covered the main working-class areas in all parts of the city. Our platform was headed "Smash the Bosses' Program of Hunger and War," and we conducted a good campaign.

Every Sunday afternoon in Washington Park on Chicago's South Side, we ran forums. Others also made speeches there, but on a Sunday afternoon the party forum had priority and we had few challengers for this privilege.

On one occasion, during an election, the Republicans—at that time traditionally entrenched among Negro voters—attempted to hold a meeting in competition with us. They were booed down, but out of this incident came an agreement for a debate the following Sunday between the Communists and Chicago's Republican Mayor, "Big Bill" Thompson.

It fell to my lot to represent the party. We knew the Republicans would come in force and try to overwhelm us. Thompson was a showman. Older readers will remember his blatant anti-British attitude and his promise "to punch King George in the snoot." We worked overtime to guarantee a big crowd of our supporters, the majority Negro workers and their wives.

When the time arrived, Thompson pulled up with a cavalcade of cars and a band. I remember it booming out an incongruous tune, considering the year and the audience, "Happy Days Are Here Again." The song was played over and over while the six-and-a-half-foot Thompson, with his broad Texas hat, stomped among the people slapping backs and shaking hands.

All I remember of my speech was that I disregarded my well-prepared notes and asked Thompson how he dared to feature "Happy Days" at a time like this. When he spoke, he was heckled and booed. He finally packed up and left, much to the delight of the crowd. This was an example of how far removed from the people these so-called astute politicians were.

The party was on the move but effective participation in struggles at the factory level was still lacking. Before the election of Roosevelt in 1932, there were many small, sporadic strikes among coal miners in Southern Illinois, dressmakers in Chicago and Collinsville, rubber workers in Mishawaka, oil workers in Whiting, nut-pickers in St. Louis, and light-steel workers in Rockford. Through the Trade Union Unity League unions, we played a role in the mining, needle-trades and nut-pickers unions only.

We directed our attention to steel, packing and railroads in order to extend our basic-industry outlook beyond mining. Our major experience was a strike in the Standard Forging Co. of Indiana Harbor. It was led by the Steel and Metal Workers Union of the TUUL. We hoped to use it as a lever to move the workers in nearby Inland Steel and the U.S. Steel Mills — a rather big order. The strike was solid for six weeks except for a small AFL craft group. After that we had to acknowledge defeat and send the workers back. But in spite of this setback, the readiness of the workers to strike if they were given leadership was clearly evidenced.

During these three years as district organizer of the party, I acquired tremendous experience, especially in orienting the party outward. I also had the responsibility for guiding the party itself to grow and develop while participating in mass activities.

At the 1932 District Convention, held in Milwaukee, we were able to report a growth from 600 members in 60 branches in 1930 to over 3,000 in 200 branches. This was a five-fold development. Our Negro membership had grown from 50 to 700, with the overwhelming majority in Chicago.

In Milwaukee we could truly point out that at the 1930 convention the predominant concern of the party was with inner activities, but that in 1932, participation in mass struggles was the central activity. Out of the latter policy had come substantial growth. However, we were still sharply critical of ourselves, especially our failure to influence the workers in basic industries and to recruit employed workers to our party. We set a goal of another 2,000 recruits by 1933.

During those three years in Chicago, my personal life was unsettled. All my energies were thrown into the activities I have been describing. There was little time for socializing, except as part of the day-to-day activity. Not only were these important years in my own political development and maturity, but they

were years when close friendships were established that have remained over a lifetime. Here I can mention only a few of them.
Dora Lifshitz was and is a remarkable woman. She was never
a full-time party or trade-union worker, but she was ever at the
service of her union and the party. In the garment factory she
was the workers' spokesman. In her International Ladies Garment Workers Union local she led the fight against Dubinsky,
Zimmerman and other right-wing officials. On the picket line
she negotiated with the police, and when that failed many a
policeman's truncheon hit her head.

In the party she was elected to leading committees; at first
on the district committee and secretariat and later on the national review commission—not because she made eloquent
speeches (she never did) but because the members felt they had
in her a real representative who would never forget them or
their problems. Her patient concern with new and young comrades was matched only by her bluntness and sharp tongue for
fellow leaders if she felt they were wrong, and especially if they
appeared to be swellheaded.

In later years in New York she was a close friend of our family, and when I was in prison, she took a special interest in the
children which continues to this day. A victim of McCarthyism,
she was deported to Poland in 1950. She refused to be a political
exile and identified herself with the political life and party activity of Poland. Today, a small grey-haired woman, she still oc-
cupies a responsible political post and refuses to retire.

Dora Lifshitz is an example of devotion to a single purpose,
the advancement of the working class to socialism under the
banner of Marx and Lenin and the Communist party. I was enriched by having her as a dear, close friend.

Another friend was Sam Hammersmark, an old-time Socialist
of Scandinavian extraction, who had come into the party with
Foster. He took a particular pride in helping young comrades,
and during my years in Chicago ran the Workers Bookshop.

There were also the two "Rocks of Gibraltar," Ray Hans-
borough and Brown Squires, associates of Claude Lightfoot.
Brown worked in the stockyards, while Ray—already ill with
TB—was unemployed. Both were modest, with no great platform eloquence but with the gift of winning support for the
party.

A party family with whom I stayed and who befriended me in every way were Dora and Manie Radin. He was a painter and she a garment worker. Not only were they very active but theirs was an open house at all hours of the day and night where scores of comrades passing through Chicago found hospitality. Then there was Bill Gebert, the district secretary. We worked well together. Because he was conscious of speaking English with an accent, I got more than my share of public appearances, but Bill was the party's political leader. Prior to being district secretary he had been the editor of the Polish paper of the party. In later years, during the CIO's organizing drive in the steel industry, Gebert worked with Phil Murray and was in charge of a big CIO propaganda campaign among foreign-born steel workers.

In the McCarthy days, because he had been arrested in southern Illinois in 1931 when he was district secretary, he was deported to Poland. There he held such important assignments in the Central Council of Trade Unions as editor of its daily newspaper, representative to the World Federation of Trade Unions (from which he attended the United Nations meeting in New York), and head of the Council's international department. Upon recovering from a serious illness, Gebert entered the Polish diplomatic service, and as I write he is known as Boleslaw Konstantin Gebert, His Excellency, Ambassador Plenipotentiary of the Polish Peoples' Republic to Turkey.

We still send each other New Year's greetings.

About the middle of 1933 the Political Committee asked me if I would be ready to go to Ohio as district (or state) secretary if their committee elected me. They stressed the importance of this assignment. While I regretted leaving Chicago, where I felt very much at home, I was willing to accept this greater political responsibility. These three years in the Chicago District, with their tremendous and varied experiences, had prepared me for the turbulent seven years in Ohio which were to come.

8

Auto Is Organized

In a country still deep in economic crisis, Ohio was one of the four or five key industrial regions. While its area was not comparable to that of Texas or California, it was nearly as large as all of England, in square miles. In 1933 Ohio was already a multi-industry state. Two fifths of its workers were in manufacturing industries, the most important of which were rubber, steel, auto, heavy- and light-machine tooling, electrical machinery and appliances, clay and glass, and coal mining.

The rubber industry was located in Akron, where 90 per cent of the rubber tires in the United States were produced. Steel was scattered in Youngstown, Warren, Cleveland, Canton, Massillon, Portsmouth, Ohio Valley and Weirton, across the Ohio River in West Virginia, but the Mahoning Valley was the most important. Auto was primarily in Cleveland and Toledo; Dayton was the center of the General Motors electrical division, which produced Frigidaires and other products, while Cincinnati was world-famous for its heavy machine-tool products. It is of interest to note that while Ohio ranked fourth among the states in the total value of tangible property, it was listed 26th in per capita wealth.

Ohio was unusually rich in its state traditions and history. One of the states carved out of the Northwest Territory, it was admitted to the Union in 1803. It became a haven for immigrants from lands across the sea, as well as for Scotch-Irish victims of Puritan intolerance in New England, Quakers who could not go along with slavery in the South, refugees from Canada who had helped the colonies in the Revolutionary War and migrant families searching for land, security and independence.

In the mid-1880s, many Germans settled in Ohio, especially in Cleveland and Cincinnati. The Bass Islands, in Lake Erie, were almost entirely settled by "Forty-Eighters" (emigres from the

German Revolution of 1848). Religious sects—Shakers, Mennonites, Moravians, Mormons—also established settlements in Ohio.

Ohio played a prominent part in the struggle against slavery as an early center of abolitionist organization and activity. The *Philanthropist*, advocating immediate and unconditional emancipation of the slaves, was printed in 1817 at Mount Pleasant. During the Civil War period, three routes of the Underground Railway, over which thousands of Negroes passed from the South into Canada, covered Ohio. Oberlin College, one of the first coeducational schools of higher learning, was also one of the busiest terminals of the railway.

After the Civil War, Cleveland's mayor, Tom L. Johnson, became famous for his struggle against the monopolies, for achieving a municipally controlled street railway and a three-cent fare, and for his ceaseless defense of free speech. The latter campaign culminated in the city's designating a permanent stone rostrum on the corner of the public square. I spoke from that historic platform many times during my seven years in Ohio.

The state was also the scene of many early and historic strikes and labor struggles. Among the national trade unions and organizations originating in Ohio were the Brotherhood of Locomotive Engineers (1863), Cigar Makers Union (1864) Federation of Organized Trades and Labor Unions (1882) and the American Federation of Labor (1886).

Ohio was the birthplace and the center of the activities of Charles Ruthenberg, one of the founders of the Communist Party. Together with Alfred Wagenknecht, he won over the Socialist party to a stand against war and support for the Russian Revolution. Eugene Debs, born in Terre Haute, Indiana, (adjacent to Ohio) was also well known in the state. In was after a visit to Ruthenberg and Wagenknecht in the local prison at Canton in 1918 that he made the speech which brought him a 10-year prison sentence.

It was, therefore, a district with a great progressive and working-class history. I came in the late summer of 1933, to transform the isolated position of the party into one of active participation in the workers' struggles. I could not then have imagined the rich and varied seven years that lay ahead.

I was met at the Cleveland bus depot by Ben Amis, the comrade who was leaving his post here for other work. We walked to his car, a 1921 Chevrolet roadster, and he asked me, "Can you drive? If not, you better learn right now since that's the only way you can get around Ohio. We don't even have enough money to travel on Nevin's buses." Nevin's was an old bus company whose fares were even cheaper than Greyhound's.

Next day I started to learn how to drive. Ben (who, incidentally, was the first Negro comrade to hold the post of district secretary) left for New York after three days. At the end of a week I made my first trip to Youngstown, 60 miles away. At that time there were no driver's tests or licenses. During those first few weeks I am sure I was endangering not only my own life but those of many other drivers. Nevertheless, from that day until July 2, 1951, when I entered Lewisburg Penitentiary, I drove a car every day without an accident.

My assignment to Ohio was part of a national effort to concentrate forces in the key industrial areas of Pennsylvania, Ohio, Michigan and Illinois, in order to establish a firm basis for the party and the Trade Union Unity League in the basic industries, while developing the organizations of the unemployed and Negro workers. In fact, Ohio had been singled out by the party leadership as "lagging behind the rest of the concentration districts."

At an extraordinary national conference in July 1933, an open letter to all party members was adopted and given widespread discussion. In very frank language the letter said that despite a number of achievements, the overall work and progress of the party was very unsatisfactory. It cited the failure to carry out an earlier decision "to transfer the center of our work to a number of the most important large factories, areas and districts"; it pointed out that despite the widespread struggles and the new forces that had emerged, "the cadres of functionaries of the party have not been rejuvenated and strengthened."

Declaring that it was "the iron revolutionary duty" to stop empty talk and to bring about the agreed-upon changes, it outlined a series of vital tasks, and said "the party must judge the activity of its functionaries and must choose its leading bodies" on the basis of whether each member and leader could be "a real organizer of mass struggles."

Among the events of the preceding year singled out for criticism, a number dealt with Ohio; for example, we had allowed the initiative in the unemployment and social-insurance campaign in Cleveland to be taken away from us; we had lost our leadership of the miners in the Ohio Valley to reformists; we had left the steel workers in Warren to themselves after their loss of a local strike; we had shown general sectarian tendencies in trade union work; and there had been little growth in party membership.

I found many loyal and devoted comrades in the district, but their activity was largely agitational and hit-or-miss. It was not rooted in the factories; morale was low; membership was in the range of 800 or 900; and finances were desperate. The comrades were supposed to be getting $10 a week, but they were lucky to average $5 or $6. Full-time workers had been given a few dollars at the end of the week, plus a basket of groceries which had been obtained from comrades who were better off. This relief-station approach was shocking and demoralizing, and within a month we put an end to the baskets and made an effort to pay everyone their pittance in cash.

Unemployment in Ohio was widespread: 242,000 were in Cleveland, a million and a half in the state. Every industrial locality was the scene of pitched battles. In the early years, these centered around relief stations and the homes of workers whom the courts were evicting for failure to pay rent. In Cleveland, where the concentration of the Negro population was greatest, some of the sharpest clashes over relief and evictions took place in the Cedar-Central ghetto.

There was still no such thing as unemployment insurance or even state or federal relief in the first days. The kind of relief occasionally available was humiliating. Some cities and counties handed out baskets to a few of the unemployed. Charity organizations, churches and *ad hoc* committees gave handouts. It is difficult today to comprehend conditions in the great depression. Starvation was widespread; wages were slashed 10, 20 and 30 per cent; evictions and foreclosures were commonplace in every street.

The limited forces of the Communists were active everywhere. Unemployed councils grew rapidly out of mass action in front of relief stations. Neighbors, in real solidarity, either prevented bailiffs from carrying out evictions or they put furniture back after an eviction and then mounted guard to protect the families. The police were ruthless at first. In Cleveland five comrades were killed in local battles — Rayford, Jackson, Oliary, Williams and Arentzi. One of these was a young Negro woman. Thousands joined the funeral marches.

With the establishment of the Civil Works Administration
and the Public Works Administration, struggles still continued
around wages and conditions on federal and state projects. Such
jobs were always very insecure, subject to the whims of congress
and state legislatures. Since the appropriations came from
federal and, after 1936, from the Ohio state government, the
protests, hunger marches, delegations, and sit-ins, usually took
place at the state capital in Columbus, or in Washington.

Up to 1935 the Ohio legislature had not appropriated a red
cent for relief. When, in 1936, all relief was turned over to the
state, the anti-New Deal Governor Martin L. Davey, and his big
business cronies said relief standards were too extravagant. The
governor introduced new legislation and threatened to bring
back soup kitchens and call out the National Guard to maintain
law and order.

The highest relief rate was in Cleveland. A family of four
got a food order equivalent to $13.60 for 15 days, or 22½ cents a
day per person. No other town came anywhere near that figure.
In answer to Governor Davey's action, Marc Grossman, director
of relief in Cleveland, resigned, declaring, "hunger will stalk
the streets of Cleveland," and "the framers of this relief bill
[which wiped half the unemployed off the relief rolls and put
the balance on an even more restricted relief rate] may well have
looked to the Hitler blood purge for their inspiration."

The Unemployed Councils were active everywhere. A rival organization initiated by the Socialists, called the Ohio Unemployed Leagues, started out with the announcement that they
would conduct themselves in a restrained and "gentlemanly"
manner, not employing the "Communist" methods of mass action engaged in by the Unemployed Councils. There was also a
third organization, the Workers Alliance, that gradually replaced the leagues in Ohio.

Our policy, both on a state and national level, was to bring
about the unity of all the unemployed. In 1936 unity was established. While the name of the new organization was the
Workers Alliance, the program and methods of mass struggle
embodied the time-tested experience of the Unemployed Councils.

The fight for unemployment and social insurance led by the
AFL Committee for Unemployment Insurance, whose secretary
was Louis Weinstock, won the support of 38 AFL local unions

in Ohio. This was only a small part of its nationwide support by 3,000 local unions, 35 central labor councils, six state federations and five international unions.

As a result of this tremendous campaign, the Roosevelt Administration in 1935 finally introduced and Congress adopted its own version of a social security measure. It covered old-age pensions and unemployment primarily, to be paid for by an equal tax on employee and employer. The rate and duration of payment were to be determined by each state. Not all wage-earners were covered in 1935. While far from ideal, it was a big step forward in establishing a radically different approach. The state was beginning to recognize its responsibility to the alleviation of national economic distress.

The Ohio Workers Alliance carried on in the good tradition of the Unemployed Councils. Statewide hunger marches were organized in 1936 and 1937, with thousands participating. Their lines of march all led to the Ohio state legislature, which was surrounded by state troopers and police. Later, in 1937, they staged a sit-down in Governor Davey's office. The CIO state convention adopted a resolution to join hands with the Workers Alliance in the fight for the demands of the unemployed.

A by-product of the big economic crisis was foreclosure. There were, in the nation, 10.5 million houses — with a debt totaling $21.5 billion. More than half of these were owned by the better-off workers whose skills had enabled them to hold more or less permanent jobs up to now. These, along with a certain number of professional people, were considered the conservative, stable section of the wage and salaried community. Nevertheless, when a wave of foreclosures and subsequent evictions swept over them, consternation and bitterness replaced the usual acceptance of government authority.

The party was quick to react. With the help of a number of Communists and left-wingers who were among the victims, the Small Home and Landowners Federation was established in late 1932. Between 1932 and 1934, it led innumerable struggles and by 1933 it had over 20,000 members. Previously such mass organizations had limited their activities to lobbying and legislative work. Stronger measures were now required. Under the leadership of a splendid comrade, E.C. Greenfield, the residents of an entire street joined together to prevent, forcibly if need be, the evictions of families from homes where mortgages had been foreclosed. People who only a few months before had been decrying the "rowdiness" and "violence" of the unemployed in fighting evictions and demonstrating for relief, were themselves fighting like tigers to hold on to their homes. The usually mild-mannered, well-dressed "backbone" of the community fought police and sheriff's deputies and built barricades. Out of these struggles, the party acquired new friends and members.

Several major struggles — some on the West Side, the St. Clair area and the Buckeye Road district — got city-wide attention. The climax came when a family named Sparonga, on Lardett Avenue, had its mortgage foreclosed and was ordered evicted. Three times the neighbors were mobilized by the Small Homeowners to put back the furniture. The courts decided this defiance of law and order had to be stopped.

Aided by the largest concentration of police ever seen, the sheriff again evicted the family. The police fought the neighbors with tear gas. Greenfield, on behalf of the Small Homeowners Federation, despite his arrest, issued a call for that evening, and by eight o'clock 20,000 homeowners were in the street. They overwhelmed the police and reinstalled the furniture and the family.

The next day Judge Powell ruled that all foreclosures would be set aside. Shortly thereafter, the Roosevelt government passed the Home Owners Loan Act. A local office was opened in Cleveland. The Small Home Owners Federation then started a fight to reduce mortgages to the amount of Home Loan bonds granted under the federal law. Of the 33,000 home loans granted in Cleveland, 13,000 went to members of the federation.

Two years later, the Home Loan Act expired and was not renewed. There were more foreclosures in Cleveland during the first three months of 1936 than during all of 1935. Some 8,000 families were threatened. With the persistence of unemployment, 20 per cent of those who had received home loans were unable to start paying back the loans. A new round of struggle developed, but it never reached the level of 1932 and 1933.

When the economic crisis eased off and some reemployment in industry began, the workers did not easily forget the lessons learned in the course of their militant struggles. The Roosevelt government, in a desperate effort to save capitalism, adopted significant reforms and made concessions to trade unions, enabling them to organize, and limiting the use of injunctions.

The employers countered with company unions, but this was not effective against the great unionizing drive that swept through the mass-production industries like a tempestuous river breaking down century-long barriers. Ohio was literally a cauldron of industrial sturggle from 1934 to 1939.

The Trade Union Unity League unions merged with the old unions. Even company unions were often turned into temporary instruments of struggle against the employers. The top reactionary AFL leaders were interested solely in organizing the skilled craftsmen. But under pressure of the workers from outside its own ranks, and a developing movement within the organization, the leadership decided to grant charters for federal locals to workers in auto, rubber and other industries. These federal locals covered the workers in factories who were not considered eligible for the elite craft unions, and who had no international union with authority to govern their affairs.

This initial organizing momentum in Ohio was accompanied by strikes in Electric Auto-Lite, Fisher Body, Goodyear, Berger Steel and others, all of which prepared the way for the establishment of the great CIO unions, for the history-making sit-down strikes in auto and rubber and for the "Little Steel" strike that swept Ohio.

The most successful response in auto, which pioneered the penetration of the basic industries, was in Ohio, Wisconsin and Indiana, actually secondary centers compared with Michigan. The first federal local was established at White Motor in Cleveland, with Wyndham Mortimer at its head. Mortimer was a Communist whom I had convinced to permit his name to be proposed for our state committee after I arrived in Ohio.

In December 1933 the White Motor workers voted 1,087 to 78 to strike, but William Green wired: "Under no circumstances permit a strike until public officials have an opportunity to adjust the controversy."

Despite this kind of sabotage by Green, workers in Ohio continued to organize in factory after factory, without a single full-time organizer. Coordination of the federal locals in the same industry was imperative to achieve unity of action. But Green forbade it. The White Motor local, led by Mortimer, ignored Green and called a conference of all locals in the Cleveland area and established an auto council. Later, this council, on the stationery of the Fisher Body local, convened its first provisional national conference, with 22 locals in attendance.

In contrast, the AFL which sent national organizer Francis Dillon into Michigan with a staff of full-timers, had not established a single local up to that time. The activity in Cleveland, condemned by Green as Communist-inspired, forced Green and his lieutenants to resign from the government Auto Labor Board, to promise a real national drive and to set a date for a national conference of federal locals in auto. At the same time, Green threatened to expel all the Cleveland locals for their militant (and effective) activity. But Mortimer, in his quiet and persistent way, night after night, and weekend after weekend, went on enrolling auto workers in the union.

In June 1934 the first national conference of the AFL federal locals in auto took place. There was a confrontation between Green and Dillon on the platform and the delegates from the factories, among whom Mortimer, Bob Travis and John Anderson—all Communists—were in the front ranks. Green and Dillon threw cold water on all proposals for militant action and opposed the establishment of a national auto union.

But 14 months later the first constitutional convention was convened and there the delegates, by a vote of 164 to 112, rejected Green's recommendation that Dillon be appointed provisional president. Despite the vote, Green appointed not only Dillon but all the other officers and the entire provisional executive board.

We had to combat the workers' demand to "send the AFL to hell" and convince them to stand united and have patience. Under the leadership of the Cleveland and Toledo locals, the fight was carried by a committee of seven, led by Mortimer and George Addes of Toledo, to the AFL Convention in Atlantic City.

The convention rejected the protest and sustained the arbitrary appointment of provisional officers by Green. However, the fight of the auto workers, plus the pressure for industrial unionism inside the AFL by the miners and clothing workers, eventually resulted in the issuance of a charter for an international union of auto workers. Industrial unionism was on its way.*

*The Committee for Industrial Organization was formed in November 1935, after the AFL annual convention of that year defeated a resolution calling for industrial unions in the mass-production industries. It was composed of eight international unions—all industrial or semi-

The Left, including the Communists, had to combat the workers' disgust with the AFL under Green's guidance. Attention was focused on the first constitutional convention in South Bend, in 1936. At that convention Dillon was again defeated. But employers and the reactionary labor leaders had not put all their eggs in one basket. A "bright young preacher" called Homer Martin had recently come upon the scene. Homer Martin had a church in the suburbs of Kansas City, where a General Motors plant was also located. He supported Roosevelt as well as the auto workers. When he lost his pulpit, he soon got a job in the General Motors factory. After being fired for union activity, he was hired to do union organizing. His great oratorical gifts made a big impression on workers—especially those from the fundamentalist South. Averse to the tedium of detail and lacking the patience needed for negotiating, Martin made his mark with his flamboyant speeches, and had come to South Bend with the ambition of rising to higher leadership.

Those members who had been struggling for the preceding three years, especially the Ohio delegates, were all for Mortimer for president. But South Bend and some other areas argued that while Mortimer was the most able, his membership in the Communist Party would be used to smear their new union.

Mortimer and other party members among the delegates asked my advice and that of the Michigan district organizer, Will Weinstone. We were both interested visitors at the convention. We told them they must make their own decision, in consultation with their colleagues, but that it was essential to start off united against the continuing opposition of the reactionary AFL leadership. The delegates finally elected Martin president and Mortimer vice-president.

Walter Reuther, at the South Bend convention praised the Soviet Union to the skies and did not hesitate to meet with the

industrial in structure. Led by John L. Lewis, the miners' unions were the most influential. The aim of the new committee was the unionization of the millions of unorganized workers in basic mass production. In August 1936 the AFL executive council suspended 10 unions for "dual unionism and insurrection," because they had not withdrawn from the CIO. During all this time, and thereafter, the CIO was active in organizing and leading struggles in the auto, rubber, steel and other industries. These unions were united in 1938, when a new federation, called the Congress of Industrial Organizations (CIO), was established.

Communists. It was we, in fact, who took the initiative in nominating him as one of the two executive board members from Michigan, even though the union had few members there.

The South Bend convention was a major turning point in auto union development, but many turbulent years were ahead. After it had been established as the United Auto Workers of America and had become the second largest union in the CIO, the union faced another great crisis when Homer Martin was exposed and expelled as an agent of the Ford Motor Co. at the April 1939 Cleveland Convention.

With Martin discredited, at least three quarters of the delegates favored Mortimer for president. Philip Murray and Sidney Hillman, representing the CIO leadership, while entering a loose alliance with the Left, nevertheless came out against Mortimer solely because he was a Communist. They proposed R.J. Thomas instead, a weak and generally incompetent person. In my opinion, the left-progressive majority made a mistake in capitulating to the pressure of Murray and Hillman. Thomas soon faded into a minor labor role, as the ambitious Walter Reuther, trimming his sails to reaction, rose to the presidency.

One of the early strikes that stirred the industry took place at the Electric Auto-Lite Co. in Toledo. This helped lay the foundation for the union, while it contributed to the general advancement of class consciousness and militancy among the auto workers. It was generally recognized that the Communists and the Unemployed Councils played a big role in winning this strike. As the party district secretary in Ohio, I remained on the scene throughout.

The Auto-Lite workers went on strike early in 1934. The company promised, if they returned to work, that it would sign a contract with the federal local in April. When April 1 came, the company refused to deal with the union and ordered its committeemen out of the office.

The strike was on. We had only three or four party members in the plant and these were older, foreign-born workers. Nevertheless, we immediately issued a leaflet pledging support. We then influenced the local Unemployed Council to call on the unemployed to help man the picket line. This example of solidarity gave encouragement to the strikers. The company then got Judge Stuart to issue an injunction restricting the pickets to 25 at each gate.

We Communists issued the slogan, "Smash the Injunction by Mass Picketing." We printed and distributed 125,000 leaflets. We marched on the picket lines with the strikers, sold the *Daily Worker*, held open-air and hall meetings and, above all, mobilized all our members and friends in other unions and in the Central Labor Council to give the strikers support.

In those early days of trade unionism, when an organization was being built anyone with experience was welcomed. Our women worked with the strikers to organize a soup kitchen. Bob Travis, a left-winger in the Chevrolet factory, was very helpful in working with the Auto-Lite strikers. He later joined the Communist Party and became a national auto union leader along with Mortimer.

Seeing the growing strength of the strikers, despite the company's success in getting a few hundred scabs into the plant, the thugs who had been deputized by the sheriff carried through a deliberate provocation. Bolts were thrown from the roof of the plant, and a girl picket was struck. A deputy slugged an elderly member of the Unemployed Council. This triggered the pent-up feelings of the strikers and their supporters. Thousands of workers counterattacked. Tear-gas bombs were freely used, but the crowd, including many who were only spectators, fought back.

In the midst of the battle the local police withdrew, since there was no love between them and the sheriff's deputies. This compelled the deputies to retreat into the plant. All through the night the battle continued, with the sheriff's men bombarding the augmented crowd of 10,000 with tear-gas and then vomiting-gas bombs.

Many were injured. In the morning, by direction of Governor White, the National Guard arrived on the scene. All day the battle continued. Two strikers were shot and killed and many were injured. Finally martial law was declared.

We then raised two slogans: "You Can't Make Auto Parts With Soldiers," and "A General Strike to Support Auto-Lite Workers."

Within a couple of days emergency meetings of union locals resulted in 53 AFL locals voting for a general strike. The company then agreed to negotiate. A five per cent wage increase was granted, together with recognition of the union. The battle of Chestnut Hill had not been in vain.

Communist prestige was high although, unfortunately, our membership among the Auto-Lite workers was negligible. The strike shook the entire community and laid the foundation for 100 per cent trade unionism and labor's active participation in political action, so far as Toledo was concerned.

After the CIO was established and the United Auto Workers affiliated with it, the workers of Michigan began to regain confidence. In 1935, 20,000 of them had joined the AFL federal locals but most had burned their cards in a huge bonfire because the AFL leaders capitulated to the auto corporations who, defying even President Roosevelt, refused to recognize the union.

The union decided to concentrate on General Motors, the heart of whose empire was Flint, with 40,000 workers. But only 100 were union members, and it was later learned that some of these were stool pigeons. Mortimer and Travis were chosen for this organizing task. Work was also progressing in other General Motors plants, especially in Cleveland and Toledo.

The early work had to be done secretly; one by one, members in each key department were won for the union. Mortimer's 40 years as a worker in the coal mines and auto factories, as well as his Communist understanding and integrity, were decisive in this situation. At an early stage, he brought the wives of the union men into the picture. Once he had a group in the factory, he built up a huge mailing list of all their fellow-workers. He then sent out a weekly letter which went to 7,000 workers at General Motors in Flint.

This work continued for six months. Conditions in the plants kept getting worse, with speedup as the major grievance. Spontaneous strikes began to break out. The plan was to strike the entire General Motors empire. The strategy was based on the fact that the basic responsibility lay with two plants—Fisher No. One in Flint and Fisher Body in Cleveland. These were the major body-building plants of the corporation. Cleveland accounted for the stampings for Chevrolets and for half the new turret-top bodies for all General Motors models.

This was a great responsibility for us in Cleveland. The workers in Fisher Body had taken the lead in both the 1934 and 1935 battles and 2,000 had been laid off. As we prepared, the union had only 300 members out of 4,500 workers. The local union president, Louis Spisak, was a weak character.

On December 28, 1936, a surprise sit-down strike started in one department and quickly spread to the entire Cleveland plant. The season had started, with the company making wage-cuts in the form of piecework adjustments. This provoked innumerable stoppages. A conference was arranged between management and the union committee for the morning of the 28th. At the last moment, the company again postponed the meeting. Feelings were so aroused and conditions so bad that they sparked the sit-down. Within two hours the general manager was in conference with Spisak and the latter agreed to evacuate the plant, resume work and open negotiations. But the other union leaders in the plant, among whom were several Communists, refused. They got in touch with Mortimer, who rushed to Cleveland from Flint. Our comrades also got in touch with me.

The workers had settled the difficult question as to whether Cleveland Fisher Body or Flint No. One would start the strike. Two days later the entire Flint General Motors empire came to a halt with the biggest sit-down strike in history.*

During the following stormy 44 days, Flint and its 40,000 workers were in the national limelight. The strike spread nationally to nearly all the 60 plants. But it was in Flint and Cleveland—about 20 plants in all, with the sit-down strike keeping them closed as tight as a drum—that the crucial battle was fought. The company used every known weapon to crack the strike—the AFL national leaders, National Guard, court injunctions, company unions, sowing dissension among the women—but all to no avail, despite some critical moments.

In Cleveland, Fisher Body was still our battlefront. Because of its pivotal character in General Motors national production, it had to be kept closed. The strike had to be organized and consolidated. Arrangements for food were imperative. While the sit-in went on, an intricate system had to be established which allowed men, on a rotation basis, to go home occasionally and still come back. A sit-in strike demanded strict discipline and organization inside the plant, including reading, games, music and classes. No liquor was permitted, and women workers

*For a detailed and authentic account of how the auto workers organized, see *The Many and the Few*, by Henry Kraus, Los Angeles, 1947. Kraus was a close associate of Wyndham Mortimer and a firsthand observer of the formation of the union.

were asked to fulfill strike duties outside the plant. In the midst
of all this, the union had to deal with every rumor and efforts
to create confusion or division, and, above all, had to sign up
virtually all the workers into the union.

There were only 300 members in local 45 (Fisher Body) when
the strike started, and few of them had any previous experience,
but these workers were ready to accept all help. We had at the
start a party shop branch of some 12 to 15 members, some of
whom were in the leadership of the local. We had been issuing a
Communist shop paper, *Spark Plug*, for years and many workers
remembered the truth of many things we had said.

Our comrades introduced me to some of the most active
non-party leaders. I remember Paul Miley, Charlie Beckman,
Bernie De Vito and others. They were so anxious to learn how
to organize things, as well as to receive ideas on how to make the
strike more effective, that it was arranged for me to meet with
the majority of the strike committee every morning. They would
come out of the factory (we thought it would be stretching things
too far for me to meet them inside the plant) and we would
get together nearby.

These daily meetings were a great school, where basic
class concepts were taught and strike strategy and tactics dealt
with, but always with the living problems of 5,000 striking workers in the foreground. Some of these workers later joined our
party, and some of those who did not have continued to this day
to play an important left-progressive role in the United Auto
Workers.

In addition to these meetings, the party branch held sessions
every other evening. Special issues of *Spark Plug* were issued.
The *Daily Worker* was sold inside and outside the factory. Support was won in other areas of the labor movement. The wives
of the workers were organized. Kitchens were established and
the strikers set up their own police force.

While this was going on, the UAW convened a nationwide
General Motors conference in Flint, immediately after the sit-
down strike was solid there. Seven of the locals represented
were already on strike. The problem was to spread the strike
and adopt demands for negotiating with the company.

The eight demands adopted were: a national conference between the UAW and General Motors; abolition of all piecework
systems of pay; six-hour day and thirty-hour week; time and a

half for overtime; minimum wage "commensurate with an American standard of living"; reinstatement of all employees "unjustly discharged"; straight seniority; speed of production to be mutually determined by each plant management and shop committee; and recognition of the UAW as sole bargaining agent for General Motors employees.

General Motors, in addition to injunctions and issuing back-to-work propaganda, organized "The Flint Alliance — for the Security of Our Jobs, Our Homes and Our Community." The company addressed all its workers, saying the "real issue" was "whether you have to have a union card to hold a job." They then declared they would not "recognize any union as the sole bargaining agency for its workers" and that employment at General Motors would continue to depend "on the ability and efficiency of the workers."

After 19 stormy days, the company agreed, under pressure, to meet the union representatives. On one side of the table sat Martin, Mortimer and John Brophy, for the United Auto Workers and CIO; on the other, William S. Knudson of General Motors, accompanied by two Wall Street directors, John Thomas Smith and Donaldson Brown. General Motors tried to double-cross the union on the truce which had been agreed upon. Twenty-five days later, negotiations started again after one of the most heroic struggles in American labor history. That week's production charts showed 28,825 units for Ford, 25,350 units for Chrysler and 1,500 units for General Motors.

While Martin was no longer there (having been sent deliberately on a speaking tour), Mortimer was still the UAW representative, together with John L. Lewis and Lee Pressman of the CIO. Lewis had had a taste of Martin's incompetence at the bargaining table and wanted no part of him.

Finally the great General Motors Corporation capitulated. It recognized the UAW as the sole bargaining agent of the workers; agreed to end discrimination against the strikers and to the dismissal of all injunctions and other pending legal actions; and conceded a five per cent wage increase. All other questions, in particular speedup and the rights of union shop stewards, were referred to negotiations that were to start at once.

Mortimer and other union leaders had to convince the sit-down strikers that the agreement should be accepted. The words of one of these sit-in strikers expressed the thinking of all when he said, before the unanimous vote of approval, "What's the use of kidding ourselves? All that piece of paper means is that we got a union. The rest depends on us. For God's sake, let's go back to work and keep up what we started here!"

And that is what they did, eventually building their union to 1.3 million members. In Cleveland the 300 union members in Fisher Body grew to a local union of 5,000. And the 15 Communists grew to a shop branch of 60. Now, many years later, I still receive letters from a member of the executive board of Local 45, recalling and praising the role of the party in that strike and the struggles that followed.

9

Akron Becomes a Union Town

Even before the Fisher Body sit-down strike, the party in Ohio had the rich experience of the sit-down strikes of the Akron rubber workers.

Akron lay 35 miles south of Cleveland, an easy one-hour ride even in our old jalopy. It was the tire center of America. There the Big Three — Goodyear, Goodrich, Firestone — and a number of smaller companies like General, Sieberling and Mohawk were all located. A typical one-industry town, everything was dominated by rubber.

As you entered the town, you smelled rubber. In contrast to the steel centers where the foreign-born or the first American-born generation dominated, Akron was an all-American town. Sixty-five per cent of its workers came from the towns nestling in the southern mountains, especially from West Virginia. Of its 255,000 population (plus another 89,000 in Greater Akron), only 31,000 were foreign-born.

Akron was also a young city. Seventy-five per cent of its people were under 40 years of age. The tire-building pits need strong, muscular men. The tire-builders were already on a six-hour day because the work was so arduous.

The workers had tried, especially in 1923 and 1926, to organize themselves into trade unions, but the company always succeeded in smashing the effort before it gained any real success. Goodyear, on the initiative of its president, Paul Litchfield, established an elaborate paternalistic company union in 1919, called the Industrial Assembly. It was provided with a theater, gymnasium, clubrooms and even a so-called university. A hospital plan was available as well as cheap vacations. The company talked a lot of nonsense about "allowing their workers a genuine voice in management." This undoubtedly held down the workers' militancy for a number of years, but the company plan was blown sky-high in 1936.

Firestone and Goodrich had never followed this Goodyear pattern which they scoffed at. But in 1933, when the rubber workers were on the move toward trade union organization, these companies quickly set up company unions. They tried to buy off a group by paying the "delegates" $15 per month, the "committee chairman" $20, and the "general chairmen" $30.

This did not deter the workers. Faced with mass unemployment, starvation and bank failures, the rubber workers had reached a point of desperation. Wages had gradually been slashed. The final straw was the never-ending speedup. In tire-building this expressed itself in what was called the "poundage output."

Using an index figure of 100 for 1914, the weight output per man rose as follows: 1922—250.56; 1929—506.25; 1930—581.03; 1931—681.05.

I know of no other industry where so many workers suffer from kidney and back trouble—a direct consequence of the heavy work and the speedup. From 1921 to 1931 there was an increase of over 21 million tires produced per year, with 7,155 fewer workers.

Between 1933 and 1935, the Akron rubber workers had one disillusioning experience after another. They had flocked solidly into the AFL when Roosevelt announced the right of every worker to join a union. They struck, they fought the police, they demanded action. As a result of a double betrayal by the labor leaders who had raised their hopes with promises and speeches, the majority tore up their union cards.

Almost alone, the Communists fought on to restore confidence. Even our people were downcast by the number of defeats. About 15 comrades, mostly Southerners, met with section organizer Jim Keller and myself.

Together we decided to combat the understandable desire of the men to say "to hell with the betrayers." We had to go back into the shops and locals and fight to maintain every local union.

The immediate demand, we agreed, must be that the AFL grant a charter for an industrial union of rubber workers (as opposed to the federal locals) to be run by the workers themselves. We resolved to organize as broad a force of men as possible committed to these ideas.

The company took advantage of the demoralized situation to worsen conditions. Layoffs increased. The men were enraged at the companies, but the great majority (the union membership had declined from 40,000 to less than 4,000) still wouldn't hear of the AFL. It was uphill work trying to build the union; repeated local union resolutions were calling for a separate rubber workers' union. Finally, Green announced the date for a founding convention. It was said that Green would come to Akron to supervise the convention personally, and that the new rubber union would have the "firm hand of the AFL in control during its formative period." Green himself declared, "I may name officers for a period, until the union is placed on an enduring basis."

September 13, 1935, was the historic day. The rubber workers elected their delegates, and despite all the tricks that Green had learned over his long years, he could neither intimidate, soft-soap nor cajole them. As the convention opened, he was handed a petition, signed by 40 of the 47 delegates present, urging him to follow democratic procedure.

Green handed them a charter. Instantly the convention turned into bedlam, for it excluded jurisdiction over all skilled trades. Green adjourned the convention arbitrarily in the midst of the uproar. Next day, with more delegates in attendance, and despite hours of maneuvering combined with threats and flowery language, the convention, by a vote of 46 to 9, defeated the proposal that Green appoint Coleman Claherty, an AFL national organizer and machine man, as provisional president.

Red-faced and furious at these "hillbillies," whom he found difficult to call Bolsheviks, Green lashed out at them for "refusing to request him to establish and finance their new International," and then he walked out. The delegates elected their own officers and executive board, all from the factories.

They now had a union of their own but without finances. They still needed to win the rubber workers back. The developments the next month at the AFL convention — remembered for a fist fight between John L. Lewis and Bill Hutchison of the Carpenters Union over the seating of the delegates from the new rubber union — created great interest among the rubber workers. Despite Lewis' past of arbitrary dictation to the miners, here was a changed leader fighting for industrial unionism. (Many of the rubber workers came from mining areas where solidarity and unionism were throughly instilled.) From this convention there emerged the embryo of the later CIO, with which the rubber union soon affiliated.

The first real sit-down strike in America started in the Firestone plant in January 1936. The men opposed a cut of 11 per cent in the base rate of the truck-tire department, and the company had fired the union committeemen. Wanting to strike but fearful of losing their jobs, they recalled the story of a foreign-born union printer. They sent a committee to hear again his experience years ago in Sarajevo, Serbia, when the printers wanted to strike, but knew the boss had a crew of scabs waiting to take their place. Said the printer, Alex Eigenmacht, "So we had an inside strike. We just sat around by our machines and, by God, nobody could come in and take our jobs and they couldn't arrest us either. We were on the job."

The committee asked, "Didn't the boss try to throw you out?" Alex replied, "He couldn't. He was afraid of hurting his expensive machinery if there was any fighting inside."

That night the Akron rubber workers did what no one in the United States had ever done before, they initiated a sit-down strike. All hell broke loose when the bosses finally comprehended what was happening. The sit-down strike in the truck-tire department spread to other departments. Men began to sign up again in the union by hundreds. The superintendent ordered them out of the factory but they refused. After 24 hours, all of Plant One was down. The company then offered to negotiate if the men would evacuate the factory, but the workers refused. As predicted, management hesitated to bring in security officers or police for fear of damage to the machinery.

Inside, the union committee, among whom were members of our party factory branch, occupied the foreman's office and issued union cards. After 53 hours, the union members in Plant Two said if there was not an immediate settlement they, too, were going on a sit-down strike.

Firestone quickly settled. They reinstated the committeemen, agreed to pay the striking workers three hours pay for each day lost, and to open up negotiations on a new base rate.

When the negotiating committee reported back, all were jubilant, saying over and over, "We are getting paid, mind you, for sitting down!" They marched out singing "Glory Hallelujah."

The union was back in business. Everything the Communists had said by word of mouth, in leaflets and at meetings, was proving to be correct.

Within a month the critical showdown came. The largest of the Big Three, Goodyear, which had just reintroduced the eight-hour day in the entire plant except for the tire-building pits, became still bolder and announced a wage cut of 10 per cent.

At three A.M., February 14, 1936, the tire-builders in Goodyear Plant Two shut off the power and started a sit-down strike in protest against the layoff of 70 men, which they interpreted as the preparation for the introduction of the eight-hour day in their department also. This was the start of one of the greatest class battles in America's history, and the first major test of industrial organization as advocated by the CIO.

After rejecting a company ultimatum to go back to work, the sit-downers were fired. But they still were in the plant. The next day the local union leaders, guided by John House, the president, took the sit-downers out of the plant. The company had agreed to cancel the dismissals. But the men refused to return, because no provision was made to rehire the 70 men who had been laid off originally.

The entire factory was astir. The local union leaders, especially House, were not only inexperienced but afraid of responsibility. Thousands of men, union and non-union, were flocking into the big union hall. The Communist Party issued mimeographed leaflets calling for union action against the eight-hour day, wage-cuts and speedup and distributed them widely.

In this charged atmosphere, Goodyear issued, as it had always done in the middle of February, its annual financial statement. This showed that the net profits for 1935 were five and a half million dollars, compared to four and a half million in 1934. The men were stung into action. That night, what was supposed to be a meeting of the 137 tire-builders who had been on a sit-down strike quickly grew to 1,500, with hundreds more unable to gain entrance. The demand for a strike now grew to a great crescendo, and the decision was unanimously reached to start that night. From the meeting they went out on a picket line to tell the night-shift men. And the strike of 14,000 men was on.

Each of the next 32 days was action-packed. In the coldest winter in years, these workers, most of whom had never been on strike before, marched in snow on the picket lines that extended for 18 miles surrounding the Goodyear plant. By the third day all three plants were closed down.

Then the battle started. Courts issued injunctions, police and sheriff's deputies battled the strikers on the picket line, the company demanded the aid of the National Guard and refused to meet the union, and a terrific newspaper and radio barrage was launched against the strikers.

In this situation, our party put all our experience at the disposal of the 14,000 strikers and the newly established trade union. We met with our own party members and all other key forces in the strike apparatus and conferred with the local leaders of the Rubber Union, including some members of the international executive board. We had regular meetings with Wilmer Tate, the left-wing president of the Central Labor Union.

I moved into Akron from Cleveland and, together with Jim Keller, lived through every minute of the strike. The first step was to get a program of demands adopted by the strikers. After the first 12 hours of picket duty, we met with the half-dozen party members who were most influential in the strike.

We worked out a leaflet which dealt with what was happening in the plants — the eight-hour day, the speedup, wage-cuts — and the swollen company profits. We brought to the foreground the question of unity and the possibility of the workers' responding with a general strike if violence and terror were used against the strikers. We called for total union organization and for union endorsement of the strike and then projected the following demands: The six-hour day; no layoffs; no wage-cuts; a wage increase of 10 per cent over the base rate; the end of speedup, and a signed agreement. This leaflet was on the picket lines and in the Goodrich, Firestone and General factories by five o'clock that day.

House was still saying the strike was not union-endorsed and "just happened" and that the only issue was the reinstatement of the 70 discharged tire-builders. That night all the picket captains unanimously endorsed and adopted as their own all the demands in the party leaflet.

At the party meeting we had concluded that the key force in the strike were the picket captains. The chief picket captain was a party leader. These picket captains were the nerve center. They knew all the trends, reactions, fears and rumors. And, through them, action could be effectively organized at decisive moments.

The picket captains met on the second day, and again fulfilling the role of the absent leaders of the local's executive committee, decided that the work stoppage must be turned into a legal strike, and that all strikers must be signed up in the union and given voting rights. Negotiations were to be opened with the company on the five demands. Picket lines were to be held solid, irrespective of injunctions, police or National Guard, and efforts were to be made to win public opinion to the strikers.

Goodyear said it would never negotiate. Tension rose as the company appealed for court injunctions and armed intervention. The Central Labor Union voted full support and promised "to take all measures within our power to defeat" any injunctions. President Sherman Dalrymple of the International Rubber Union threatened "industrial paralysis affecting the entire city" if injunctions were issued. But the full court of six judges issued a sweeping injunction prohibiting mass picketing. Fortunately the police chief and the sheriff disagreed on shooting their way into the picket line. The company was still able to rally 2,500 workers against the strike, and these men were used in every way. The strikers christened them "Red Apples," and that term became a permanent part of the rubber worker's vocabulary to describe company-minded men.

At this point John L. Lewis and the CIO moved in. The steps they advised—making the strike official and signing up everybody into the union—were carried out.

As the strike seesawed back and forth, a dangerous point was reached around the 14th day. The federal government sent in their so-called ace arbitrator, Edward McGrady. He was now an assistant secretary of labor but had previously been an AFL organizer, which didn't endear him to the rubber workers. His technique was to promise the world to the strikers, if they would just return to work and allow negotiations to take place. At one point, even some of the CIO people wavered on this issue. McGrady's proposals had become a delicate matter because the company had at first rejected them, and the union leadership thought they would win public opinion if they accepted.

Again the picket captains were the decisive force. They made it clear to the leaders of the new union and the CIO officials that the strike would remain solid and they flatly rejected McGrady's scheme. At a strikers' meeting in the Armory, addressed by Dalrymple, Powers Hapgood, John Owens and Rose Pesota, and chaired by John House, the men booed McGrady's name and, to the amazement of the CIO officials (who hastily beat a retreat on McGrady), sang "Let's hang McGrady to a sour-apple tree."

The thing that had turned the tide was the information the party had provided the picket captains and the workers about McGrady's sellouts at Industrial Rayon Co. in Cleveland and in Toledo.

On the 23rd day, the company finally realized it had to negotiate. After several days of talks between the company and union leaders, Goodyear declared that its final proposals for a settlement were as follows: (1) All employees of the Goodyear Tire and Rubber Company, as of February 12, 1936, shall return to work without discrimination or interruption of service record; (2) management of the company will meet with any and all employees individually or through their chosen representatives; (3) notice will be given to representatives of the employees affected of changes in wage rates before they are posted; (4) in the tire division, the company has adopted the 36-hour week, six-hour shifts. Any change in these hours per week or per day below 30 hours or above 36 hours a week will be by arrangement with the employees in the departments or divisions affected; (5) lists of contemplated layoffs will be made in duplicate by the department foreman, one copy will be retained by the fore-

man and the other copy will be kept in the office of the labor
department; both lists will be available for inspection.

These proposals were accompanied by a big barrage from the
newspapers, the radio, ministers and civic officials who insisted
that now was the time to settle. And four weeks of strike had
had a negative impact on some of the less active strikers and
their families.

The party leaders then met with all our comrades who were
active in the strike. At the beginning there were sharp disagree-
ments on what to do about the company proposals. After long
discussions and much talk by Jim Keller, myself and Bill Ricketts, the head of the picket captains, it was decided that we could
not advise an out-of-hand rejection of the company proposals,
unsatisfactory as they were. We must prevent public opinion
from being turned against the strikers.

Bill Ricketts said, "Instead of just voting 'no' to Litchfield's
offer, why, we accept some of the points, the harmless ones, and
the others we reject. Then we adopt a resolution saying the committee should go back to the Goodyear Co. and talk it over some
more. That way the newspapers will say in their headlines.
'Union Wants More Parleys,' or something like that. Akron will
see that sounds sensible, and the union won't be blamed for
prolonging the strike."

It was decided that we would propose that the union accept
the second and the third points. The company had already
given the union a signed memorandum that they recognized
the right of union committees as well as the International Union
president to negotiate on questions of hours and wages as ap-
plying to the second point. On the first point, it was decided to
add a clause that the men return within seven days. On the
fourth, the amendment called for the six-hour day to apply to
all workers. It was stipulated that the fifth point state specifically
that one of the triplicate copies goes to the union.

The picket captains endorsed these proposals. Then came the
local union meeting, with 4,000 inside and at least another
thousand crowding around outside. Our inside information
was that the CIO and the rubber union leaders were divided
among themselves on what to do. They had finally decided
not to speak, but to leave things in the hands of the strikers.

As they waited for the negotiating committee to arrive and
report, the workers from the Southland sang hymns, patriotic

and popular songs. Finally, the committee arrived and reported on what the company said was their final offer. Silence greeted the report, till Bill Ricketts got the floor and submitted a resolution indicating what was to be accepted and what amended. With great cheers, the meeting unanimously adopted Bill's motion.

The first newspaper headline was "Two Points of Peace Plan Accepted. Company Terms Partially Met." Later editions revealed the next moves of the enemy. The company broke off negotiations and declared the strikers had rejected their proposals in full. That night they organized a vigilante outfit called the "Akron Law and Order League." On its behalf, ex-Mayor Sparks went on the radio and called on all citizens "to gang up upon the out-of-town radical and Communists leaders," saying, "It is this handful . . . of labor agitators, radicals, Communists, red orators . . . [that] . . . came into Akron determined to make the rubber city 100 per cent union or to wreck the industry." Goodyear contributed $15,000 to the Law and Order League.

In the lynch atmosphere that was being created, it was decisive to maintain the unity of the strikers' ranks and the common front between ourselves and the CIO leaders. I made it my business to talk to Central Labor Union president Tate, CIO leaders John Ownes, Leo Krzyski and Rose Pesota and various leaders of the United Rubber Workers of America.

Tate went on the radio and answered Sparks. The union took the radio for nine continuous hours, with National Secretary-Treasurer Frank Grillo in command, all through one night, interspersing announcements, news, music, warnings and speeches. These countermeasurers subdued the company hoodlums. The next day the company resumed negotiations with the union.

While the new negotiations were going on, two of our leading comrades who were picket captains argued for letting all the picket captains see and hear an official spokesman of the Communist Party. With great modesty, these two comrades, who had carried the burden for five weeks, pointed out that without party leadership the strike would have been lost. It wasn't fair that the picket captains should get all the credit when actually the party leadership was in great measure responsible.

We finally decided that Jim Keller, our Akron organizer, would be the speaker, if the picket captains accepted Bill Ricketts' proposal to invite him. By a big majority, the invitation was extended. Keller spoke for about 20 minutes, congratulating them on their great victory. He said, "I have seen a lot of strikes, but I have never seen men who went on the picket line in the worst blizzard in the history of northern Ohio and stayed there for 32 days in cold and rain and against threats of violence until they won a great victory." At this point he was interrupted and one captain said, "I thought you guys was against the settlement. I got a leaflet here where you Reds call this a sellout."

Keller explained this was a leaflet issued by the Trotskyites and repudiated it in its entirety. But the question opened the door for an explanation of our party's attitude toward the agreement, which was to be voted on next day. Keller explained it clause by clause and how, with union organization, it could be built on.

He not only showed what it meant to rubber workers but added. "They're waiting in steel and in auto. When they hear you've won, they will be on the march." He concluded, "I hereby predict that if—and I know you will—if you fellows take the picket line back to the tire machines and the mill room, the Goodyear strike will be America's new declaration of freedom. Your strike, which you fought so bravely, was the first page of CIO history. It will not be the last. You are the new pioneers."

The next day the strikers voted for an amended agreement. They marched in a massive public parade throughout Akron, past the Goodrich and Firestone plants, into the center of town and past the Mayflower Hotel, where the rubber officials held their luncheons and banquets, and then past the more humble Portage Hotel, the scene of so many union conventions. Across the street from the Portage Hotel, in the Everett Building, was the party office flying a big banner outside the window congratulating the Goodyear workers on their victory.

With the strike won in Goodyear, the union took in thousands of new members. Within a year, and after another big strike at Firestone, 70,000 workers were in the rubber union. This was virtually complete organization. The great sweep in rubber resulted in expanded union crusades in Akron and in nearby Barberton. The workers of Babcock & Wilcox Boiler Co., the Columbia Chemical and the big Diamond Match Co. in Barberton all flocked into the unions, as did virtually every worker in Akron, including the girls in Woolworth's.

From organizing unions we went on to politics. In 1936 a local Farmer-Labor Party was formed, with a full slate of candidates, headed by Wilmer Tate. The slate was disqualified on technical grounds. By 1937, recognizing that Akron and Summit County could not go it alone and had to adjust themselves to the general picture, the Farmer-Labor Party became the broader and more powerful Labor's Non-Partisan League. It swept the county against the reactionary Liberty League candidate, Governor Martin L. Davey,* carried every ward for Roosevelt except one, and in the democratic primaries nominated its candidate for mayor and 10 out of 11 of its councilmanic candidates.

From Washington, William Green denounced the rubber workers. He instructed the central labor body to expel the rubber locals, but Wilmer Tate successfully defied Green three times. Finally, with the establishment of local CIO councils, Tate took the initiative by establishing a coordinating committee that functioned for years, with joint Labor Day parades and joint supporting activities for all strikes. The atmosphere was such that these rubber workers, once having experienced effective methods of class struggle, were inspired to move into other fields. Two thousand union members came to hear the story of the Republican Loyalists in the Spanish civil war; President Dalrymple was the main speaker at a "Save China: Boycott Japan" meeting; and the Communist Party held meetings with 500 to 750 people attending. The union established an excellent educational department to meet the demands of its members for classes, lectures and libraries.

These Southern workers, before their revolutionizing experiences in the great battles of those years, had been fair bait for every religious demagogue. Reared in the fundamentalist South, they had many of the prejudices of poor whites. While they brought into the trade unions certain forms that stemmed from their religious habits, such as opening meetings with prayers and interspersing hymns, they also changed the content, much as the Negro people have done throughout the years.

---

*Davey became the first Ohio governor unable to gain renomination by his own party.

When the employers brought in every variety of preacher, from Dr. Frank Buchman of Moral Re-Armament to the Rev. Gerald K. Smith of Louisiana, they all met with rejection by the rubber workers. The use of religion for the protection of profits was no longer a viable tool there.

From the beginning, it was no easy task to influence, indeed to be accepted by these Southern workers with their years of hostility to foreigners, Negroes, Jews and, above all, "Bolsheviks." But, by exercising patience and skill, we succeeded. While the major consideration was the advancement of correct policies and tactics, there was another objective—winning to the party and its Marxist policies 15 to 20 key Southern workers who carried these policies to hundreds and then to thousands.

From their homes in the shadow of the great stinking rubber factories, hundreds joined our party in Akron. Factory party branches were built in the Goodyear, Goodrich, Firestone, General and Mohawk plants as well as in Diamond Match and Babcock & Wilcox. And among those in our ranks were many of the picket captains whose contribution was so decisive in winning the Goodyear strike. But our influence went beyond that, extending to members of the international executive committee and key staff members.

We always endeavored to use a most flexible line of approach. The activities of our members—putting into operation the decisions we had arrived at democratically, promoting public activity such as leaflets, public meetings and radio speeches— were combined with a constant exchange of views with members in the top leadership of various unions and their political organizations.

In 1935 I was privileged to be a member of our party delegation to the Seventh World Congress of the Comintern, where the great Georgi Dimitrov made his historic report, "The United Peoples' Front Against Fascism and War."

This event had great political significance for me and our later work in Ohio. But it was also the beginning of a personal association which brought me much happiness over the subsequent years. In Moscow I met Mae, who was working in a publishing house, and whom I had known in the Young Communist League. We formed an attachment which led her to Cleveland, where we were married in March 1936. For the next year we shared an apartment with Helen and Carl Winter. At that time we still tended to disparage such conventions as a honeymoon, so all our honeymoons came in later life.

The next two years were the start of a rounded-out family life, in which love and respect combined with party activity to create the kind of harmony which has a pervasive influence on every aspect of one's life. Mae was active in the local party, giving particular attention to membership work. Unable to find regular employment, she worked on a WPA writers' project, doing editorial work. Many weeks her WPA wage, $15 a week, was greater than the pay I received from the party.

The 1938 state convention of the party was to be held in Akron, on May 14 and 15. The night before it opened, I took Mae to the hospital in Cleveland with labor pains. But since I had to make the report to the convention during the opening session, there was nothing to do but drive to Akron. Mae urged me to forget her and to concentrate on the convention.

Just ten minutes before I was introduced, a phone call came through that I was the father of a boy—our Bob. The convention chairman, Yetta Land, thus had a human interest item to announce when she introduced me. The delegates got up and cheered and I, in my self-consciousness, didn't even stop to thank them, but started right in on my report. As soon as I was through, I drove back to the hospital to see Mae and the baby and then dashed back to the convention in Akron. When it came time for her to come home from the hospital, I was already at the party's national convention.

The arrival of Bob brought many joys and some problems. Mae had to stop working, and the district committee decided I must receive $15 a week to maintain a family. Each stage of Bob's development was of great interest and brought us much joy.

In those years, odd though it may seem today, I considered it a waste of good time to travel to Columbus or Cincinnati during the day, so I always drove at night. Arriving in the morning, I would put in a day's work without any sleep. I did the same whenever I had to go to regional or national meetings in Chicago or New York.

The great struggles developing all over Ohio involved my being away from home a good part of the time. This meant an additional burden on Mae, who was left alone at home with the baby. These added responsibilities were characteristic of much of our married life — reaching their highest point during my trial and imprisonment. Mae, like the wives of so many other leading comrades, carried more than her share of what should be the joint responsibilities of married life.

10

The Little Steel Strike

Organizing steel was the basic objective in Ohio. Workers in the industry made up 30 per cent of those employed in manufacturing in the state. On a national scale, one-third of all steel workers were employed in Ohio. Steel mills were scattered throughout the state in Youngstown, Warren, Canton, Massillon, Niles, Mansfield, Steubenville, Cleveland, Lorain, Portsmouth and Yorkville.

Not only did steel have the largest number of workers to organize, but they were up against the toughest and most brutal of monopolies. This history of the labor movement is marked by the steel workers' heroic struggles, too many drowned in blood.

The obstacles to be surmounted were great, but past setbacks and defeats built up a storehouse of experience that was to prove invaluable. William Z. Foster's leadership in the only previous national steel strike (1919) had created a background of good will toward the party. With the attainment of unity, the foreign-born and Negro workers in the industry were to play a decisive role in the struggles that lay ahead.

Moods of struggle and determination to organize were developing among the steel workers, who were bitter at the low wages and intolerable conditions (average hourly earnings were 65 cents for skilled workers and 47 cents for the unskilled). The influence of the New Deal and, above all, the new hope arising from the establishment of the Committee for Industrial Organizations influenced us to urge the Steel and Metal Workers Union to merge with the existing skeleton AFL organization.

the Amalgamated Association of Iron, Steel and Tin Workers, headed by a dyed-in-the-wool reactionary, Mike Tighe. Its total membership in 1935 was 9,000 — mostly the top skilled workers in the rolling mills. By effective work, especially in the Youngstown area, we were able to influence a number of Amalgamated lodges, who developed a successful movement for a progressive policy nationally, based on a two-fold approach: first, the preparation for a union-organizing drive in the steel industry and winning over the Amalgamated national convention to this end; and second, the election of rank-and-file steel workers to national leadership in order to insure adherence to this policy. The movement was successful in part despite Tighe's expulsion of the militants, including some Communists. The Amalgamated national convention was won for a national organizing drive.

Tighe succeeded in sabotaging the convention's decision for nearly a year. Finally, in June 1936, the Amalgamated agreed to accept the half-million dollars offered by the Committee for Industrial Organization (still a committee within the AFL) to help organize the steel workers with the proviso that a CIO steel workers organizing committee would be established to include representatives of CIO unions and the Amalgamated. By November of that year, the AFL convention illegally expelled the unions that constituted the CIO committee.

The establishment of the Steel Workers Organizing Committee, headed by Phil Murray, changed everything. By the time of the expulsions, the Amalgamated had grown from 9,000 to 82,000. In another year it numbered 500,000. How was this brought about, and what role was played by the Communists?

A sizable apparatus and a staff of organizers were established by the Steel Workers Organizing Committee. While Lewis made sure the top posts were filled by his own men, when it came to the 200 organizers, both Lewis and Murray made every effort to enlist Communists. In Ohio our entire party and Young Communist League staffs in the steel area were incorporated into the staff of the committee. This included Gus Hall, in charge of Warren and Niles; John Steuben, in charge of Youngstown, and many others.

This was a year of intensive activity. It must be said that organizing the steel workers in those early days had no glamor about it. It was a hard, slogging process. Many previous defeats, followed by reprisals, still brought fear to many workers. For each enthusiast, there were several loath to take the plunge.

In the first months, members were recruited into the Steel Workers Organizing Committee one by one. The previous experience of our comrades was of great value. A mill was laid out in a diagram, according to departments and the number of workers employed in each. The task was to establish a core of secret union members in one department after another, without the company's knowledge. This meant establishing contact with a key worker on his off-shift. At first the men didn't want to be visited in their homes till after dark, so that neighbors would not get suspicious.

The conscientious organizers worked day and night for months. Many of the mine union "pie-cards" had never known or had long forgotten this type of organization. This resulted in a certain amount of ill will and friction which we had to smooth over.

To supplement the basic work in the mills, the party encouraged the setting up of special conferences of Negro and foreign-born organizations. The latter were especially important in Ohio, where a large percentage of the steel workers belonged to fraternal, sports and social clubs based on their various languages. This brought me in touch once again with my old colleague, Bill Gebert, who had been appointed by Murray to be responsible for this work.

Trade union activity developed on the background of a mounting offensive by big business against Roosevelt and the New Deal, which found one of its expressions in the Liberty League. The President had won the 1936 election with the full support of the CIO. He had made far-reaching promises to fight poverty and the monopolies, to see that the trade unions had full rights and to institute a system of social security and other reforms.

The hard work of the 200 organizers on the staff and the nearly 5,000 volunteer organizers — another technique that grew out of Communist experience — was aided by the nation-wide radio oratory of John L. Lewis. He characterized the anti-union campaign of the American Iron and Steel Institute as "a declaration of industrial civil war." He went on to charge that "although the industry had produced thousands of millionaries and hundreds of multi-millionaires among bankers, promoters, so-called financiers and steel executives, it has never throughout the past 35 years paid a bare subsistence wage, not to mention a living wage, to the great mass of its workers." He closed with an appeal to "the workers in the iron and steel industry who are listening to me tonight to throw off their shackles of servitude and join the union of their industry."

The pulse of the battle against the monopolies was quickening on both the industrial and political fronts. The defeat of General Motors after the heroic sit-down strike was not lost on U.S. Steel, the largest of the steel monopolies. Lewis asked for the opening of negotiations for a contract with the Steel Institute. This was rejected, but it was soon evident that division existed in the institute.

The big breakthrough came when U.S. Steel signed an agreement with the steel workers on March 2, 1937. The mere threat of a national strike enabled the union, which now had 150,000 members, to win a great victory. The agreement provided for a ten-cent-an-hour wage increase, an eight-hour day, a 40-hour week, seniority, and grievance committee machinery. It covered all 240,000 workers employed by U.S. Steel.

Overnight things began to happen. Tens of thousands joined the union. By October of that year agreements had been signed by 431 companies employing 500,000 workers. But the bitter-enders of the Steel Institue, the "Little Steel" companies who accounted for one-fourth of the industry's production, arrogantly refused to sign up.

The president of Republic Steel, Tom Girdler, who led the combination of Republic, Youngstown Sheet & Tube and Inland Steel, declared he would resign and retire to grow apples before he would sign an agreement with the CIO which, he said, meant "handing America over to Communism." The union had no recourse but to strike all the plants of Little Steel.

For us in Ohio this meant much sweat and blood. Of the 65,740 workers employed by Republic and Youngstown Sheet & Tube companies, 50,410 were in Ohio. Inland Steel's 11,500 workers were all located in Indiana and there were no Bethlehem mills in Ohio. White the CIO was justifiably shouting from the housetops about its national victory in the steel industry, Ohio remained the salient on the battlefront where the war continued to be real and bloody.

The strike was called on May 26, 1937, and was practically solid. For two months Ohio was the scene of great activity. The strikers kept the mills closed tight, using the famous flying squads of selected strikers with cars and motorbikes in order to protect any threatened weak spot in the miles-long area that had to be covered. Reserves were brought up when John L. Lewis called out 10,000 coal miners from mines owned by Little Steel. At the same time the CIO started organizing activity among the iron-ore workers in the mines of Little Steel, and the Maritime Union started similar activity on the ships and barges that transported iron ore.

Little Steel employers admitted afterwards to having spent $44,000 for guns, tear gas and bombs in their determination to defeat the strike. The first murders took place in Youngstown, a month after the strike began. It was woman's day on the picket line. At the gates of one of the Republic mills, the police fired tear gas into the crowd of 200 women who were picketing. This precipitated a six-hour pitched battle, in the course of which two strikers were shot dead. Before the strike was over, four other strikers were shot and killed in Massillon, Cleveland and Canton.

There were immediate demonstrations of solidarity. The Teamsters Union in Youngstown declared a general strike. The Brotherhood of Railroad Trainmen stopped switching service at all Republic plants. The AFL Central Labor Council in Youngstown protested. At Warren, in answer to an appeal from Gus Hall, the central body went on record for a general strike and 6,000 workers actually walked out. Similar actions took place in other cities.

At the end of two months, the situation became very serious. The employers had maintained their offensive. They combined violence and the frame-up of trade union leaders (Gus Hall was falsely accused on a murder and dynamite charge) with an announcement that they would grant wage increases but would never sign a contract with the union. The workers and their families were in more and more difficult circumstances. There were signs of weakening among many workers who were not in contact with the union. The number of waverers increased when the issue was presented to them as "continuing the strike merely to sign a piece of paper," a clever word-of-mouth canard circulated by industry to sow doubt and dissension.

In all areas of the state various law-and-order committees were set up by the employers. Then back-to-work movements were announced under phony names. The companies, led by Republic Steel, proclaimed in big full-page ads that they would reopen their mills.

The situation became very tense. Police, deputy sheriffs and hired thugs were all lined up to open the mill gates. Four thousand rubber workers from Akron, hundreds of steel workers from the mills of U.S. Steel in Ohio, and some auto workers started toward Youngstown. All roads were blocked by armed police. Hundreds of workers were jailed in a few hours' time. The active steel union members were all lined up on the picket line, ready for battle.

In response to great pressure, President Roosevelt at the last minute made an appeal that the mills remain closed and asked Governor Martin L. Davey to send in the National Guard. Union leaders, in particular those from the mine workers, were under the illusion that they had the sympathy of the governor.

After staying up all that night, in constant touch with developments in the Mahoning Valley, I watched the Ohio National Guard march over the bridge to take positions at the mill gates. The strikers, understandably but mistakenly, cheered and hailed their arrival as a great victory. I felt then that this reliance on Davey and the National Guard was a serious mistake, but at such a tense moment, we decided not to say anything publicly for a few days. But we did sound the alarm among all party members.

During that week, there was a frenzied increase in the company-inspired back-to-work movements, abetted by all the newspapers and other civic forces. Before the week ended, Davey had revealed his true colors and said that the National Guard would be used to allow anyone who so desired to return to work. With this betrayal, the backbone of the strike was broken. Each day more and more men returned to work.

At this point there was considerable chaos. A substantial minority of the workers continued to consider themselves on strike. They tended to denounce everyone who returned as a scab. Due in large part to the influence of the party, the Steel Workers Organizing Commitee stayed on the job after the strike. They had to reorganize their work after picking up the pieces but, as a result of their continued and consistent efforts, Little Steel and Tom Girdler were forced to do what they said they never would do—sign an agreement with the union two years later.

To face up to a defeat is difficult for everyone, including the party. Its position in steel was different from that in rubber and auto, where the party leadership was in close and intimate contact with the entire union or strike apparatus.

In steel, everything was tied up tightly by old-time union leaders, especially those of the United Mine Workers. Communists played an important role on the staff, but they were subordinate to the major policy-makers. While the general orientation of the CIO and the steel union was correct, their main weakness was neglecting the great mass of workers involved. This was especially true in the Little Steel strike. Some of our own comrades, while doing a splendid job, tended to ignore the broader political implications of the strike, neglected certain basic strike strategy, ignored the party committees and were too selective in party recruiting.

Speaking on the complexities of the defeat before a party convention in the winter of 1937, I said, "Many of the workers who returned are not hostile to the CIO. I was told, and we know, that many workers come and want to pay their dues and the money is refused. In Canton, Massillon and Warren, the official line of the local union is to call everyone back in the mill a scab. This incorrect line is tearing apart workers' organizations such as the International Workers Order and other fraternal organizations, where good workers, after the strike, returned to work and are now being expelled and branded as scabs. We must correct these situations."

Among the many party comrades who played a prominent role in the Steel Workers Organizing Committee was Gus Hall, today the outstanding leader of the Communist Party of the United States. I have already made reference to our first meeting when he was a teenager up in the iron range. Following his strike leadership in Warren he became the party organizer for the entire Mahoning Valley; subsequently he was state secretary of Ohio, then national secretary, before becoming general secretary.

To this day there is on my desk a paperweight which I treasure and which always reminds me of Youngstown. After I was sentenced to prison in 1949, I received a gift from Youngstown—a small steel ingot, highly polished, with the inscription: "To Johnny from the C.P. of Youngstown. 1949."

Along with the dramatic events in auto, rubber and steel, our work among the unemployed went forward. The Roosevelt administration, while easing off the economic distress, by no means provided full employment. It was not within the capacity of capitalism to make a substantial recovery, until the European war brought armament orders.

After the initial success of the Unemployed Councils, led by Communists but largely non-Communist in membership, other political forces tried to establish competing unemployed organizations. The left-Socialists Rev. A.J. Muste, Louis Budenz, and Arnold Johnson* built the Workers Alliance. Other socialists and liberals, in company with some former Communists associated with Jay Lovestone, set up the Unemployed Leagues.

After a few years the three merged, taking the name of Workers Alliance. The two main leaders in the Ohio merger were Andy Onda of the Unemployed Councils and Arnold Johnson of the Alliance. Johnson came into our party at about this time and in 1940, succeeded me as Ohio state secretary of the party.

On the trade union front, friendly relations developed between the official party leaders and the rising new nonparty CIO leaders in rubber, auto and steel. When it came to the old-line miners and clothing union leaders of the CIO, establishing close working relations was a lot more difficult, but the exigencies of the situation, combined with common immediate class struggle aims, overcame these difficulties in nearly all cases.

These relations took on different forms for different people. Once the ice was broken, John Owens, president of the Ohio District of the United Mine Workers and later president of the Ohio CIO Council, was friendly and we got on very well. About once a month I would visit his office in Columbus. Our talks

---

*Muste, a pacifist, became a leader in the American peace movement and made notable contributions to the campaign against the invasion of Vietnam; Arnold Johnson, who came from a theological and academic background, became a national leader of the Communist Party. Louis Budenz became a prime exhibit in the government collection of stool pigeons whose fabrications provided a lucrative income.

covered all immediate economic and political problems in Ohio. Owens would seldom permit a drift to more fundamental questions. But in all my dealings with him he was forthright, kept his word, and treated the party with respect. Owens is now the national secretary-treasurer of the miners.

Much more difficult was the Steel Workers Organizing Committee director for northern Ohio, William Donovan. His office also was open, but he always seemed fearful and brought our meetings to a close as quickly as possible. Donovan had an erratic temperament that grew worse with the years. His life was to end in suicide.

Meetings with Leo Krzyski, Rose Pesota and other Socialist trade unionists were of a different character. They were roving CIO organizers. As old-time Socialists and left-wingers, they adopted the attitude that we were comrades, but there was always the undertone that we each knew the motives of the other and that while we were working together now, we were not trusting each other too far. To achieve a working relationship with sections of the AFL leadership was much more difficult. In Cleveland we eventually established friendly relations with Trent Longo of the Painters and two main leaders of the International Ladies Garment Workers.

In 1936, when we were campaigning for a Farmer-Labor Party, we met with such trade union leaders as Kroll of the Amalgamated Clothing Workers, in Cincinnati; Wilmer Tate, of the Akron Central Labor Council; Francis Gerhardt of the AFL federal local in the Diamond Match Co., in Barberton; Reisinger, regional organizer of the UAW; Eagle and Callahan of the rubber union's international executive board, and Coleman Taylor, of the newly organized United Electrical Workers. It was gratifying to note that they did not hesitate to sit with representatives of the Communist Party in preliminary conferences to establish a Farmer-Labor Party, nor to accept me as a member of an initiating committee. In fact, there were on the Ohio Promotional Committee for a Farmer-Labor Party representatives of eight Central Labor Councils, the ILGWU, the ACWA, and the Socialist Party, in addition to those cited above.

In 1935 we decided to make a concerted effort to bring about a united May Day action between the Communists and Socialists. The Socialists were fewer in number, but their names still commanded a certain influence. With the upsurge of labor, they were striving to gain a new lease on life, and they had some influence in sections of the trade unions.

After prolonged negotiations we finally reached agreement. With the official participation of a few trade unions, the two organizations of the unemployed, the International Workers Order, the Workmen's Circle, the language groups, the Young Communists and the Young Socialists, we had a parade. Nearly 1,000 marched through downtown streets to the public square. There, Leo Krzyski, representing the Socialists, and I, representing the Communists, were the principal speakers.

Other examples of local united front action included the campaign for social insurance, the Committee to Aid Spanish Democracy, the Small Home Owners Association and the National Negro Congress. In all these activities the party did not hide its identity and it conducted its own independent activities, such as the outstanding campaign to defeat Governor Davey and our work in the trade unions organized by Labor's Non-Partisan League.

When the fascist General Franco led an army revolt against the legally elected Republican government of Spain on July 18, 1936, the first blow of World War II was actually struck. Before long the troops, airplanes and guns of Hitler and Mussolini were in Spain helping Franco. The British-French-American governments, under a phony neutrality act, actually aided Franco and the fascists by preventing arms from reaching the Republican government — the Loyalists, as they were known.

Realizing the threat of fascism to the entire world, thousands of volunteers responded to the call for help to save Republican Spain. From the United States, over 3,000 responded and took their places in the Lincoln, Washington, and Mackenzie-Papineau battalions. Among these were 150 from Ohio, over half of them members of the Communist Party. They included five members of our district committee and many other active comrades. Their enlistment and transportation overseas were accomplished without publicity or fanfare, since the Roosevelt administration during the first year of the war tried to prevent all help to Republic Spain.

Each of the 150 volunteers deserves equal recognition, since it was their concern for democracy and their understanding of the political issues that sent them to Spain. They knew that if

the fascists were successful, their own country and the entire
would be engulfed in a terrible war.

One of the volunteers was the late David White, a party member. His father, Governor George White, had a typical politi-
cian's viewpoint and had ordered out the National Guard in
the Toledo Auto-Lite strike. Despite a background of wealth
and an education at conservative Princeton University, Dave
White found his way to Marxism. From Spain he wrote to us:

"A curious irony has occurred to me. I was sent to Princeton
partly because of my father and uncle, of course. Partly, also,
because of the important and useful contacts I would doubtless
make. This reason was of course never mentioned. Well, it
didn't work. I picked up a few friends and let the rest slide.

"But I break away from my accustomed life and come to
Spain. Lo and behold, during the trip and since I have been
here, I meet rafts of important and influential people — people
beside whom the Park Avenue bond salesmen and Chicago
wheat buyers and bankers' sons pale to thin, thin shadows.
People who have done important work in the world, who believe in something and have proved it, who have life and color;
people from all over the world by whom the world is to be built
anew."

Many of these comrades never returned. They were killed on
the various battlefields of Spain. One of these was Joe Dallet.
Joe's death had a strong impact on the workers of Mahoning
Valley, among whom he had established such strong ties in the
struggles of the unemployed and the early battles in steel. Within a few days we organized a memorial meeting in Youngstown
attended by 1,500 steelworkers, Negro and white. Spokesmen
from the SWOC, the AFL Central Labor Council, the NAACP,
the Communist Party, and the International Workers Order
all commented on various aspects of Joe's life. Even the local
newspaper, the Youngstown *Vindicator*, which had denounced
him in life, respected him in death. It wrote:

"Those who have to do with public affairs frequently have
found themselves disagreeing sharply with the causes which
Joe Dallet championed, but all of them came to respect the
rugged honesty of his character and some of them, at least,
came to regard with real affection the earnest personality which
looked so straight-forwardly out of his brown eyes.

"Whatever may be said of Joe's ideology as a Communist worker, certainly he had a steadfast devotion to an idea, which he pursued without regard to the consequences for himself. That he should fall in battle for the cause he cherished, at the head of a charge which he felt was in behalf of liberty and justice to man, is thoroughly typical of his character."

Among my treasured possessions are two books sent to me by comrades in Spain. One is in Spanish and called *Un ano de las Brigadas Internacionales*, and the other in English in the *XV International Brigade*. The inscription on the latter reads: "From the 20th Century Abolitionists—Ohioans fighting in Spain that Spaniards shall never be slaves of Hitler and Mussolini; that America shall never be subjected to the most terrible slavery of all, fascism."

It is dated June 6, 1938, and signed by John Gates, Frank Rogers, Henry Mack, Abe Lewis, Sandor Voros, Jack Cooper and Dave Gordon. It is this Johnny Gates that I choose to remember. Not the shadow that retained the name but no longer the substance, and who deserted the party in 1957.*

During the war in Spain, the North American Committee to Aid Spanish Democracy, as well as its affiliate, the Medical Bureau, were active in Ohio raising many thousands of dollars and shipping tons of food and clothing to the children of Loyalist Spain. Our party in Cleveland during a one-week drive collected $1,200. In the Ohio Valley, the committee chapter functioned on a very broad united front basis, with Adolf Pacifico, the miners' district president, as chairman. There were groups of Spanish people in Cleveland and Canton and each of them sent fully equipped ambulances to Spain.

The party tried to utilize every election campaign to speak to new thousands of people. To arouse our own members and achieve maximum publicity for our election platform and candidates, we held state nominating conferences.

*Gates, editor of the *Daily Worker* in the postwar years, was in later years unable to withstand the government's pressure against the party. After unsuccessfully attempting to persuade the party to adopt a reformist program, he separated from the movement and, like a number of this kin, faded into obscurity after making obeisance to the class enemy.

Typical of the kind of programs we presented at the plants is this extract from our 1936 platform: improve and enforce the minimum wage law; support the relief standards bill; institute federal social insurance; provide free textbooks in all elementary and high schools; reduce overcrowded classes; establish greater school appropriations; abolish the Reserve Officers Training Corps in all schools; outlaw the Black Legion, repeal the Criminal Syndicalist law; abolish compulsory arbitration in labor disputes; revise election laws, including the newly adopted Civil Rights Act; repeal of sales tax; institute tax exemption of individually owned houses up to $5,000 valuation; pass moratorium laws to protect small farmers and house-owners against foreclosures and evictions.

Over the years our best known and most popular candidates were Andy Onda, Yetta Land, I.O. Ford, Ben Atkins and Anton Krchmarek. In later years Arnold Johnson also became a well known candidate, polling substantial votes for the Cleveland School Board.

An outstanding election campaign was conducted in Ward 30 of Cleveland in 1937. This was the largest ward in all of Ohio. Cleveland elections were called "nonpartisan" which meant the party label of each candidate was not printed on the ballot. The two candidates with the highest votes in the primary went to a final ballot.

Our party had considered Ward 30 a concentration area and contested it for many years with Krchmarek. Beginning in 1934 we ran Andy Onda. In 1937, when the party was in the midst of all the big industrial battles and was developing public mass activity on electoral issues (we worked out a very effective tax program for Cleveland and sent delegations with it to the city council), Onda won in the Ward 30 primaries. A terrific howl came from every reactionary quarter, and they in turn tried to intimidate all the New Dealers and progressive forces.

Since Onda was the Cleveland party secretary, the three newspapers, the church, the machines of the Democratic and Republican parties, and sections of the trade union leadership all united with one aim — to prevent the Communists from going to city hall. We, on our part, countered this with broad united support for Onda, based on a fighting policy. He got the endorsement of Labor's Non-Partisan League, the Independent Voters League, the CIO Industrial Council and some AFL locals and language organizations.

A tremendous campaign was conducted, against great odds. When the votes were counted, Onda had 6,452 against 6,833 for his opponent. While we lost by 381 votes, the comrades were elated and the class enemy stunned. It would be interesting to know the real count, for the election machinery was in the hands of our opponents.

Feeling ourselves a part of the developing mass movement, and being very much under attack from the forces of reaction, it was decisive that we increase our activity on the public scene. The party sent delegations to the state legislature or to sub-committee hearings and to many city council meetings. Some were heard and some were thrown out, but the people knew we were there.

We also fought for our right to the radio in Cleveland and other cities in the state. I remember speaking several times over Station WGAR, in a series we called the Voice of Progress. In Cincinnati the party had a weekly broadcast over Station WCPO. In Akron there was also a regular weekly broadcast, while in Youngstown, Toledo, Columbus and Wheeling, West Virginia, we had occasional broadcasts.

Another thing we fought for was our right to answer all attacks in the newspapers. At the beginning we were just ignored. However, as we became more of a force, we made some headway. I recall the, Cleveland *Press* ran a series of articles entitled "Communism and Its Program of Infiltration." The author was a hack journalist, Anthony De Cola, to whom I had given a lengthy interview. There were so many distortions that we demanded space to answer. We finally were given an entire newspaper column, in which I was able to present our party's views.

On another occasion the Cleveland *Plain Dealer* had written a particularly dirty story. I protested and demanded an interview with the editor, Paul Bellamy. He was the son of the famous author Edward Bellamy, who wrote the book *Looking Backward*, which we all read when I joined the movement. We had a long, interesting conversation, in which I chided him about betraying his father's ideals. He didn't like that and tried to justify himself. While I didn't dissuade Paul Bellamy from continuing to be the main newspaper voice of capitalism in Cleveland, he did agree to print a correction of his story. In subsequent months he always sent his son to interview me on anything important involving the party.

We also began to get invitations to forums and debates, in which we tried to involve as many comrades as possible. When it came to state-wide events, it usually fell to me to represent the party. I remember a debate in Columbus (I think it was sponsored by the American Legion) with a prominent civic personality named Wilkins. The hall was packed and the questions were unending. Some of the Legionnaires threatened to become belligerent but were restrained. In later years Wilkins became a United States federal judge.

Antioch College in Yellow Springs broke the academic ice and organized several forums, with gatherings in some professor's house afterwards, where discussions went on until the wee hours of the morning.

Within six months of my arrival in Ohio, we were confronted with the necessity of getting an appropriate hall for the Seventh National Convention of the Party. We broke new ground and got the Prospect Auditorium. But in 1939 we decided to face the challenge of filling the main Cleveland public auditorium, which seated 10,000. The speakers were General Secretary Earl Browder, Cleveland Secretary Andy Onda, John Gates, who had just returned from Spain, and myself. With much sweat and toil we achieved an audience of between 6,000 and 7,000, which did not escape notice in the papers the next morning. This was another example of setting bold objectives and then working very hard to achieve them.

As the party became more of a public force—at a time when there was increasing concern over the growth of Hitler fascism—we also broke through into the field of white-collar workers and professionals. Of great importance was the initial help of a long-time newspaperman, Bill Davey, through whom we organized a large branch of newspaper men and women. They all were very active in the American Newspaper Guild, and for many years the Cleveland Guild was an anchor of progressive policy.

At the same time we organized a very active branch of artists. We also won some lawyers and doctors to the party. During this period we tried to win party members from among the staffs of various colleges, with only a minimum of success. However, among those recruited was Hy Lumer, now the editor of the Marxist monthly, *Political Affairs*.

In 1937, on the occasion of the 18th anniversary of the party and the 150th anniversary of the United States Constitution, we had brought out, under the editorship of Carl Winter, a yearbook, *Ohio Marches Toward Peace and Progress*. It was a masterful historical and a superb technical job—an accomplishment of which the party in Ohio can always be proud. In 1939, on the occasion of the 20th anniversary of the party, another yearbook, *In Pursuit of Happiness*, was issued, under the editorship of A.W. Mills. While lacking the meticulous historical and technical detail of the earlier work, it was another important contribution to the Ohio party. Both these yearbooks were invaluable to our many new members and helped to establish the party as a serious force in the community at large.

Another important activity was centered at the Cleveland Workers School and its branches.

The comrades who carried on the work at all levels throughout the years are, of course, too numerous to mention. But let me talk about at least four of them here—three men and a woman—plain people who became party leaders with great mass influence. I cannot take credit for recruiting any of them, but I did see in each of them the kind of ability our party needed in its leadership, and I did everything in my power to cultivate that ability.

Andy Onda, for instance, was a man who offered a particular kind of challenge. The son of a Czechoslovakian family which had settled in Pittsburgh, he was big and strong and had been toughened in the steel mills of Pennsylvania and Ohio. When I arrived in Ohio, he was unemployed and active in the Unemployed Councils. Demonstrating great talent for leadership, he soon became one of the local and state leaders.

Courageous, tough and outspoken, he faced and met many serious tests in the daily struggles and in the hunger marches. At the same time he was thirsting for political knowledge. We spent long hours discussing things that puzzled him. I recommended books for him to read, and then we thrashed out the points he raised. Of prime importance were discussions about working with people. There never was any problem about a correct approach to Negro people, but he carried over from his peasant family a lot of backward attitudes toward women, and this remained an acute problem for a long time.

Against the wishes of some of the comrades, I won support for his election to party leadership, where his presence was tempestuous, to say the least. He had ingrained hostility toward "intellectuals," and he wanted action without talk, so our leading committees were at times hectic. On occasion, I myself would have doubts as to whether I was correct, but I plodded on. The combination of patience and entrusting him with responsible assignments, together with collective work and friendly social relations, finally resulted in his becoming an outstanding leader and public spokesman for the party. It was a blow to all of us when he was cut down by a fatal disease in the prime of life.

I have already described Wyndham Mortimer in his role as national leader of the auto workers' struggles and an outstanding early leader of the United Auto Workers Association. The memory of Mortimer in Ohio is coupled with the name of another shop worker, Bernard McGroarty. As a result of my efforts, both of them had been elected to the leading party committees in Ohio. While both were good examples of what is sometimes called "worker-intellectuals," each were in their own way active mass leaders in the trade union movement.

Mortimer was originally a coal miner who, when I arrived in Ohio, was working as a machinist in the White Motor Co. He organized the workers into the union and was their recognized spokesman. While still working at the bench, he spent his weekends and evenings helping to organize other plants.

McGroarty was a stereotyper by trade. Active in his union and industry, he became a recognized Left leader in the Cleveland Federation of Labor. Never a full-timer, he devoted much of his spare time to various union activities. When the American Newspaper Guild organized the newspapermen, he was a great help in explaining the role of unionism to these writers, who had never before had any such experience.

Both "Mort" and "Mac," active as they were in trade union work, always recognized the decisive importance of the party and never shrank from the demands of their roles in leadership. Both were extremely modest, never showed any prima donna tendencies, and were always ready to accept tasks, no matter how humble.

With both of them in top party committees, the integration of Onda into collective leadership became easier. They were industrial workers who worked with their hands and led

workers' struggles, but they were also well acquainted with
Marxist philosophy and political theory. Onda could not dis-
miss them as "intellectuals," and their patience contributed
much in shaping the "rough diamond."

Unfortunately all three have passed away. Mortimer died at
82 years of age at the end of August 1966. In reply to a letter I
sent his daughter, she wrote, "My father valued your friendship
through the years and enjoyed his visits with you in London."

Mrs. Yetta Land, originally a cigar maker, became by self-
education one of the first woman lawyers in Cleveland. Early
in life she was a Socialist but then she joined the Communist
Party. Well known for her readiness to defend civil liberties and
Negro rights cases when few others would touch them, she was
professionally respected in the courts for her alertness and
her determination to convince jury or judge of the soundness
of her case. She always had a warm, comradely approach. Never
looking on herself as an authority on party policy, she set an
example to many other professionals and artists in her readiness to join in any party task, however humble or dangerous.
She ran as the Communist candidate for many elective offices
and served as Ohio state chairman over a number of years.

At the end of 1940, the Central Committee decided that I
should leave Ohio and come to the party center as national
organization secretary. The preceding ten years, three in Chicago and seven in Ohio, had been the richest of my life in political experience and in leadership. This in no way minimizes
what had gone before or was to come after. But being in the
midst of historic mass struggles that shaped the character of
events for years ahead, and seeing the party in Ohio grow from
800 to 4,800 members brought great satisfaction. At a big affair
held to bid me goodbye, there were many messages from party
committees and leaders and from non-party leaders in the trade
union movement. The Ohio party chairman, Yetta Land, said:

"As I recall the banquet of seven years ago welcoming our
new state secretary, I can still see the questioning look on the
faces of those present. They seemed to study the young comrade
who was to chart the course of the Ohio Communist Party in
its duties and obligations to the masses in their struggles for a
better life.

"By his reserved but scientific, patient, loyal guidance and
leadership, Comrade John Williamson has more than fulfilled

the highest expectations of the most critical party members. He leaves in Ohio a host of devoted comrades and friends who have learned to love and respect him as a leader, a comrade, and a friend. To us he will always be 'Our Johnny'."

I left Ohio at the end of 1940 with mixed feelings. It had been a most satisfying place to work. The party had made progress and was a political factor to be reckoned with; hundreds of my comrades were not merely co-workers but warm friends; and I was happily married, with a home and family.

At the time, I felt honored, if apprehensive, at my new national responsibilities.

11

Communists and World War II

In January 1941 I found myself back in New York City, with the conviction that although it was the central headquarters of our party, New York was not the center of working class power. My feelings about this were to persist throughout the years. The Midwest—Illinois, Michigan, Ohio and Western Pennsylvania— where steel, auto, engineering and machine tools, rubber and transport dominate the scene is the real working class center. This is no way to minimize the importance of the great metropolis, which so often had stood out nationally as the hub of progressive development.

The period from September 1939, when Hitler attacked Poland, to June 1941, when Hitler invaded the Soviet Union, was a difficult one. It happened that on September 1, the very day Hitler struck at Poland, we were holding a big national conference in Chicago to celebrate the 20th anniversary of the founding of the party. The central committee on that occasion characterized the conflict as "an imperialist war . . .between rival imperialisms for world domination," pledged itself to fight to "protect and improve living standards, democratic liberties and the right to organize and strike," and urged the forging of an alliance of workers, poor farmers and middle-class "against the economic royalists and imperialist warmakers." The central slogan adopted was "Keep America out of the Imperialist War."

It was the period of the "phony" war when for six months neither side made any military move against the other. The Finnish-Soviet War, which lasted from November 1939 to March 1940, had been used to whip up further anti-Soviet hysteria. This had already taken on a serious anti-Communist character after the Soviet-German non-aggression pact the preceding month.

During this period, the party general secretary, Earl Browder, as well as William Weiner of the International Workers Order, and Harry Gannes of the *Daily Worker*, were arrested and charged with various technical violations of passport regulations. Bill Schneiderman of California had his citizenship revoked (it was restored in a historic United States Court decision in 1943), and many other comrades were arrested. Before I left Ohio I was already functioning in such a way as to minimize the possibilities of arrest.

Browder was expected to go to prison at any time (he was finally sent to Atlanta in March 1941). So when it was decided that I become national organization secretary, it was thought advisable to refrain from announcing this publicly. In fact, I got a private job with a firm whose owner was friendly. My work was supposedly outside the office, so I showed up only two or three times a week, to "make reports" and establish myself with the office staff as being attached to the firm. But most of my time was devoted to the party.

While Browder was in prison, Bob Minor was elected acting general secretary, and he and Foster worked closely together during this period.

By June 1941, when Hitler invaded the Soviet Union, the political atmosphere began to change, and after December 7, when Pearl Harbor was attacked and the United States entered the war against Hitler Germany, there was an even greater change. The prosecution of the party had ceased, although Browder was still in prison, and the entire party leadership was once again functioning openly.

Within a few hours after Hitler's attack on the Soviet Union, we rounded up everyone for a political committee meeting, where we adopted a statement that condemned the Nazi invasion of the USSR and called for "full support and cooperation with the Soviet Union in its struggle against Hitlerism."

Six days later the Executive Committee approved a report by Foster which said in part:

"Hitler's attack upon the Soviet Union changes the character of the world war, and thereby makes necessary changes in our party's attitude toward the war. Previously the war had been a struggle between the rival imperialist power groupings. . . . But now . . . it is not only that the life of the first socialist country is at stake—the democracy and national independence of every people are jeopardized, not the least that of the United States. . . .

"While supporting the Roosevelt Administration in all blows that it may deliver against Hitler, we do not forget the imperialist character of our government nor its imperialist aims in this war. . . .

"We must work to make our government's policy a program of democratic struggle against Hitler and Hitlerism."

Five months later we convened a very large and representative party conference in the Fraternal Hall in New York City. In the midst of the discussion on the morning of the second day—December 7—we got the news of the Japanese attack on Pearl Harbor. The conference was recessed for an hour, while the political committee went into session.

Bob Minor made a memorable report that day for the political committee, and submitted a public statement which denounced the attack and said the fate of all nations and peoples had "been thrown into the arena for determination by military means." The party "pledges its loyalty, its devoted labor and the last drop of its blood in support of our country in this greatest of all crimes that ever threatened its existence." The next morning's *Daily Worker* had a full-spread headline, "Everything for Victory."

By May 1942, Roosevelt freed Browder after one year of a four-year prison sentence, declaring "that the commutation of his sentence which brings about his release at this time . . . will have a tendency to promote national unity." Whether the adroit Roosevelt was already taking an odds-on chance that as a by-product of this action Browder would undergo an ideological change—as he did two years later—will of course never be known.

It was during the all-out activity to win the war against Hitler fascism that our party grew to 80,000 members. The *Worker* circulation exceeded 100,000. In 1941 and 1943 we elected Pete Cacchione to the New York City Council with the highest number of first-choice ballots of any Brooklyn candidate, and in 1943 extended our electoral victory to Ben Davis's election to the city council from Manhattan.

In later years the two major parties in New York united to abolish the democratic voting system of proportional representation to make it easier for Communists to be excluded from the City Council. This was only one of many schemes devised to make the election of Communists extremely difficult and to create excessive requirements to bar the party from the ballot. Those who assert that Communists put no reliance on the electoral process never mention the farcical legalities that make democratic elections a virtual impossibility. The Communist Party is not the only victim; all third parties and independent candidates throughout the United States are faced with hampering election laws. And even when they gain a place on the ballot, they are discriminated against by press, radio and television.

Among the 80,000 party members were 15,000 comrades in the armed services; many of them had enlisted. It was by deeds that we threw ourselves into the war against fascism, and no segment of the American population had a finer record than that of our party in World War II.

In 1944 there was a development that did great harm to our movement—the dissolution of the Communist Party as such, and the establishment in its place of the Communist Political Association. In January the national committee adopted a report and recommendation presented by Earl Browder. It proposed calling a convention which would "adjust its [the party's] name to correspond more exactly to the American political tradition and its practical political role." The report said there was "not the same compelling fundamental reason why the organization should bear the name 'Communist'" but, on balance, recommended it should call itself something like "American Communist Political Association."

There was, of course, much more involved than a change of name. This book is obviously not the place for a complete account and analysis of the issues and struggles that ensued. But the political roots of this move were grounded in an erroneous estimation of the coalition of forces that had joined in national unity against the fascist war. This estimation confused international diplomatic agreements among the United States, the USSR and Britain with class peace within the capitalist countries. It attempted to revise Marxist theories of the cyclical and general crises of capitalism, and even went so far as to cooperate with "free enterprise" in the assumption that it would work effectively in the postwar period. Thus the decisive position of the working class and the leading role of its party were liquidated, both in immediate struggles and in the fundamental struggle for socialism.

How wrong we were is proved by the pages of postwar history, with the imperialist activity of the United States government extending to global dimensions, stubbornly obstructing agreements on peace, colonial freedom and the self-determination of nations.

Nevertheless, the Browder position had become that of the national committee, with only Foster opposing it in the political committee. In May 1944, the party convention unanimously voted to dissolve itself and form the Communist Political Association. The convention met in the tense atmosphere of the eve of D-Day, the invasion of Hitler-occupied Europe and the opening of the second front, for which we had so long fought and struggled.

A year later we received the April 1945 issue of *Cahiers du Communisme*, the theoretical organ of the French Communist Party, containing an article by Jacques Duclos, its deputy general secretary, "On the Dissolution of the CPUSA." The gist of his long article was that our policy amounted to "a notorious revision of Marxism on the part of Browder and his supporters." It was an ideological bombshell. Amidst shock and confusion in our leadership, there soon began to crystallize a group that conceded we had departed from Marxist principles, despite our good intentions. After continuous meetings during the next two weeks, in which Browder continued to defend his policy, the National Board rejected his position. Finally, the National Committee decided to convene a special convention for July 26-28, and immediately to open up the pre-convention discussion in the party (a formality, since it was already raging). It adopted a draft resolution recognizing our errors. Browder, who remained obdurate, was removed as general secretary; a temporary secretariat was elected of Foster, Dennis and myself.

Meeting in a politically super-charged atmosphere, the convention reconstituted the Communist Party, rejecting the revisionist errors of Browder. An enlarged leadership was elected, which still retained the core of the old leaders who had renounced Browder's position. Instead of a general secretary, a national secretariat was elected, consisting of Foster, Dennis, Thompson and myself. Although at the convention Foster went out of his way to emphasize that even before Duclos' article some of us "were beginning to express directly opposing views" to Browder, there can be no excusing the leadership, including myself, from the grave responsibility for our mistake.

We took a beating as a result of the revisionist line we had followed and when, after profound and soul-searching re-examination and months of discussion and struggle, the party was reconstituted, one-third of the members had been in the organization less than a year and we had lost a number of them. There was even greater damage. The independent political activity of the party had decreased; *Daily Worker* circulation declined because our branch apparatus had been dissolved, sales of theoretical literature dropped off and dues payments went down. The virtual abandonment of our concentrated work with youth was to create an absence of new sources of leadership in the years to come. Neglect of the problems of the Negro people and the cessation of organizing efforts in the South undoubtedly slowed the pace of the freedom movement which arose later. The class-consciousness of trade unionists was blunted, and there was a decline in the industrial and trade union composition of the party. Some of the returning veterans were thrown into confusion by the turmoil within the party.

The crucial problem now confronting us was to carry through the most fundamental party reappraisal, aimed at rooting out the revisionist concepts that had eaten into the program and practice of the party. We had to reconstitute the concept and form of the Communist Party while maintaining our win-the-war policy devoid of distortions, avoiding panic or chaos within our ranks and striving for maximum unity.

When Browder, in the face of eventual unanimous opposition, obdurately held to his revisionist thesis, there was no alternative but to remove him from the party.

In the 12 months following the reconstitution of the party, our first responsibility was to popularize the convention decisions while we were proceeding with the reorganizational task. This was not merely another change of name but an important ideological effort to reestablish in theory and practice the precepts of a Marxist-Leninist party, while simultaneously reacting to and participating in the major political developments of these months.

During that year we recruited 15,000 new members, of whom nearly one-third were Negro workers; we organized 400 shop and industrial branches, of which 100 were composed of exclusively new members; and reconstituted the party in the south where 1,146 of the 2,159 members were new to the Party. The membership responded to the reorganization in a wave of enthusiasm, and we were back on the right track.

12

Division in the CIO

At the plenary meeting of the national committee in July 1946, Bill Foster proposed the election of Gene Dennis as general secretary, and this was unanimously approved. At the same time, Henry Winston, returned Negro veteran and former leader of the Young Communist League, was elected national organization secretary and I, national labor secretary.

The next years found me concerned with the turbulent postwar strike struggles and, even more important, with the growing attacks upon the party and other Left forces in the trade unions. These developments took place against the background of the postwar world offensive of United States imperialism, its atom-bomb diplomacy against the socialist world, the Marshall Plan and the Truman Doctrine — in a word, the unleashing of the cold war. At home, this was accompanied by the anti-Communist hysteria, reaching its height in the McCarthy era, which hit out at everything progressive and democratic.

In resistance to these attacks were a number of effective strikes, a new upsurge of the Negro people, the Wallace campaign for the presidency on the Progressive Party ticket, the Peekskill battle and the heroic peace movement.

The peace forces held a conference of 5,000 delegates in Chicago and collected nearly a million signatures to a petition calling for an immediate conference of the big powers, controlled disarmament and destruction of all weapons of mass annihilation. Many signatures had previously been collected for the Stockholm Appeal through the committee, whose chairman was the late Dr. W.E.B. Du Bois. Dr. Du Bois was arrested as a foreign agent and later acquitted. In all of these activities, Communists participated with maximum involvement.

The corporate interests launched a drive to halt the progressive trend represented by the CIO and to try to bring both the AFL and CIO into line with the policies of monopoly capital. They had no problem with the AFL leadership. On foreign policy, the ALF officialdom outdid the Truman administration in opposing democratic changes in the world. On domestic issues they shamelessly condemned the strikes conducted by CIO unions, claiming that strikes resulted in rising prices. "All American workers", they said, "would be better off today" if they had been "willing to accept smaller increases."

Of course, this in no way represented the feelings of the workers in the shops and factories organized by AFL unions. But the American worker in much of labor history has been forced to act against both the bosses and his own top leaders.

Probably nowhere else in the world has the ideology of capitalism penetrated the high officialdom of labor so deeply, and part of this ideology inevitably rubbed off on the rank and file, especially when the issue did not involve a direct relationship to bread and butter. Unfortunately, many youth see labor only in the image of these leaders and have no acquaintance with the rank and file. Hence they neglect the tedious work of establishing relations with workers. Thus, some progressive movements tend to be lopsided, with white-collar, professional and academic groups in total leadership.

With the CIO, things were more difficult for the reactionaries. They would have to reverse convention policies, and try to isolate left-wing leaders from hundreds of thousands of rank-and-file members who had elected them. This would require the

destruction of the Left-Center alliance of leadership, which had
been the cornerstone of the CIO's progress since its founding.
A many-sided program was put into operation that brought
into play the government, the employers, the AFL Council and
the Catholic church. A combination of cajolery and threats was
directed at Murray. A hysterical campaign was unleashed
against the party and all Communist or left-wing trade union
leaders, to cover up the employers' offensive against the trade
unions and the workers' struggle to obtain better conditions.
Typical of the threats to Murray was a comment in the Pittsburgh *Press,* which said bluntly: "It is high time President Phil
Murray of the CIO stopped giving aid and comfort to the Communists of that organization . . . and worse, he·has helped keep
them in power by opposing efforts of the anti-Communists to
oust them."

The next three CIO conventions—Atlantic City, 1946; Boston, 1947; and Portland, 1948—were the scenes of struggle
throughout which we fought at every stage for a policy of
united action on the economic front, despite the sharp differences that existed on issues like the Marshall Plan, the Truman
Doctrine, the World Federation of Trade Unions, the Taft-
Hartley Act, and others.

At the 1946 Atlantic City convention, the main policy was
still essentially progressive. Demands were made by such leaders as Emil Rieve and James Carey, supported by all the capitalist propaganda machinery on the outside, that the convention
lump Communists and fascists together, characterize Communists as foreign agents, and call for a purge of all Communists
from the affiliated unions.

On that occasion, the Left (of which the Communists were a
part) fought tenaciously to expose the fact that the device of
red-baiting was being used to weaken and split the CIO. They
tried to make it clear that their chief concern was a united CIO,
which alone would be able to resist the growing anti-labor attacks inside and outside of Congress, but they also insisted that
if any attempt was made to bring the Rieve-Carey proposals to
the floor, they would be vigorously fought, regardless of consequences.

A special subcommittee of the convention was established,
which met in almost continuous session for 36 hours. The forces
of the Right, including the Social Democrats and the Associa-

tion of Catholic Trade Unionists,* and those of the Left each stood their ground; delegates were about evenly divided. Philip Murray and his Center forces held the balance of power. Murray demanded a compromise; if it was not reached, he threatened to resign as CIO president.

After hours of haggling and bitter controversy, the Right was defeated but it was at the expense of a compromise formula which the Communists and the left-wing knew was both erroneous and unjust. It said that the convention went on record "to resent and reject efforts of the Communist Party or other political parties and their adherents to interfere in the affairs of the CIO." Murray nevertheless declared at the convention: "I should like it to be distinctly understood that I am definitely opposed to any form of repression in this movement of ours. There should be no misunderstanding about that."

And when it came to executive board elections, the Murray Center forces joined in electing left-wingers and Communists, including Ben Gold, a member of the party's national committee.

There has been much subsequent debate on whether support of this compromise was correct. I think that under the circumstances no better alternative action was possible. The main resolutions were progressive. These included the wages fight and the struggles against anti-labor legislation, poll tax, Negro discrimination and the House Un-American Committee. They favored political-action committees and the establishment of joint farmer-labor committees; support to the World Federation of Trade Unions; aid to Greek workers; a progressive peace policy based on Big Three unity, and opposition to the draft.

The unity of the CIO had been preserved, despite unprecedented maneuvers and much outside interference from reaction to split it. The task now was to fight for the implementation of the policies adopted.

*It is a curious twist of history that Msgr. Charles Owen Rice of Pittsburgh, one of the leaders in the anti-Communist Association of Catholic Trade Unionists, is at present a strong opponent of the war in Viet Nam and an advocate of a "detente with Communist Asia." He has become associated with the kind of united front that in these earlier years he sought to destroy. Undoubtedly, this is a reflection of the worldwide upheaval within the Catholic church.

The aim of the Right to oust the Communists was defeated. How they felt about it was expressed in the *Jewish Daily Forward*, which said: "Philip Murray betrayed the right-wingers. They had a right to expect help from him.... It would have been better if the anti-Communists had accepted Murray's challenge and permitted him to abdicate."

The Communist Party was opposed to interference in the affairs of the trade unions. Whenever or wherever any local party organization veered away from this practice, it was not only criticized but corrected. I dealt at length with this question a few days after the CIO convention when I stated:

"The aim and responsibility of the Communist Party is politically to influence all workers, including trade unionists, but never to interfere in the affairs of the unions. There is a big difference between *political influencing* and *interference*. The first is our responsibility and natural right as a political party. The other would lead to confusing the role of the party with that of the trade unions, and would bring with it division instead of unity and strength. To influence workers politically, both in the shop and in the community, to understand and support the program and the policies of the Communist Party is our right and responsibility. We can argue and debate our policies among the workers, and contrast them with the policies of the Democratic, Republican, or Socialist Parties."

In the 12-month period between the Atlantic City and the 1947 Boston conventions of the CIO, events developed rapidly; the cold-war drums were beating louder and Truman's atom-bomb diplomacy sank to a new low; the anti-labor Taft-Hartley Act had been adopted and anti-Communist splitting efforts were being carried on within the CIO wherever the Right was in control; prices were skyrocketing without compensating wage increases. While the workers were very restless, the fear of a developing economic crisis and of atomic war was also evident.

It was in this atmosphere that both the AFL and the CIO conventions met. The CIO, meeting in Boston, still stood out as the progressive sector of the labor movement. By and large, its official policies, expressed in some 40 resolutions, gave leadership to the struggle. This was one result of rank-and-file pressure and the skillful work of the Left in the convention committees.

The two central issues were the Taft-Hartley Act and foreign policy, especially the recently announced Marshall Plan.

The convention adopted a model fighting resolution against the Taft-Hartley Act, which stated in part:

"The act represents a triumph of repression. It is a direct step toward fascism. . . . No right was too fundamental, no activity of workers too basic to escape the act's hatchet. . . . We would not merit the name of free Americans if we acquiesced in a law which robbed American workers of the right to strike, to picket, and to engage in those concerted activities which are the life blood of our movement. . . . Nor will we permit the blackmail, the threats and the smears of legislative hatchet-men operating through the House Labor and Un-American Committees to divide or deter us.

"From this day forward we dedicate ourselves to the mission of obtaining a repudiation and forthright appeal of this infamous Act."

But this resolution was already undermined by the prior action of certain CIO leaders who indicated their readiness to have their unions sign the anti-Communist affidavits. They saw this as a way to help them fight the Left forces in their own unions. The resolution was further undermined when Philip Murray, although declaring that he was "unwilling to file an affidavit that I am not a Communist," nevertheless added he could understand that other affiliates might feel ready to sign and "there certainly is nothing in the policy [of the CIO] . . . which either inhibits or prevents those organizations from exercising that right."

It is not too surprising, therefore, that the proposed foreign policy resolution was a compromise, but one which the Left felt it should support, especially since it did not endorse either the Truman Doctrine or the Marshall Plan. In fact, it called for "a fulfillment of the basic policy of our late President Roosevelt for unity of purpose and action" by the United States, the Soviet Union and Britain within the United Nations. It stressed that "failure to accomplish this necessarily means dissension and strife in the world." It also called for "universal disarmament," for "complete demilitarization and utter destruction of all vestiges of fascism . . . and complete elimination of cartels in Germany," and for "discontinuance of production of atomic bombs and outlawing of atomic weapons."

The forces of reaction, however, did not give up easily. In concert with their red-baiting allies inside the CIO, they planned a flank attack, aimed at simultaneously putting public pressure on Murray and forcing his hand as a "loyal American." It was arranged that General George Marshall, Secretary of State, should address the convention. In a carefully staged visit and speech, Marshall combined a calm, deliberate analysis of the issue of help to the war-stricken nations of Western Europe with a strong appeal to American patriotism.

It was staged so that Marshall arrived and spoke just prior to the debate on the foreign policy resolution. The debate that followed was the sharpest in CIO history. All of the right-wing whooped it up for Marshall and Truman. In the face of a growing hysteria, Irving Potash and Joe Kehoe, members of the international executive boards of the Fur and Leather Workers Union and the American Communications Association, respectively, spoke in support of the resolution and boldly challenged the entire reactionary concept of the Truman Doctrine and the Marshall Plan. Many other Left and progressive members, stunned and confused by what was taking place, failed to take the floor. Murray finally arose and pledged his personal support to the Marshall Plan and the entire reactionary foreign policy of United States imperialism.

When the foreign policy resolution was adopted, the headlines at home and abroad interpreted Murray's speech as CIO endorsement for the Marshall Plan. Needless to say, there was considerable confusion and great bitterness against Murray in the ranks of the Left. In the following months there also developed the first betrayals of top left-wing trade union leaders.

Never before was there a CIO convention like the one in Portland in 1948. A new majority, led by Murray, Reuther and Rieve, was in control. While Murray remained the chief spokesman, Reuther and Rieve were in command. To the accompaniment of anti-Communist slander and hysteria, a right-wing program was adopted, and the first organizational measures were taken against the Left. Nevertheless, the left-wing forces brought before the convention a comprehensive progressive policy and fought for it. For the first time in CIO history, the recommendations of the committees on resolutions and on officers reports were not unanimous.

The reactionary program of this new right-wing majority was expressed primarily by its support of the Truman-Dulles foreign policy and its desertion of the Roosevelt-CIO policy of American-Soviet collaboration as the cornerstone of peace. This led to its unqualified support of President Truman and the two-party system, its rejection of a third party and the imposition of a political straitjacket for all CIO affiliates. It aimed at a wage policy that was anemic, lifeless and class collaborationist. And it declared war on the Left and progressive forces wherein all democratic procedures were to be ruthlessly violated.

The offensive against the Left found early expression in the lifting of the charter of the New York CIO Council; in the issuing of a 60-day ultimatum to the Farm Equipment Union that ordered it to merge with the auto workers; and in giving the executive board power to move against the jurisdiction of the executives of international unions which did not accept CIO political dictates.

The left-progressive minority at the convention, comprising 11 unions, put forward a positive position on five issues: the need of a real peace policy instead of the bipartisan administration cold war policy; an estimate that the partial trade union support to the Progressive Party and Henry Wallace was a contribution in the election campaign; condemnation of the raiding of progressive unions by right-wing unions, which included in some cases the use of the Taft-Hartley Act; criticism of Carey's testimony before the House labor committee as an unprincipled attack on the United Electrical Workers; and the declaration that labor could not rely on the good will of politicians but only on its own strength and militant struggle.

While there were still weaknesses in the united fight of these 11 unions, nevertheless they were advancing and fighting for a program that represented the interests of all the workers.

Portland was the third CIO convention I had watched from the visitors' balcony. In each, the forces of monopoly capitalism made headway in weakening and splitting the great CIO fortress of working-class power. What a difference from the days of united action in the sit-down strikes of General Motors, Goodrich or Goodyear Tire and Rubber companies, or the battles of Little Steel!

Why had the left-progressive forces not been able to prevent this set-back? What mistakes had been made? My principal conclusion was that we had not devoted sufficient time to building party strength and organization in the factories and among the rank and file, and had not done enough to develop class understanding and socialist consciousness. Important as it was to have Left leadership, combining Communists and left-progressives, it became equally clear that, in the face of a united political attack, this was possible only if there was an adequate party membership, with strong ties and influence at the rank-and-file level. Furthermore, our attention had been concentrated on CIO members, despite our theoretical recognition that with "the AFL representing 60 per cent of the organized working class" it was especially necessary "to improve our work among AFL workers."

The months following Portland were devoted to open warfare by the new majority against the 11 industrial unions under left-progressive leadership and against the left-progressive forces inside unions like auto and steel, in which the right-wing now had a firm grip, or in unions like maritime and transport, in which former Left leaders had capitulated under combined attack.

At the Portland convention it was Reuther who shouted at the left-progressive forces: "You are not going to be tolerated forever. . . . Make up your minds either to get clear in the CIO or clear out of the CIO." Now it was Murray who proposed at an executive board meeting that all board members must conform to majority political policies or resign or be kicked out.

In August 1949, as part of the preparations for the disastrous split of the CIO in Cleveland, the official paper, the *CIO News* devoted an entire front page to an attack on the party, using as a basis of the attack a report in the January *Political Affairs* in which I reviewed the CIO and AFL conventions. It was decided that I should reply publicly to Murray.

In "A Letter to Philip Murray" in *The Worker*, I quoted chapter and verse: how Murray had sung the praises of Truman, who had promised to repeal the Taft-Hartley Act, to initiate civil rights legislation and to feed the hungry of America's wartime allies by means of the Marshall Plan. I pointed out the stark betrayal only nine months later. I then took up the charge of "changing the Party line" by citing what Murray had said previously on four key questions—foreign policy, attitude to Truman, autonomy of CIO unions and rights of Communists in the CIO—and pointing out his present complete about-face on each of them. Here is part of what I wrote:

"Communists have worked in alliance with you in the past, and would do so now, on the basis of a minimum program representing the economic and political interests of labor and that would allow democracy and autonomy in the affairs of the CIO. When Communists and left-wingers were in alliance with you from 1935 to 1946; when you welcomed the cooperation of Communists in organizing the unorganized; when you hired scores of Steel Workers Organizing Committee organizers and directors whom you knew to be Communists—we were no different than now. Then, as now, we believed in socialism and you believed in capitalism. Nevertheless, we were able to work together on the basis of a fighting militant trade union program.

"Brother Murray: The main concern of the Communists today, as ever, is to promote the united action of labor in defense of its economic and political needs. We are sharply aware of the dangers facing the labor movement. We see clearly the arrogance of the employers, their refusal to grant the just wage and contract demands of the unions, and their preparations to weaken or smash the unions wherever they feel the unions are weak. And the employers don't make any distinction between the workers of right- or left-led unions, when their profits are involved. . . .

"We stand as uncompromising today as ever for the unity of the labor movement. We are particularly firm in our stand for a united CIO, for a united wage fight, for a united front to repeal Taft-Hartley. We are against splits, against secessions and against expulsions. We believe that there is room in a trade union for differences, especially on political issues."

As one Scot to another, I finished off with an appropriate quotation from Robert Burns, "Oh, wad some power the giftie gi'e us, To see oursel's as others see us."

While no answer ever reached me, I learned from other sources that Murray was furious, because the letter stated the simple truth.

Two months later, carried away by a wave of jingoism and the onset of the McCarthy hysteria, and hoping to quell the growing demands of the membership for a wage fight, Murray and

Reuther turned the 1949 Cleveland CIO convention into an orgy of red-baiting and anti-Communist slander. The climax came when the CIO was split by the expulsion of 11 unions, with 900,000 members. This was followed by wild scenes of international union-splitting, abetted by the employers and the government, while the AFL raided both groups of CIO unions indiscriminately.

13

Surrender to Taft-Hartley

The preoccupation of the CIO leadership with smashing the coalition that had brought the organization enormous gains, and the continued division of labor into two major national bodies paved the way for the Taft-Hartley Act. Although anti-labor legislation was not a novel device in the United States, the approach and techniques of the Taft-Hartley Act were new. Under the guise of helping the workers and adhering to the Roosevelt era's endorsement of labor unions, the act, by placing all these rights under the supervision of a government board, undermined the right to organize, to strike, to collect dues and to choose officers. The board was empowered to lay down the rules and to conduct elections for the choice of a union and to poll the membership on whether to strike. This was government interference with a vengeance!

More specifically, the act abolished the closed shop, established a 60-day cooling-off period before strikes could be called; outlawed mass picketing and secondary boycotts; permitted employer interference in the unionization of their plants, and revived court injunctions in labor disputes. It excluded certain workers from the right to collective bargaining, while it favored craft unions over shop or industrial organization. In addition, it required the filing of financial statements and prohibited political expenditures by trade unions as well as the expression of political views in their publications. Unions were subjected to being sued for "unfair labor practices" by employers, and all union officials were compelled to sign affidavits stating they were not Communists.

This sweeping anti-labor legislation was a class answer to the workers' postwar militancy and strikes. Its aims were to weaken the fight for higher wages and better conditions, to make strikes more difficult, to render impossible organizing drives by either the CIO or the AFL in the South. It served to implement United States foreign policy and to obstruct the development of a third-party movement. It was designed to stimulate further divisions in the ranks of the trade unions and to isolate the left-wingers and Communists by prohibiting them from holding union office.

While both the CIO and the AFL opposed the legislation separately and developed considerable activity around the issue, they absolutely refused to join in united action. Murray rejected protest stoppages as a means of struggle. When the AFL and CIO unions in Los Angeles got together and organized a motorcade to Washington, with the expectation that it would snowball as it proceeded, it was disowned by both Green and Murray as an innovation of the "Communists."

Furthermore, with the 1948 presidential elections looming, all the trade unions were partially lulled by the expectation that Truman would veto this legislation of the Republican-dominated 80th Congress. Such optimism was fatal. The party pointed out its pitfalls and continued to fight resolutely.

President Truman played a double game. He vetoed the bill, declaring that it was "deliberately designed to weaken labor unions," that it "would deprive workers of legal protection of fundamental rights," "that it would threaten fundamental democratic freedoms." But although the administration had the democratic votes to sustain Truman's veto, they were never mustered. In fact, half the Democrats joined with the Republicans in overriding the veto and making the bill the law of the land in June 1947.

Labor was stunned. Both the CIO and the AFL said it put the workers at the mercy of the employers. The CIO said that it "represents a triumph of repression . . . and . . . is a direct step toward fascism." William Green characterized it as "a slave measure, un-American, vicious, and destructive of labor's constitutional rights."

Still calling for repeal, it was not long before opportunism, rivalry between AFL and CIO unions, the anti-Communist virus and, above all, the top leadership support of United States imperialist policies, resulted in the capitulation of the unions, one by one.

The AFL convention, while condemning the act, meekly submitted to it by authorizing its officers to sign the anti-Communist affidavits and to file financial reports. The main opponent of this action was John L. Lewis, who declared the Act was "the first ugly, savage thrust of fascism in America . . . [brought] . . . into being through an alliance between industrialists and the Republican majority in Congress, aided by those Democratic legislators who still believe in the institution of human slavery."

But Lewis was defeated and took his union out of the AFL. In sharp language he exposed the contradiction of the convention's calling for the repeal of the Taft-Hartley Act while proposing to comply with it, declaring:

"What a paradox! How much heart do you think that will give the members of our organizations out in the industrial centers of this country when they see their great leaders, with all the pomp and ceremonials of a great convention, kneeling in obeisance before this detestable and tyrannical statue? . . .

"The leaders of our movement are to be the first of our mighty hosts of 8,000,000 members to put their tails between their legs and run like cravens before the threat of the Taft-Hartley bill. . . .

"I am reminded of the Biblical parable, 'Lions led by asses.' "

The CIO convention, although sharp in condemnation of the Act, left it up to each of its affiliated unions to decide upon a course of action. This meant surrender.

The Act was used ruthlessly against all workers, but its main targets were the non-complying unions and workers who went on strike.

The struggle to repeal the Taft-Hartley Act then started. While fully supporting this action, the party also pointed to the right-wing trade union leadership's accommodation in deed to the law. We outlined a more comprehensive battle against Taft-Hartleyism, while striving to strengthen the front of non-complying unions (made up of 14 or 15 CIO unions, the Mine Workers, Typographical Union and others).

During the 1948 presidential elections, Truman promised the repeal of the Taft-Hartley Act, while he maneuvered, with the help of the top trade union leaders, to cut down the vote for Wallace and the Progressive Party. But, once elected, he betrayed that promise. Instead of repeal, he offered a few amendments which still left intact the essential features of the Act, under a new name. He received support for his position from some trade union leaders.

The Truman amendments were accepted by Congress, and this anti-labor legislation continues to be invoked over and over again against the workers and the trade unions. Nearly two decades later, the first legal breakthrough was made in the Archie Brown case which invalidated the act's prohibition against Communists holding trade-union office.

But the Communists who still held trade union elective positions in the late 40's, from national officers to shop stewards, faced a difficult problem. Should they resign their trade union positions under protest, or resign from the party and hold on to their union jobs? Because of the political atmosphere, most of our people who held national trade union posts were not publicly known as party members, although they fought for party policy and defended the party's rights. In the factories of the basic industries, a public avowal would mean dismissal. And there was the belief in some quarters that party objectives and the workers' interests could be best furthered if Communists stayed in their elected trade union posts.

In this connection, the case of Max Perlow, national secretary-treasurer of the CIO Furniture Workers Union, comes to mind. After refusing to sign the anti-Communist affidavit for over a year, his union's executive board, faced with increasing losses of membership to the raiding AFL Upholsterers Union, decided they could not hold out any longer. Perlow announced that he was regretfully resigning from the party to fulfill the requirements of his union to comply with the Taft-Hartley Act. In the statement he issued for publication, he said:

"It is no secret to our membership that I have been a member of the Communist Party for many years. It is because of the teachings of this party that I have decided to devote my entire life to the cause of the workers. I came to the conclusion that there can be no higher privilege, no greater principle, than to serve the working people. . . . It is not true that the Communist

Party advocates the overthrow of the government by force and violence. . . .

"I am forced to sign the affidavit or give up my work in the service of the membership. . . . I decided to sign the affidavit and not allow this vicious law to bar me from continuing, to the best of my abilities, to serve the membership of our Union. . . .

"I feel that I owe it to all of you, in good conscience, to make it clear that I stand upon my constitutional right to believe that socialism provides the one real answer to the economic problems of our time. . . . I stand upon my constitutional right to believe that Marxism is the best expression of the hopes and aspirations of mankind."

A number of letters came to the *Daily Worker* asking for a party opinion on this action of Perlow. I was designated to answer and I wrote:

"The whole purpose of the anti-Communist provision in the Taft-Hartley Act is to separate Communist leadership from the mass of workers. In this particular situation, apparently, Perlow saw no other way to prevent this from happening than by the course he took, while explaining his actions and beliefs to his fellow union members and to the workers at large.

"Some ask, as you do, whether this is the precedent for all to follow. In our opinion, the answer is no. On the contrary, the precedent to follow by all non-complying unions is the effective and consistent winning of the rank and file against Taft-Hartley compliance as, for example, has been done in the ILWU, where over 95 per cent of the workers voted in a referendum against compliance.

"Precisely during this period of attack, Communist trade unionists must work in such a way as to strengthen their relationships with their fellow unionists and avoid isolation from the trade union movement and its members. . . .

"Irrespective of what individuals may do, the leading role and regular and proper functioning of the party as an organization is indispensable, if we are to give effective leadership to the working class and its allies in the various struggles."

A number of comrades resigned their trade union positions rather than give up party membership, but the greater number preferred to hold on to their union posts and resign from the party. Despite their original good intentions and proclaimed loyalty, too many in the stormy years ahead found themselves politically rudderless. Once the political compromise was made, some carried this into accommodation with the employers on union principles.

Now, with the benefit of hindsight and my experience in Britain, I think that we should have been more emphatic that membership in the Communist Party, with everything that it implies, provides the best opportunity to influence and lead the workers at all levels, especially in factory and local unions. If one is forced to make a choice for a temporary period, the values of party membership (ideological clarity based on Marxism-Leninism, organized contact and discipline) are decisive.

I have already related how the Communist Party unfurled the banner of struggle for full political, economic and social equality for the Negro people as far back as 1924, and remained in the forefront of this many-sided fight, even when it stood almost alone.

It was largely attributable to the influence of the Communists that in its first years the initials CIO had an almost magnetic attraction not only to Negro workers, but to the broadest sections of the Negro people. This was because it spoke out boldly on Negro democratic rights, established its own anti-discrimination committee, and supported all legislation favoring freedom.

In those early CIO days, many of the unions who were identified with left-progressive leadership waged a battle within their own membership for equal pay and upgrading for Negro workers and their right to hold trade union office. In some cases, union discipline had to be enforced to translate democratic constitutions and convention resolutions into action. When the Communist Blackie Myers, a white leader of the National Maritime Union, declined renomination for the CIO executive board to make room for Ferdinand Smith, the first Negro to sit on that body, it had a big impact.

By 1947, however, new problems had arisen in the relations of the Negro workers with the trade unions. Approximately 850,000 Negroes were trade union members, divided roughly as follows: 400,000 in the AFL and 450,000 in CIO unions. After the initial breakthrough of the CIO, the AFL intensified its activities. In the organizing drives in the South during 1946-47, the AFL was actually making greater progress than the CIO in reaching Negro workers, with the exception of the good work done by the CIO Food and Tobacco Workers and the Furniture Workers unions.

In all its literature the AFL pointed out that its founder was an immigrant Jew (Samuel Gompers) and that the name "American Federation of Labor" was actually proposed by a Negro delegate from Pittsburgh at its first convention. It was also a fact that the oldest and only nationally known Negro trade union leader was the ex-Socialist A. Phillip Randolph, who headed the AFL Pullman Porters Union.

The CIO had promised much but the years passed and there still remained a gap between promises and results. This was dramatized at the Boston CIO convention, when a Negro delegate from the tobacco industry in the South spoke in support of a really far-reaching resolution on Negro rights, and said:

"Too long have the Negro . . . workers . . . heard a lot of words read to them. It is time for action, and I am now wondering if the CIO is going to do . . . some of the things by action. You talk about political action and you talk about politics. How can there be any action when the Negroes in the South are not allowed to vote? . . . . We no longer look to the government in Washington for protection. It has failed. Today we are looking for an organization that says they are organized to fight for the freedom of all men regardless of race, creed or color, and that is the CIO. . . .

"You have got to get up and do something in action . . . and not by mere words."

At the end of 1947 the party held a special national conference on the problems of the Negro people. There were two reports — one by Ben Davis on "Building the United Negro People's Movement," the second by myself on "The Trade Unions and the Negro Workers." My report particularly addressed itself to the new problems that confronted the CIO as "the section of the labor movement that has already won the confidence of the Negro people." It seems to me now that this was a one-sided approach, especially when the facts showed the AFL had almost as many Negro members as the CIO, despite the much better resolutions of the CIO.

We singled out three things that particularly jeopardized the developing unity of the Negro people's movement with the trade unions, as well as the prestige of the unions among the

Negro workers. These were that the unions were not waging a satisfactory or consistent struggle to retain the economic gains won by the Negro workers in industry during the war; that, too often, within the trade unions, there was a formal approach to the question of equality of the Negro members in the actual operative leadership; and that not enough was being done to translate into life the good resolutions on equal rights, to overcome the denial of voting rights in the South, to achieve equal opportunities for education and housing and to struggle against the whole system of Jim Crow segregation in restaurants, railways, movies, hotels and buses.

A bit of a storm blew up among some of our top national comrades holding posts in national unions at my criticism of the slow progress in electing Negro workers to top posts and committees. While the average Negro worker knew that in many AFL unions his fight to attain equality in leadership was tied up with the general struggle for a progressive policy, he could not understand why this should be so in the CIO unions.

Our report showed that a survey of 23 CIO unions revealed 12 of them to be without a single Negro among their national officers or on the executive boards. These included the three largest unions — steel, auto and electrical. The unions that had elected Negroes to top positions were in the following fields: maritime, longshoremen, food and tobacco, transport, fur and leather, marine cooks and stewards, rubber, farm equipment, shipyard, and public workers.

We showed how the employers and all the forces opposed to the unity of Negro and white workers were trying to take advantage of this situation to divide the workers. This was confirmed by the fact that some Negro papers hailed the Taft-Hartley Act and supported a campaign to drop out of the unions or to withhold dues under the slogan, "no taxation without representation." In general, a stay-at-home trend had been developing among Negro workers when it came to union activity. Within the trade unions the most conscious Negro union members were organizing Negro caucuses.

As I write this in Britain nearly 20 years later, with the great Negro freedom movement sweeping the country, and when I think of how this powerful movement is transforming the political life of America, I feel proud of the early contributions the Communists made in helping to lay its foundations. The

Negro people have demonstrated that it is organized mass action that is decisive in achieving their demands, as the Communists have always maintained.

Throughout my years in the party national office, I spent half my time visiting the districts in connection with campaigns and party organization. Especially rewarding were my annual trips to the Pacific Coast, which combined public meetings, radio talks and intensive meetings with all party committees. I had worked out a pattern for the western trip, allowing one week each in Seattle, San Francisco and Los Angeles, and dividing a fourth week between Portland and Denver, Salt Lake City or Butte. No cities compare with Seattle and San Francisco for scenic beauty and surroundings. Both seemed to retain some of the youthful frontier spirit of the Far West that still expressed itself in the labor movement, especially among the lumber workers of Washington and the longshoremen of San Francisco. Much more often these trips took me back to Ohio and Chicago, where the daily work I came to do was enriched by comradeship with so many old friends and comrades.

Since I have been in Britain, I have received occasional letters or messages from comrades in Cleveland's Fisher Body plant, Akron's Goodyear plant and from active trade union leaders in Chicago. One day, a few years ago, I got an invitation from the national secretary of a well known British trade union to attend a reception at his house. It happened that his wife, who was from New York and was now a labor councillor, had studiously avoided me since my return to Britain, even though she had belonged to one of the committees established to help Paul Robeson get his passport. The reason for the invitation was that my host was receiving an American trade union delegation, one of whose members years ago had been an active section organizer of the party, and who wanted me invited to the reception. On another occasion, the grandson of an active party member in Cleveland when I was district secretary, came to visit me when I was South Essex district secretary. He was interested in learning about the British labor movement.

During these years in the national office I must have spoken to hundreds of public meetings, indoor and outdoor. But nothing could be compared to a Madison Square Garden meeting. It was the largest hall in New York, seating approximately

20,000. While the overriding job was to get the place filled, it was also a feat of organization to get everyone seated with the help of an army of ushers, who also sold literature, took the collection and maintained order if there were provocative interruptions.

The Communist was the only political party that could fill the Garden on the basis of a straight political appeal and an admission charge. On top of that, a Garden collection was always sure to net a considerable sum. Others filled the Garden for similar occasions with big entertainment programs, free admission and, in the case of the Democratic Party, machine pressure on the job-holders.

In such a mammoth hall, ringed with several tiers of seats that reached up beyond one's sight, it was a most difficult job for the speaker to establish and maintain contact with the audience. Everything was planned to split-second accuracy. The bane of every party organizer in charge of a Garden meeting were those few comrades, like Bill Foster and Bob Minor, who would never write out a speech and, as they got carried away with the response of the audience, would go far beyond their time. Bob was even more guilty of this than Bill.

Of the eight or nine times I spoke at Madison Square Garden, the opening session of the 14th national convention stands out. The national committee had been arrested under the Smith Act a couple of weeks prior to this and released on bail. This meeting, therefore, was also in the nature of a protest against the arrests. The meeting was jammed and the police closed the doors. My role was to introduce a party manifesto appealing to the people to organize mass protest movements against the anti-democratic actions of the reactionary 80th Congress.

I had prepared what I thought was an appropriate speech, in my own words and style. But we had "gone modern" in the party center, and had a comrade in charge of publicity, the late Marion Bachrach. On the eve of the Garden meeting, the Department of Justice loosed another of its fake sensational spy scares, the confessions of one Elizabeth Bentley, whom none of us had ever seen or known. The newspapers were full of "Beautiful-Blonde-Tells-All" headlines.

Marion, an excellent writer, felt called upon to reply to these headlines. So at the point in my written speech where I was hitting back against the attacks of monopoly and stating "they are trying to arrest progress by arresting the leaders of the Communist Party," Marion had inserted, "they are trying to keep the people from thinking about their troubles by feeding them thriller-dillers about 'beautiful blondes' who turn out to be homely brunettes, and 'spy-rings' that never happened at all."

The reaction next day of all the brunettes to this comment convinced me never again to allow publicity experts, even as talented as Marion, to interfere with my own style and presentation of a speech.

During the years of 1949 and 1950, two leading British comrades visited us unannounced. First, Arthur Horner, at that time national secretary of the Miners Union, was on trade union business in the United States. Having completed this, he stopped in to see us before his ship sailed.

It was a Sunday and the only place open was the *Daily Worker*. The office phoned me and I made arrangements to meet him and then take him to visit Bill Foster, who was ill but able to move around. In the course of driving him to Foster's house, I answered Arthur's questions about the American trade union movement. At one point I denounced in appropriate terms "Tsar" Joe Ryan of the East Coast longshoremen, the only trade union official in America elected to a life term of office.

To my surprise, Horner told me that he himself was elected for life (up to compulsory retirement at 65 years of age) in the British Miners Union. My astonishment was such as to almost wreck the car. The discussion lasted till we reached Foster's house, but neither of us convinced the other of his opinion on that subject.

The other visitor, about a year later, was Bill Gallacher, the Communist member of Parliament from Scotland, accompanied by his wife, Jean. One day, as I walked from the party offices to the *Political Affairs* office at the other end of the corridor, a man and woman who looked familiar were sitting in the reception room. I looked again and recognized my old friend and comrade, Bill, whom I had last seen in Moscow at one of the Comintern sessions.

After appropriate greetings I upbraided him for not notifying us of his arrival. With his usual modesty he said since he was not on official party business but only visiting relatives in Chicago, and since he knew how busy we were, he didn't want to bother us. After introducing him and Jean to everyone, we showed them around the building. He immediately inquired about all features of American life and the party's position on them.

He and Jean went sight-seeing in New York and visited many friends, old and new, some of whom he remembered from his long experiences as a party and trade union leader and MP in Britain. It was surprising how these contacts reached into all walks of life, including the arts.

We were anxious to share Gallacher's great experiences and talents with the party, especially since our movement was under heavy attack and we were in the midst of our nine-month-long Smith Act trial. Gallacher told us that before getting his visa he had been made to promise he would hold no public meetings or propagate communism in the United States. We worked out a plan, to which he agreed, that if he spoke about Britain to an invitation meeting of New York active members this would not violate his pledge. We did not, however, depend on the State Department's acceptance of our interpretation, and so we arranged the meeting for the night before he was due to sail.

Without a single public announcement, 3,000 party actives gathered in the Manhattan Center. The evening was all Gallacher's and he was in excellent form. He paced up and down that big platform. The audience was alternately silently intent and then howling with laughter. I would have sworn that the majority did not understand half of what they heard in Bill's rich Scottish brogue, but they got into the spirit of the event. After speaking for over an hour, he answered questions for another hour. We all enjoyed his great contribution, and Gallacher was the talk of the party in New York for weeks afterward.

We were ready to take him to his hotel after such an exhausting night, but he insisted upon accepting an invitation to visit a Broadway star—who would have been scared to death to meet an American party leader—and I found out the next day that he and Jean were up till 2 A.M. Here again, we saw a party leader who was a man of the people, respected everywhere for his rugged, forthright and honest personality, a comrade whose rich experience and knowledge were known throughout the world, and who up to his death a few years ago, when he was in his 80s, was more active than many people half his age.

I was not to see him again till I arrived in Glasgow on May 12, 1955, where on the station platform he headed a large delegation to greet me and my family. He stood in front leading everyone in singing the International.

At about this time, Gene Dennis was serving a sentence of one year for boldly expressing his contempt of the House Committee on Un-American Activities.* He had challenged its constitutional authority, charging that its Southern members were holding office illegally since their Negro citizens were disfranchised. The National Committee had to decide on a temporary replacement for the general secretary. Upon Gene's recommendation, we unanimously chose Gus Hall and elected him national secretary. Gus came from Ohio where he was state secretary and, together with Winston, Robert Thompson and myself, constituted a secretariat.

Our lawyers were able to keep Gene in the local federal detention prison because of the need for legal consultations on the pending Supreme Court appeal from our Smith Act convictions. Each week for 11 months I visited Gene in West Street jail, together with one of our lawyers, and we discussed, under the heading of legal business, all pressing questions. Since we were sure the lawyers' visiting room was bugged, we carried on a lot of our conversation in writing, a practice that requires great patience.

Both Gus and Gene had records as devoted Communists and courageous fighters against the class enemy as well as in defense of party principles and unity. Both were industrial workers with little formal education, who had through much self-education, reading and participation in working-class struggles become worker-intellectuals and fine party leaders.

In those days Gene was the patient type of thinker, with a good grasp of Marxist-Leninist theory, somewhat slow to make up his mind; once having arrived at a conclusion, however, he fought for it tooth and nail. It was not easy to know Gene intimately, but when you did, you got to know him as a man of real warmth and comradeship who had complete disregard for his personal cares. Possessing a wonderful mind and an effec-

---

*The committee chairman, J. Parnell Thomas, was subsequently convicted of stealing government funds.

tive pen, he was never a great speaker. The truth is that he went through a nervous upheaval each time he had to address a Madison Square Garden meeting.

Where the two men differed was in secondary things. Gus was a very warm person, easy to talk to and gifted in finding a common language with his listeners while putting across the most complex political argument. Gus also had that characteristic of Foster's — an ear or a feel for what the factory worker or man in the street was thinking at a given moment. Reading Gus's reports, speeches and articles here in England these last years, I see a tremendous growth in his comprehension of Marxist-Leninist theory and its application to American conditions. Gus is a worthy successor to Gene as general secretary and the party has been politically richer for the contributions of both.

From our arrival in New York City in 1941 until 1955, when I was deported, we lived in two different houses, both in Washington Heights. Our son Bob went to nursery school and then through all the various stages of schooling, including attendance at Bronx High School of Science and the first year of college at Cooper Union.

Our family grew. A second son, Glen, was born in 1943. He was a "blue baby," and medical science had not yet learned to handle such cases. Dozens of times each day the baby turned blue and had to be held, head down, before he regained normal breathing. After four months he died. As always seems to be the case in our family crises, I was on a trip to the districts when this happened. On the train between Cleveland and Detroit, the conductor passed through shouting my name, and handed me a telegram informing me of the sad news. I rushed back to New York by plane to be with Mae and Bob.

Four years later Neil was born. After bringing the baby from the hospital, he became critically ill. Our doctor, a family friend, was very considerate and devoted much time to saving Neil's life. It was a great relief to have him restored to good health after several weeks.

While these were years of strenuous work and, starting in 1948, of persecution, trials and imprisonment, they were also years when our family was happy and life was rich. The main responsibility for the house and raising the children fell on Mae, because of the load of work I had to carry, including many evening meetings and out-of-town visits.

This was the case in the homes of most party leaders, despite our belief in equality and joint responsibility for the house and for raising a family. As Bob grew older, I did find time to take him to an occasional baseball game, a circus or the rodeo. Nearby was Fort Tryon Park where many a pleasant Sunday morning was spent. When Neil reached a comparable age, I was sitting behind steel bars and concrete walls, and his knowledge of his Dad were the quarterly visits to Lewisburg Penitentiary, where even he had to go through the "electric eye" to make sure he didn't smuggle in any dangerous weapons.

14

Prosecution and Imprisonment

Political persecution is not new in the life of Communists and others fighting for social progress. Its forms and intensity vary with circumstances and the relationship of class forces.

Nevertheless, the first experience of arrest, trial, hearings, prison or deportation is always new to the individual concerned. Like a man on the battlefield who is ordered to go over the top for the first time, he never knows how he will react until it happens.

My own experiences were very much like those of my colleagues. We were not confronted with tragic ordeals like those of the Rosenbergs, or the victims in Nazi concentration camps or today's martyrs in Mississippi. Of the many party leaders arrested, tried and sentenced under the Smith Act, only one became a traitor. The overwhelming majority stood the test in battle, even though a few, after being released from prison or released by appeals court decisions have subsequently given up the struggle and looked for an easier life.

On the morning of February 10, 1948, as I left our house at 4500 Broadway in upper Manhattan to go to work, I was quickly surrounded by five burly plainclothesmen who tried to hustle me into a waiting car. I resisted and demanded to know who they were. They identified themselves as agents of the FBI and of the Immigration Department. By this time people were stopping on the street to see what was happening, which was precisely what I wanted.

I insisted upon going back to the house to notify the family, knowing Mae would immediately let the party office know. They were not sure whether to agree or not, but finally two of them remained downstairs while three accompanied me up-stairs. Mae answered the knock with eight-month old Neil in her arms. Surrounded by my captors, I informed her of what was happening. I was confident I would be home that day, and I assured her I would be out on bail in a few hours. But it was to be a month before I saw home again.

I was then taken downtown and from there to Ellis Island by ferry. This was the celebrated entrance gate to America through which millions of immigrants from Europe had arrived. One end of the island was now a government detention center for stowaways, illegal entrants awaiting return, and aliens ordered deported who could not raise bail. On the other end of the is-land was a government hospital.

I was locked up in a solitary cell. Before the day was over, it was clear I wasn't going to get out on bail so easily. I was in-formed that I had been arrested as an "undesirable alien" be-longing to an organization that believed in "overthrowing the United States government by force and violence." Attorney General Tom Clark (now on the Supreme Court) ordered that I be held indefinitely without bail.

On the island was also the well-known anti-fascist fighter and German Communist leader, Gerhardt Eisler. He wanted to leave the United States, but was being held under bail awaiting trial. Charged with contempt of the House Un-American Com-mittee, he was denied bail and held for deportation.

In the next 30 days three other left-wing national trade union leaders were arrested under deportation charges and brought to Ellis Island: Ferdinand Smith, national secretary of the Mari-time Union; Charlie Doyle, an international vice-president of the Gas, Coke and Chemical Workers Union; and Irving Po-tash, international vice-president of the Fur Workers Union and a member of the Communist Party national board.

Attorney General Tom Clark's decision to deny us bail was both unprecedented and unconstitutional. If he could get away with his claim that the courts had no power to grant bail, it would mean that no court, no judge, or due process of law could be invoked in such cases in the future. Since deportation proceedings dragged out for years, it would also mean that Ellis Island would become a virtual concentration camp for anyone the administration wanted to get rid of.

An intensive court battle started for the right to bail, supplemented by a growing wave of protests. A positive advantage was the agreement among the five of us on the Island that our cases, while being fought individually in the courts, should be tied together in the public campaign waged by the American Committee for the Protection of Foreign Born.

Each day some new legal move was made, but they all led to a dead end—no release on bail. There was a wave of trade union support for those of us who were well known in the labor movement. Even before the three CIO leaders were arrested, I received hundreds of letters and wires from trade union locals, central labor councils and national leaders—especially from Cleveland, Akron, Youngstown, Toledo, Chicago, Flint, Detroit and New York. CIO President Philip Murray publicly protested on behalf of Smith, Doyle and Potash. Picket demonstrations took place in various cities in front of federal government offices. A delegation of trade unionists visited Washington to protest. A public protest meeting was held in New York with Maritime Union Vice-president Frederick Myers, Food Workers Union leader Charles Collins, singer Lena Horne, artist Rockwell Kent, labor councillor Connolly and the Rev. William Spofford.

During all this time there was virtual press silence, except for the *Daily Worker*, which made the story front-page news. A box was carried daily listing in large figures opposite our names the number of days each of us had been held and denied the right to bail.

On the Island we were at first locked in separate cells and allowed only a half-hour of exercise daily. We were not permitted to visit the library or to eat with the other "detainees." Through the grapevine we kept in touch, although we never saw each other. Finally, after two weeks' fight on the inside and outside against this obvious harassment, we were put together in one large cell. While still separated from the other prisoners, our exercise time was extended to one hour, we were allowed the food sent in by our families and we even got a radio. The authorities liked to stress that we were not prisoners, only detainees; we didn't occupy cells, only "cabins." But whatever you called it, we were denied our freedom and locked up behind steel bars. While we could see the Statue of Liberty from the roof where we got our daily exercise, the location was such that the statue had her back to us—a piece of irony that was not without its propaganda value.

Taking advantage of the easier regulations for detainees (in comparison with prisoners), I conducted an intensive campaign for freedom from the Island. I personally answered every letter or telegram. I wrote letters to the press. When Truman made a nationwide radio broadcast invoking the name of Jefferson, I had a fine opportunity to answer him with effective chapter-and-verse quotes from Jefferson relevant to our fight for freedom.

When we were alone in our cells each of us read until our eyes ached. Once we were together and the regime became less rigorous, we discussed many things, including how we could force action. We got to know each other better; exchanged food received from home and news about our families. My oldest boy Bobby appeared on a radio quiz program for his school, and we all listened and were proud when he answered all questions correctly and his team won the prize. All of us fell in love with Ferd Smith's beautiful little granddaughter, Stephanie. And we had many laughs when Eisler, in friendly quarrels, accused Doyle of liking only banal songs like "I Am My Own Grandpa," an accusation which Doyle, with his Irish wit, hotly denied.

We finally decided to take drastic action when Judge Conger after interminable delays refused bail to Eisler, Doyle and myself. We decided to go on a hunger strike for as long as we were held without bail. Fully aware of the seriousness of such an action and its consequences, we prepared to make it effective and tried to anticipate the reactions of our jailers.

We wrote a letter to Attorney General Clark, which he refused to release to the press, in which we charged he was trying "to bury us alive," because we were fighting against the anti-labor activities of the Truman administration. We pointed out that no one was safe if Clark's action was not defeated, and we concluded, "We notify you that as of the morning of Monday, March 1, we are starting a protest hunger strike."

The next morning we refused to leave our cell to eat break-fast. In the next hour every official, up to the superintendent, visited us, but we were adamant. They placed a guard inside the cell with us 24 hours a day. He even accompanied us to the toilet. The day before we had given all our food, candy and fruit to 10-and 11-year-old stowaways from Greece. That morn-ing we went through the cell with a fine-tooth comb to make sure nothing was left. As we anticipated, the officials on the first day said the hunger strike was a hoax and claimed we had hoarded food in our cells. They soon dropped that canard when we released through our lawyers our letter to Clark and also gave some information about the Greek children who were being held.

During the next three days they tried every maneuver to break the hunger strike. We were taken out individually and offered food; big, savory meals were brought to our cells. We were suffering from hunger pangs but we ordered them to remove the food, threatening to throw it at the guards. Then they tried a trick which backfired and brought an end to these provocations. Smith and I were summoned to the post office. I was given a package filled with fruit, and Smith a package containing a roasted chicken. We refused to accept them and asked that the packages be given to the child stowaways. They then came up with a post office regulation which said that only detainees could legally receive post through the United States mails. The officials suddenly insisted they couldn't touch it legally.

We had a sharp session, during which our voices could be heard all over the place. We insisted that the food be given to the stowaways. They refused. Finally the assistant superintend-ent showed up (I'm sure it was his idea originally), and he took me to his office. Knowing he was supposed to have a liberal background, I told him to stop playing games, that he was deal-ing with people who took this serious action only because all other avenues had been denied them, and that we would hold him personally responsible for any more of these provocative moves, which only worsened our physical condition.

He still insisted that the new food arriving by post—either sent before our announced hunger strike, or since by some well-meaning supporters—could not be given to the child stow-aways. He even said we made them all sick with the rich food we gave them the day before we started the hunger strike. We compromised and agreed that it would be put on a table where anyone could get it. I always suspected that the guards qualified as "anyone."

On the morning of the fourth day, attended by the superintendent, a doctor and my good friend and lawyer, the late Mrs. Carol King, we were all transferred to the hospital. Since there were no barred windows there, two guards covered us 24 hours a day. The first three days had been the worst. Later the hunger pains and headaches subsided. We felt tired and spent a lot of time on our cots from then on, conserving our strength.

The head of the hospital visited us daily. We served notice on him not to try forcible feeding or we would take legal action against him. The poor man was apologetic and did everything he could for us—which was nothing. We agreed to be weighed and have our pulse taken daily.

The news of our hunger strike broke through the press silence and became headline news. The New York *Post* declared editorially: "[These men] have been imprisoned not because they have committed any hostile act...but because they hold what the Justice Department believes to be 'dangerous thoughts'."

The liberal daily, *PM*, had a full-page editorial signed by Max Lerner, declaring our imprisonment was the government's way "of trying to harry the Communists out of whatever strongholds they still retain in the trade unions...and ...these are not ordinary deportation cases but a political maneuver." He also declared our hunger strike "a valid protest... that dramatizes the injustice."

Many protest demonstrations were organized that week. In New York over 7,000 gathered with placards outside the Immigration Building at Columbus Circle and then marched down Broadway to Times Square. Pictures of these thousands appeared the next day, including one of my ten-year-old Bobby with a big sign "I want my Dad." Smaller demonstrations took place in Chicago, San Francisco, Detroit, Cleveland, Los Angeles, Pittsburgh and elsewhere. A picket line marched in front of the White House.

On the fourth day of the hunger strike, the first breakthrough came. Potash was released on bail. The CIO had sent their national counsel to appear on his behalf and, under the pressure that built up, the judge found a technicality to cover his release on bail, pending appeal. On the fifth day, three of us—Eisler, Doyle and myself—were hauled back to court where our lawyers had started *habeas corpus* proceedings. This was a five-hour ordeal, since we were denied water, the only thing that had passed our lips for the preceding 110 hours. Nevertheless, it was an important part of the battle.

As we waited to enter the courtroom, we were besieged by dozens of reporters and photographers, which insured even greater publicity for our case. When we entered the courtroom, packed to capacity with our friends and families, everyone stood up. The court attendants were startled, since there was no sign that the judge was entering to open the session. Then it dawned on them what had happened, and they ran around like startled rabbits.

Joe North wrote the next day: "I don't know whether the attendants understood, but everybody else did. These prisoners are greater than those who sit in judgement of them. That's what this scene meant."

While our lawyers fought well, Judge Bondy denied the writ but reserved decision on the application for bail, pending appeal to a higher court. We were returned to our hospital cots on Ellis Island.

The next day—Saturday, March 6—was the sixth of our hunger strike. All our families visited us, including Eisler's world-famous musician brother, Hans. Reflected in the faces of our loved ones was great concern at our loss of weight and anxiety over how it was all going to end.

After the visits, exhausted by the events of the preceding two days, we lay down on our beds. Late in the day we were visited by the assistant director, accompanied by a doctor. He told us to pack up; we had just been granted bail. Eisler, very skeptical because of previous experiences in prisons and concentration camps, asked how we knew he was telling the truth. The assistant director protested loudly that he wouldn't joke about things like that, and then said in exasperation, "Because of you, I've had to come back here all the way from home, to see you officially leave. The rules are that no one leaves Ellis Island on Saturdays or Sundays."

Finally convinced, we ate a bowl of soup and drank some orange juice, and the ferry took us back to New York. A hundred people met us with shouts of victory. They had been in the courtroom that afternoon when Judge Bondy found "the power" to grant us bail. We were rushed to a doctor on Park Avenue who found that we were not in bad condition, aside from losing weight (I lost 18 pounds). After two days' rest we were back in circulation.

During the judge's public appearance on the bench that afternoon, telegrams were stacked over a foot high on his desk and were still being handed him as he signed his order. Proof of the power of mass pressure (and how it can sweep away legal technicalities) was the fact that legally Ferdy Smith's case was not even before Judge Bondy that day, but when the release on bail came, it included him with the rest of us.

Our hunger strike and the splendid support of tens of thousands of people gave us temporary freedom and defeated Tom Clark's efforts to establish a concentration camp for left-wing aliens. It took another five years before the same kind of thing was tried again, but this time it was part of the infamous McCarran Act.

In a pamphlet written after we were released, we said in a joint statement: "Six days of hunger strike are quite an experience. But the greatest experience for us all was the solidarity of the people on the outside. This we will never forget."

On July 20, 1948, I stepped off a plane from Los Angeles, very tired. It was a hot, sultry humid New York day with the temperature in the 90s. The plane had run into trouble over Oklahoma and we were late in arriving. When I got home, I phoned the office to say I was back but was going to get some sleep. In a couple of hours the office phoned me to say I must come at once—an emergency.

I went reluctantly, without shaving and in shirt sleeves, thinking I would be back in an hour. The following story had been leaked to us: It seemed that a grand jury which had been in session for months trying to hang a Red label on several prominent New Dealers had failed in the attempt. In desperation, on the last day of the jury's legal existence, it was now about to indict the Communist Party's national leaders, in order to help Truman rebut the Republicans' charge of "20 years of Democratic treason."

A group of us—Foster, Dennis, Winston, Davis, Stachel, Thompson and myself—were discussing this in Dennis's office when the door burst open and a dozen men rushed in. They identified themselves as FBI men, and then identified each of us officially. We were handcuffed and taken outside, where the street had been barricaded off. Separate cars were provided for each of us, with an intricate system of inter-car radio communication.

At FBI headquarters we were each stripped and interrogated separately. I refused to answer any questions except my name and address. They kept up their barrage of questions till I lost my temper. After being mugged and placarded with numbers, we were locked up till they could get a judge to come from home to convene court. (A picture of me unshaven and looking like a desperado was used by the Hearst press for years.) Then we were all charged under the Smith Act on two counts: first, a conspiracy indictment alleging we organized to advocate and teach the violent overthrow of the United States government by force and violence at some unknown time in the future; and second, a membership indictment alleging that we belonged to an organization, the Communist Party, that taught and advocated the overthrow of the government by force and violence.

We were released late that night on $5,000 bail each. The remaining members of the national committee — Hall in Cleveland, Winter in Detroit, Green in Chicago, and Potash and Gates who were on vacation — were arrested during the next few days, brought to New York, charged and released on bail.

The nine-month-long Foley Square trial of the party's national committee that started in February 1949 became well known throughout the world. It was the longest criminal trial in the history of that court. Books have been written about it. The trial record totals more than five million words, bound in 20 big volumes. I have a set packed away for posterity.

The judge, Harold Medina, was a 20th century reincarnation of the infamous Judge Jeffries of the English Bloody Assize. He was deliberately chosen because of his violent class bias and his bitter anti-Communism. And his every act for nine long months reflected this.

Before the trial started we challenged the entire jury system in New York as being rigged, and we forced the chief judge to admit it. Up to that time the great majority of jurors were in the so-called blue-ribbon category — "respectable," middle-class Anglo-Saxons. While Medina rejected our motion, which took a month to hear, the result of our challenge was a formal change in the stacked, class composition of jurors.

The government evidence was contained in dozens of books by Marx, Engels, Lenin and Stalin, plus the fictitious testimony of stool pigeons. Most of the witnesses had been blackmailed into being "stools" by government threats to prosecute them for some earlier misdoing. Medina held that books of Marxist political theory were competent evidence, comparable to the introduction of burglars' tools as evidence in a trial for robbery.

On the opening day of the trial 400 uniformed police were at the Foley Square courthouse. Over 1,000 protesters formed a moving picket line. For months, 300 to 400 workers showed up daily at lunch time to picket and demand our freedom. At the end of nine months, when we were found guilty, Medina took delight in denying us bail. We spent ten days waiting in the New York Federal Detention Prison on West Street – an old brick building, in which iron cages occupied the middle of the floor space, with a corridor running all the way around for the guards (it resembled animal cages in a zoo). Then we were brought before Judge Medina for sentencing.

The government prosecutors and judge made a spectacle of this occasion. Nearly a thousand armed police were in and around the courthouse. Inside, the courthouse was ringed with burly United States marshals. Behind each of the defendants was another marshal. Thus the government demonstrated its fear of socialism. Medina and United States Prosecutor John F. Xavier McGohey played their parts with an eye on the press and on advancing their careers. Medina, haughty and sardonic, exuded hatred as he declared that he wished he could sentence us each to ten years, but would have to limit himself to the legal maximum of five years in prison and $10,000 fine. He then swung around and said, "I have some unfinished business," and sentenced each of our six lawyers to jail for contempt of court, the penalties ranging up to six months.

The atmosphere was such that not a single judge would grant us bail. Neither would the United States Court of Appeals. Finally, after five weeks in the West Side jail, the appeal went before United States Supreme Court Justice Jackson, who released us on bail totaling $260,000. Four of us – Dennis, Potash, Stachel and myself – were each put on $30,000 bail, and the other seven on $20,000 each.

The entire trial was a political frameup. The only evidence concerning me, for example, consisted of the already well known fact that I was a member of the national committee and secretariat of the party. This was buttressed by the introduction of printed copies of speeches, articles, reports and pamphlets that I had made or written, and that had been distributed widely. In several of these I made reference to individual reading or class study of many books, including such Marxist classics as *The Communist Manifesto, Imperialism,* and *Foundations of Leninism.* Evidently our "conspiracy" consisted of membership in the national committee of the party. From the entire stable of FBI informers, not a single criminal act on my part was even alleged. My activity had been a public record for 30 years. The same was true of my co-defendants, against whom the government failed to charge any overt act.

The political character of this conviction and jailing is underscored in various court opinions. Circuit Court Chief Judge Hand said: "It is not for us to say whether such a prosecution makes against the movement or . . . only creates more disciples." United States Supreme Court Justice Frankfurter questioned the "wisdom of the assumptions underlying the legislation and prosecution." Justice Jackson said, "I have little faith in the long-range effectiveness of this conviction, to stop the rise of the Communist movement." Nevertheless, all of these judges affirmed our conviction, and the affirmative decision of the circuit court stated, "We must not close our eyes to our position in the world at this time. . . . The status quo, hastily contrived in 1945, was showing strains and stresses not originally expected."

United States Supreme Court Justice Black asserted in his dissent that we were "not charged with non-verbal acts of any kind" and were "not even charged with saying or writing anything designed to overthrow the government." And Justice Douglas said, "I repeat that we deal here with speech alone. . . . To make a speech unlawful because two men conceive it is to raise the law of conspiracy to appalling proportions. Even *The New York Times* said editorially, "The decision of the Supreme Court upholding the conviction of the eleven Communist leaders is one of the most momentous in the recent history of that tribunal. . . . This undoing of the Communist Party has been achieved only by a violent upheaval in our judicial concepts."

Nevertheless, the United States Supreme Court by a vote of six to two upheld the conviction on July 2, 1951. We were each send to different federal penitentiaries, manacled hand and foot, as befitted "dangerous" men.

Medina and McGohey each got judicial promotions as rewards. McGohey and his staff were just political hangers-on of the Tammany machine. Their names are already forgotten. Medina was different. He was a fully conscious representative of capitalism and one of its intellectual props within the judiciary. The choice of Medina had been made to assure a combination of vindictive class consciousness with a thorough knowledge of the law and alertness to prevent any too-obvious legal errors.

Carl Winter and I landed in the Lewisburg Penitentiary, in a small town of the same name in northern Pennsylvania. All government authorities and prison officials stoutly maintain that in America there are no political prisoners. This is a fairy tale. Actually the conditions of the political prisoner are more punitive than those of other prisoners.

When you cross the threshold of a federal penitentiary, you shed not only your handcuffs, leg-irons and clothes to don prison blues; it is the intent of the authorities to have you also shed your personality, ideas, initiative, dignity and the ability to think and act. The first step in that direction is the assignment of a number by which you are known from then on. My number was 19353. It appears on your cell door, clothes, shoes and letters — and you are called by it. You can only pass from one place to another with a pass listing your number, the time you left and arrived along with the signature of the guards and the control center.

For weeks after your release from prison, the jangle of keys and the glare of flashlights is vividly with you for one learns to live by the blare of bugles, bells and whistles over the loudspeaker system. Your locker is constantly being shaken down by the guards; at least twice a day you must go through the "electric eye" to make sure you have no metal on you. For the first month you live in quarantine while they give you dozens of injections. Separated from the other prisoners, you are supposed to be getting conditioned to your new life. At the end of the month you are sent into the prison population.

Lewisburg had 1,400 prisoners, the great majority under 25. About 300 were from the army — mainly from Korea — serving sentences of ten years to life. Once we were safely locked behind the 30-foot walls, the very first words uttered to us were, "You have no rights here, only privileges." How true this was from that moment on until March 1955!

You get assigned to either a cell or to a dormitory that houses about 42 inmates. Carl Winter and I lived through both cells and dormitories. There are pro and con arguments on the "merits" of each, even among political prisoners. You get "work" and "dress" clothes, consisting of trousers and shirts. The work clothes are torn and unshapely; the "dress blues" are used only for visits, the cinema or Sundays. Everyone is assigned to some work. Lewisburg had a branch of Federal Industries Inc., comprising a metal fabricating plant and a clothing factory. The former made and sold all types of lockers for the armed services and other branches of government; the latter made pants for the army and for prisons.

About 350 prisoners were employed. They worked hard and received slave-labor pay, from $17 a month in fourth grade to $37 in first grade. Most were classified in third or fourth grade. Despite this, employment was much sought after because of the pay and, even more, the chance to earn "industrial good time"—extra days off your sentence each month. The Smith Act prisoners were denied the right to apply for industry and thereby deprived of good time.

Carl and I were assigned to the mechanical maintenance department—he, as clerk in the paint shop, and I to what was called mechanical repair (a combination of machine-shop, sheet-metal and welding work). After six months of work on the bench, I was given a clerical job, although it was never officially listed as such because of the officials' fear that they would be accused of coddling the Communists if two of them were given such work.

The foreman in the maintenance shops were a notch above the others; they had to have been qualified craftsmen before assuming the duties of foreman-guard. The clerk's job was to requisition material and to keep and give out all tools. Once a month an inventory was taken. All requisitions, orders and so forth were in his hands, so he had a typewriter available. I had two foremen in succession and was treated by both of them more decently than they treated many others. Their attitude was that as long as I did the work, they didn't care what

I did with the rest of my time. Only, they warned, don't expect us to save you if you get caught by one of the snooping guards (hacks).

Since the clerk's job could be done effectively in about one hour a day, except at the end of the month, I had lots of free time. This became a real problem, as you will see later. If the foremen had all their records and paper work in first-class shape, they were ready to leave you alone. This was our *quid pro quo* arrangement.

During these years, discrimination against Negro prisoners was still officially practiced. They were housed separately, ate in separate dining halls, sat in separate sections of the auditorium and had separate barber shops. Ben Davis's splendid fight in the Terre Haute Penitentiary, challenging this discrimination, electrified the prison world when the grapevine spread the story of his lawsuit against the government.

When Ben Davis arrived in Terre Haute he constantly protested the Jim Crow discrimination. He was penalized by being shifted from job to job, till they had him mopping the floors. He then decided on a court case against the government. After months of delay in making available to him the necessary law books for reference, and additional months lost because of the need to submit the case through the hands of the warden and Washington, the brief reached the court. Ben was then punished by being put into "administrative segregation"—locked up in the "hole" for 24 hours a day but given his food allotment.

The case was finally set for 15 days before his scheduled release. When he arrived in court, handcuffed, the United States Attorney asked mockingly, "What are you doing here, Davis? Why don't you go home?" That was the way he was informed that the government was releasing him 15 days early rather than risk exposure of their rotten Jim Crow system. The court then dismissed his case because he was no longer in custody. Furthermore, he could not have been subject to segregation because he was in "administrative segregation for his own protection," on the date the brief reached the court and thereafter. This was the same penitentiary where a few years later Henry Winston was also harassed and penalized, and where neglect by prison authorities led to his present total blindness.

Three other features of prison life are worth mentioning. They are the daily routines of the count, court call and hospital line. The holy of holies in prison is the count. You are counted at least ten times a day, mostly standing at attention. The count of each cell block or workshop is then phoned in and added up at the control center. You continue standing until the all-clear signal sounds. Since some of the hacks couldn't even count, endless confusion would result.

When the occasional escape occurs, it is usually discovered at count. After a dozen recounts, while everything is held up, it may finally be established that someone is missing. Then confusion is rampant. Everybody is locked up and all normal activity is suspended. All the hacks go out beating the bushes to try to find the missing prisoner.

While I was there, the first escape from inside the prison occurred (other escapes were from the farm or from other outside jobs). Three lads had prepared the escape by sawing the bars in advance. They made off in the middle of the night in a dense fog. The trio got over the wall by use of a ladder. Within a month they were caught; one, perhaps two, were shot to death in the process.

With their escape, all hell broke loose. For four days we were locked up. The guards, who were supposed to check each cell bar with a hammer, were suspended, as was the man in charge of locking up all ladders. A new electrical device was built all around the walls, but birds would set it off when they perched on it, and for a few months there was real bedlam until that was straightened out.

Another daily event is court call at 8:15 A.M. The court is composed of one of the associate wardens and two lieutenants. The victims all stand outside and go in alone to hear the charges and to be sentenced. Punishments range from loss of various privileges, loss of good time already earned, a shift in job or quarters, or confinement in the hole—"punitive segregation." This meant being locked up alone in a dark cell, stripped of all your clothes and with a sort of coverall, no bed or mattress, and reduced food rations for a week to a month.

In Lewisburg I had several experiences on court call, usually on some framed-up charge of destroying prison clothes or having something in my locker a superpatriotic hack thought I wasn't entitled to. Once I was charged with "conducting political propaganda." On that count I was given a warning. When political prisoners came before court call, the officials didn't find it so easy to get away with charges, since we could never be intimidated.

The other daily event was sick call, which formed after lunch. For 1,400 men, there were two doctors and a staff of a dozen United States Health Service orderlies (with no medical qualifications except as male nurses in the navy). The bulk of the work, including injections, was done by inmates. It was considered a cushy job, because you could get more food and also medicine that could be exchanged for cigarettes. On our hospital line we usually were seen by the chief of these health service orderlies. He was a vicious, cruel character who treated all prisoners like dirt and accused them of malingering. He tried to prevent the men from seeing the doctor and handed out aspirins as a cure-all.

This orderly was also a loud-mouthed anti-Communist, who displayed his hatred of us and tried to incite us by provocative remarks. It was a constant battle. Despite my efforts to keep in good health, my ear became seriously infected. The inmate tried to be helpful and syringed out the ear with every conceivable medicine available, but it kept getting worse. Sleep was impossible. There was a horrible discharge. I complained to the family, and they and my lawyer wrote sharp letters. Finally, the prison doctor called in an outside ear specialist, who said everything that had been done was wrong. In a week he had cleared it up. But it kept recurring in later years.

Knowing that the aim of the ruling class was to try to weaken the party by decapitating it, all of us undertook, within the limits permitted, to take every measure possible to preserve our health — which we had never done on the outside. Consequently, we took advantage of every opportunity to walk and get fresh air. We never missed stockade, as free time in the yard was called. During the winter months, stockade was reduced to two hours on Saturday and three hours on Sunday, weather permitting. During the rest of the year the time was four hours on Saturday and Sunday and during the summer one to two hours in the evening. We insisted upon our walk even if it was raining, much to the annoyance of some guards.

Since the food was overwhelmingly starchy, we also created a movement for the commissary to sell apples or oranges. This was considered unheard of but we broke through, and for six months of the year fruit was sold. Incidentally, in federal prisons, absolutely no food or anything else can be sent in from the outside. You were allowed to receive $10 each month as commissary money. Commissary sold cigarettes, tobacco, crackers, candy, razor blades, combs, watches and, as a result of our pressure, oranges and apples. Cigarettes and tobacco were the major products sold, not only because prison strain and frustration increased smoking, but because cigarettes were the accepted currency of prison exchange.

The objective of every political prisoner, aside from maintaining his health, is to keep alert mentally and to react politically to all national and international events, thus demonstrating to prisoners and officials that his ideas can never be jailed and that his morale is unimpaired. And, of course, to utilize all available time in as constructive a way as the many restrictions and the special political discrimination permit.

How to keep your mind occupied is a constant challenge. We were denied the right to carry on any research, far less write books. We were entitled, if the warden approved, to buy one daily newspaper and one weekly magazine and I got *The New York Times* and *U.S. News and World Report*, while Carl Winter received the New York *Herald Tribune* and *The Nation*. So we would have long political discussions during stockade, especially at weekends, based on the news in these papers and magazines. There was also a weekly movie.

We made maximum use of the library. Because we were denied the privilege granted to all others to have two books (approved, of course) sent in monthly from the publisher, we resorted to every possible ruse. Other prisoners were cooperative. The guard in charge of the library had a staff of prisoners as his clerks. One of these each quarter prepared a list of proposed books for purchase, which the guard was then supposed to go over and submit as his own. If the accession clerk was friendly or cooperative, and with the help of a carton of cigarettes, he would fit in some worthwhile books on his list. We never tried to get Marxist books, since that would be pushing our luck too far and jeopardizing these inmates. Only once did we get a book by a Communist on the list—*The Scalpel and the Sword* about Dr. Norman Bethune. Since the bulk of the books were of the mystery or sexy variety, this title easily slipped by all the officials, none of whom were too well read to start with.

Lewisburg Penitentiary boasted of its enlightened policy; a system of classes was taught by prisoners who had college experience and were approved of as safe. There were also available correspondence courses with a state college. Another way to keep usefully occupied was to take such courses. I took two in English, one in elementary math and one in Spanish.

The biggest problem was to keep busy during work, when seven of the eight hours hung heavy on my hands. I dug up in the library a "Typing—Self-Taught" book. For a year I banged away two or three hours a day practising the touch system. Other hours were spent figuring out how to convey ideas and proposals in a normal family letter, or composing letters of protest to the appropriate officials, or writing to my lawyers. The latter opened the door for a fight to get certain trial documents or related legal opinions on which to advise the lawyers how we thought our case might be reopened or, in my case, how to fight deportation.

The foreman-guard didn't object to my reading in my spare time, but I wanted the books most when I was in the workshop. I would set up my book in front of the typewriter and stick a requisition form into the machine. This meant keeping one eye on the door through which the roving guards appeared. Once or twice I was caught in the act. My biggest problem was to convey the reading material from my cell to the workshop. I wore a surgical belt because of a slipped disc, and we had to go through an electric eye. That meant no books could be smuggled inside my shirt or coat. But that obstacle, too, was overcome by cooperative inmates.

Of course, there is a lot of time-consuming prison routine—clothing change, showers, commissary, meals and going back and forth to work. All this has to be done at scheduled hours and involves queuing up under the constant supervision of guards.

The lifeline of a political prisoner is sustained by letters and visits from his family. That is the one living link with the outside world, and into it are contained all of one's love and concern for wife and children and for other comrades, in and out of prison, and one's interest in political developments.

You were allowed a two-hour visit monthly with approved people—in my case, my wife and children. In New York you were separated by a heavy glass partition and spoke through a telephone-like apparatus. But in Lewisburg there was a visiting room where we faced our visitors under the supervision of one or two guards for the entire room. Because of the remote location of the prison, Mae's visit from New York meant traveling by several trains a good part of the day, staying overnight in a hotel and visiting me in the morning, so as to get back that night and go to work next morning.

These visits were expensive and emotionally disturbing. Opinons vary about visits, even among political prisoners. I felt they were most valuable. Mae never missed a visit all those years. We both felt it correct for the children to make occasional visits, to know where their Dad was and to explain why, the scope of the explanation depending upon their age.

During the first year there were a couple of visits when Neil, then four years old, had experiences that reflected the brutal application of prison rules to children. When he was shoved through the electric eye, to which all visitors had to submit, it rang loudly and scared him. The cause was a toy metal motor car he was holding. The guard insisted on taking it from him and, with childlike stubbornness, he resisted. Finally, persuaded by his mother and older brother, he got through the eye, but that visit was spoiled for everyone because he was so upset.

On another occasion, the guard categorically refused to let this youngster bring into the visiting room his drawing book and crayons. Could he possible think that four-year-old Neil would carry on an illegal correspondence with me during the visit?

A big occasion was Christmas. We "politicals" were never given extra visiting hours, as most were, but it was the one time in the year when we were allowed a four-pound package from the outside. It had to be limited to four items—hard candies, chocolate, crackers and dried fruit—all in the original wrapper. You can imagine what love and emotion went into the annual package from the families to each of us inside.

During my years back in Britain I have been asked hundreds of times, "How were political prisoners accepted by the other inmates?" Despite the constant barrage of anti-Communist propaganda that all Americans, prisoners included, were subjected to, we were treated with great respect by the great majority of inmates. The kind of violent and murderous attack of which Bob Thompson was the victim came from a handful of prisoners—in most cases incited by guards—and did not reflect the general attitude.

When six of us first arrived in Lewisburg (four were hold-overs, to be sent on to Atlanta, Terre Haute and Leavenworth by the next prison bus) and marched single-file into one of the big dining halls for our first meal, a terrific cheer went up. From all sides came shouts of "Hello, Gene!" (this from men who had known Gene Dennis when he previously served a year's term in New York for contempt of congress). Guards came running but immediately all was quiet, as if nothing had happened. This reflected the feeling of the inmates that we were people who had challenged the state, which pushed everybody around, and that we were being mistreated — in prison language, "bum rapped."

In general, however, the way you are treated by most of the inmates depends on your attitude. The rats and depraved homosexuals must be demonstratively ignored. You must recognize you are going to live among these people for months or years, just as if you were in the armed forces or any other confined group of people. You must be friendly, do your share in everything, be ready to help, keep confidences and, above all, avoid any action that could be misunderstood as high-hatting or appearing superior.

At one time when Carl Winter and I were having our regular walk in the circular cinder track during stockade, we became conscious of two groups shaping up for trouble. We found out that a number of inmates who were particularly friendly with us had served a warning on a small group, which had consistently cursed us and tried to provoke us so they would have an excuse to "cut us up." Our defenders had told the hoodlums to stop it "or else." This was the day when they were scheduled to do battle on our behalf, if necessary.

After much persuasion, we convinced them to avoid the battle, although we expressed our appreciation. We pointed out this would only play into the hands of the provocateurs and officials, who would like nothing better than to charge us and our friends with precipitating riot and mutiny. Reluctantly they consented but they were not convinced they were doing the right thing. They made many wisecracks (they didn't know or worry about the fine legal distinctions in our indictment) about "these two guys who were jailed for 'advocating force and violence' not letting us use a little violence on those bastards who are bothering them."

The lowest breed in the prisoner's book is the stool pigeon or rat. At Lewisburg David Greenglass, whose lying testimony sent his sister, Ethel Rosenberg, and her husband, Julius, to the electric chair, was not only hated by the inmates but was not safe in their midst. He was constantly protected by the guards. He washed by himself, ate on the diet line, had his hair cut by a guard and not a prisoner barber, and during all the years I was at Lewisburg never once ventured into the yard.

The majority of the guards were interested only in completing their 20-year employment and then drawing their pension along with working at other jobs. However, there was a sadistic minority who hated all prisoners, and most of these were also viciously anti-Communist. During the week of the Rosenbergs' execution, one of these anti-Communist guards (he later committed suicide) remarked to an inmate as Carl Winter and I were walking in the yard: "Doesn't it make you sick to see these two Communists walking there alive while the Rosenbergs fry?" In less than half-an-hour the inmate came and told us of this provocation.

Another example of indirect provocation was an article in the weekly mimeographed prison paper The Lens of February 22, 1952. Since this was Washington's birthday, the editorial was allegedly about the president but was actually an incitement against us. It said that some people in America "claim membership in the revolutionary brotherhood to which Washington belongs," that "American Communist puppets are preaching revolution which, if successful, would bring us under the complete domination of a foreign power," and that the leaders of the American Communist Party are telling "bold lies." It referred to the "vile stench which these people try to hide by identifying themselves" as true revolutionaries. While this appeared under the signature of the crawler who served as editor, it was clear that it was administration-inspired.

In Lewisburg—and this was the experience elsewhere with other Smith Act victims—a Communist leader was looked upon as a sort of Solomon able to answer all questions and problems. Fortunately, Carl Winters had far more formal education than I, so when it came to complex questions of science and math, I would always pass them on to him. Many letters, parole applications and the legal correspondence of other prisoners had our touch on it. We even had to give advice on intimate family problems and to try to settle quarrels brought to us.

Among the professional criminals, especially those of Italian extraction, there is a graded hierarchy. Their top rank felt that as national Communist leaders, we were really VIPs. (Hadn't we been in front-page headlines and pictures for months?) When Frank Costello, top man of the Italians, came briefly to Lewisburg, our Italian friends fell all over themselves introducing us to him.

The type of people you find as prisoners could well be the subject of a separate book. One of the inmates at Lewisburg was Alger Hiss, stalwart anti-fascist New Dealer who had been framed. He conducted himself with modesty and reserved dignity and was held in high respect by the majority of the inmates, in contrast to the treatment given Greenglass.

Toward the end of the term, William Remington, convicted of a perjury charge based on denying membership in the Young Communist League or party while employed by the government, also arrived in Lewisburg. We did not know him, but we knew he was a victim of a frame-up and the McCarthy witch-hunt. But during his trial he proved himself a weakling and evidently thought he would benefit by denouncing the Communist Party. (He still got three years.) When he arrived at Lewisburg, he continued his anti-Communist statements, directing them personally at me. This only isolated him, and he got the cold shoulder from most. He then associated with the handful of known rats. During the week that Alger Hiss was released, and the press revived all its attacks on him, Remington was found murdered. The exact reason will never be known. But the *Daily Worker* and our party spokesman correctly condemned this foul murder and pointed the finger of responsibility at the government and its justice department and prison officials. Elizabeth Gurley Flynn asked, "Are political prisoners sentenced to death when they enter American federal prisons?"

There are endless stories of different types of inmates. One argued he "was a different type from all these other prisoners and shouldn't be here at all." He said it wasn't his fault if someone was so stupid as to pay him money for "a warehouseful of steel rods in Ohio," which he sold even though they didn't belong to him.

The cleverest con men were both Canadians. They also sold things that didn't belong to them. One was the library accession clerk for a while. He bet us a carton of cigarettes he could get a book by Mao Tse-tung (advertised that week in *The New York Times* book section) into the library. He put it on the next list for purchase. The library hack questioned it; but the Canadian con man went to work on him in such a subtle fashion that when he finished the guard was convinced that he was really appallingly ignorant not to know about this "famous Chinese philosopher." He let the book stay on the list but it got pushed farther up the line. We so appreciated his success that we gave our Canadian friend half a carton of cigarettes anyway, particularly since he had been more successful with other titles.

15

From Prison to Deportation

There is no doubt that Smith Act prisoners were denied privileges granted to criminal inmates. The franker officials admitted this in conversation but, of course, would never put it in writing.

Discrimination against us was manifested by refusing good time, in denying us the newspapers, magazines and books we had been accustomed to reading, in denying us the better housing quarters we were entitled to, in barring correspondence with anyone but family, not to speak of purely malicious actions like terminating our visits on the dot, while others could have from one to two hours' extra time. Hundreds of cards sent us at Christmas or on birthdays were withheld; even the special letter I wrote to Bob Minor's wife, Lydia, when Bob died was rejected.

Of my many experiences, four will illuminate this discrimination. Although prison rules state you are entitled to have ten people on your list of correspondents, I was never able to get a single name approved beyond my wife, my oldest son and my mother. Similarly, prison rules state that after six months, if you have no disciplinary violations on your record and if you are recommended by your foreman, you are entitled to meritorious good time (MGT). This means two days a month remission of sentence for the first year and four days a month for subsequent years. In our case it would have meant serving four months less time. I was recommended for MGT four times but it never was granted.

At the beginning there was a frank admission that it was because of "the nature of your case," and the fear that some radio commentator would make an issue of it. Finally, Washington made a new ruling: to qualify for MGT you had to show "evidence of a sincere desire to become a useful and law-abiding member of society upon your release." Subsequently, the authorities fell back on this ruling to explain why we had to serve the extra four months.

There was a humorous side in my being kept from receiving books. The prison rules say you are entitled to buy two books a month, if they are approved beforehand and come directly from the publisher. During the first six months I succeeded in buying eight. Then suddenly the door was closed, and in the succeeding years I never was allowed to buy another book. Every request I submitted was rejected out of hand.

Among the books that had been rejected after the crackdown were *The Frontiers of Economic Knowledge* (the author was President Eisenhower's economic adviser); and *The Decline and Fall of British Capitalism*. Finally, I requested permission to buy the *U.S. Statistical Abstract*, which was based on United States census figures and printed by the Government Printing Office. After a four-month delay I was called up and told that Warden Humphrey had again rejected my request.

Having been made aware through the grapevine what the decision was, even before I was called up, I determined to protest emphatically and to press vigorously for an explanation. It was clear the authorities felt themselves on weak ground, since they stalled for four months. Finally I was told that "this book itself is all right, but any book you get will be used by you for your own purposes." The official then went on to say, "You know, there is a rule against continuing in prison the kind of activity you engaged in on the outside." Since we were jailed for our ideas, he was going to try to stop us from thinking in jail. This made perfect sense to him.

The explanations for this blantant political discrimination varied from one official to another. The more honest of them didn't approve of it. I had one associate warden tell me that all my complaints were justified, but I might as well recognize that "murderers will get these privileges while they will be denied to you." He even said he had been overruled by the "top" in wanting to grant them to me.

When Director of Prisons Bennett made his annual visit I demanded to see him (he always saw about 25 prisoners to prove he was listening to all sides). During the third year this was finally granted. Everyone was in a dither when Bennett visited. The guards had the 25 he was to see waiting in a line in their dress blues half an hour before he even arrived. When my turn finally came, I presented with all my skill my many experiences of political discrimination.

This man had been appointed by Roosevelt and once considered himself a liberal, but he had changed his colors to carry on under Eisenhower. He fumed and spluttered and then shouted, "You have not changed your views. Why should we grant you MGT and release you out on the street one minute before we have to?" Very calmly but pointedly I told him he was the source of the political discrimination. I indignantly rejected his talk of "changing views" and said he well knew that Communists don't betray their principles. Red-faced, he told me the interview was concluded and none of my complaints were justified.

Seemingly our voices had penetrated through the wooden door because the next day it was a topic of conversation everywhere that the Communist had told off Bennett.

In contrast was the treatment given to the American Nazi agent, Douglas Chandler, who was also in Lewisburg. Chandler was a pal of the infamous Lord Haw Haw, whom the British executed as a traitor. Chandler, who called himself "Paul Revere" on the Nazi Radio Berlin and carried on the same traitorous work for Hitler as did Lord Haw Haw, only received a prison sentence. Unlike the Communists, who gave everything they had to the fight against Hitler and now found themselves in prison in the United States, this traitor had a job as a teacher, lived in the best quarters, ate on the diet line (they even brought chicken for him because he claimed he didn't eat red meat), and was given every privilege we were denied. I heard he was later given a presidential pardon.

Another example comes to mind. During the first year we were in prison there appeared a double-page spread in *The American Weekly*, a magazine supplement of the Hearst Sunday papers with a circulation of millions. The article was written by the top stool-pigeon of the day, Louis Budenz, who had once been an assistant editor of the *Daily Worker*.

His article was headlined "How to Spot a Red Spy." Budenz spewed forth the usual stale lies of "a Communist network," "orders from Moscow" and all associated fables. The villain of the article turned out to be "a party bureaucrat, John Williamson . . . limited in education and culture." The writer described how a young man had come to see me "with awe," and when "ushered into the presence of Williamson found a squat, blond-haired, bespectacled man, with an abrupt manner." I was then alleged to have said to him, never having seen him before, "We want alert young men like you. . . . Someone will visit you shortly with an important commission from the party." You can imagine the rest. With all stops out, this "alert young man" became a Moscow agent who betrayed America and practiced espionage.

Such scurrilous slander reflected the atmosphere of the time. I immediately wrote my lawyer denouncing the story as "a lie and an invention of Budenz' mind." I instructed him to "file a suit for damages against Budenz and the publishers . . . (which) would point out the vicious, slanderous, lying and damaging character of this article and its false accusations and implications concerning my role and activities." I also asked him to issue a public denunciation of the article in my behalf, since a prisoner has no such rights.

After four and a half weeks, this letter to my lawyer was returned with an official note saying, "The Director (of Prisons) returns the attached letter to you. He requested you be informed that civil action is not permitted while you are under federal supervision." So millions of people were allowed to read and believe this blatant lie, while I, in federal prison (called federal supervision), was denied the elementary right to sue for libel.

By this time Carl Winter had been transferred to another prison to appear as a witness in the trial of his wife, Helen, also a Smith Act victim. In his place Maurice Braverman of Balti-

more had joined us. After the murder of Remington, always
alert to the threat of frame-up or malicious instigation, our
lawyers immediately visited us and demanded that Washington
transfer us.

On December 13, I was notified through the grapevine that I
was being shipped that night. I was listed to go to Danbury,
Connecticut. Long before the guards came to move me (they
don't tell you in advance), I had disposed of all my stuff to other
inmates and had sorted out the personal property I was going
to try to take with me. Fortunately there was an easy hack on
duty and nearly everything went through.

With a dozen others scheduled to leave the next morning, I
was locked up in an isolation cell. In the morning, we were
handcuffed and piled into the prison bus. In a special iron
grille, where he could not be reached, a guard sat with a gun.
A lieutenant from Danbury was in charge. He asked me if I
knew Jack Stachel (one of the 11 in our trial who had been sent
to Danbury because he had just suffered a heart attack). I was
always suspicious and kept everything on an official level. On
the trip one of the prisoners got very ill. The lieutenant then
unlocked my handcuffs and asked me to try to take care of
him until we left him in New York.

Late at night we finally reached Danbury—"the gentlemen's
club," as the get-tough newspapers and journals called it. But
I, together with a Negro prisoner, was put into the hole without
any explanation. This meant all my clothes were taken away and
I was given an old pair of coveralls. It also meant no blankets
and not even a chance to stretch my legs. No one would explain
anything. I demanded to see every official in the place, but it
was after 10 P.M. and no one was available. I was livid with anger and slept little that night as I planned my next moves.

At 6 A.M. I demanded to see the warden. Finally, at 8:30, I was
taken before the associated warden. I entered an emphatic
protest at the treatment accorded me. He explained that since
neither he nor the warden were on duty when I arrived, no
one else wanted to assume the responsibility for assigning such a
dangerous character to the ordinary quarantine area. He would
straighten it all out and I would be on my way to quarantine in
five minutes.

I then asked about the Negro lad who had been sent with me
to the hole. Why was he there? His further explanation out-

raged me. Without a thought, he blandly said, "We had to make
it appear to the other prisoners that two of you were involved,
so we just shoved him in along with you." At the first opportunity, I reported to the Negro lad what the associate warden
had said and apologized for unwittingly being the cause of his
going to the hole.

Danbury was considered a lesser custody prison than Lewisburg, but my two-and-a-half months there were in fact worse
for me. The only positive factors were that the shorter distance
from New York City made Mae's visits less arduous for her, and
I also had a chance to see Jack Stachel, who had been in Danbury throughout his sentence. We had opportunities for long
talks before our release on March 1, 1955.

I was locked up in a maximum security cell, a cage with bars
on all four sides. My transfer meant learning a new job and
establishing new relations. Three weeks of this time I spent in
the prison hospital. Here I saw a well-known doctor—in prison
for an income-tax offense, I believe—actually take over the
running of things. He treated the ailments and operated, but
of course it was the signature of the official prison doctor that
appeared on all documents.

Let no one think that serving time is easy. Each day is served
in full, all 24 hours of it. As the days pass into weeks, then into
months and years, the Communist serves his term in pain and
anguish, as does his family. Most of the wives, including my own,
had to find work in order to live. This was not easy, since the
FBI visited employers as soon as they got a job and, nine times
out of ten, they were fired. Even under such circumstances, a
few independent-minded employers told the FBI to go to hell.
The public was not aware of this, for the press exercised its
freedom by suppression of news.

Each family was confronted at home and in school with a
combination of isolation and harassment in this atmosphere of
McCarthyite fear and intimidation. In neighborhoods where
our wives had been active and had cultivated the friendship of
neighbors, things were easier. Only one neighbor boycotted
our family while a dozen came and offered help in caring for
the children when Mae had to go away. Shopkeepers offered
goods at cheaper prices and found other means of expressing
their concern—but all on the quiet.

In addition to working and raising a family under such political conditions, and worrying about what was happening in prison and what lay ahead for the family as far as further prossecution was concerned (in my case another trial for membership in the party and a deportation warrant), the wives were the representatives of their husbands in relations with the prison and Washington authorities. Mae was actively fighting both Warden Humphrey and Director of Prisons Bennett on each of the acts of discrimination against me.

She conducted, in agreement with the party leadership and our lawyers, an intensive campaign to bring pressure on the board to grant parole. Scores of prominent people sent letters demanding parole but my three applications all came back, "Parole Denied."

The wives formed the Families Committee of Smith Act Victims. With the party wholly or partly underground during these years, a lot of work fell on these families committees. They organized house meetings and affairs and sent speakers to organizations. Much money was raised. It went for a multitude of uses: the $10 monthly commissary allowance for each prisoner; fares for visits; sending the children away on summer holiday; printing literature about our case and demanding our release; paying for medicine for certain of the wives who were ill, and for other necessities.

The committee played an important role in initiating a campaign of open letters to the President demanding amnesty. It gave full support to other activities for amnesty, including a national conference, which was held on June 14, 1952, at St. Nicholas Arena in New York City. Our wives proved to be very effective. All the greater loss to the movement (and perhaps a reflection on their husbands) that too many of them were retired again to the background, relegated to the more routine local party tasks, after our release.

The hardships for the wives and children of the four political refugees were even greater. These refugees did not enter prison on July 2, 1951, but went into hiding. Subsequently, Gus Hall and Bob Thompson were caught, but despite all the boasted ability of the FBI, Henry Winston and Gil Green were never picked up. They surrendered voluntarily after the first seven of us had served our sentences.

No one will demur at my singling out the late Lil Green. For
four years she and the three children never saw Gil, even behind prison bars. Then three years were added to his original
sentence of five, so that for the succeeding six and a half years,
they saw him only in prison. During all that time she was harassed brutally night and day by the FBI. Employers were intimidated into refusing her jobs. After several years of this, the
comrades determined to spirit her into the country with her
children for a rest. But the second night after their arrival a
searchlight played on the cottage all night. The "dogs" were
back and that holiday was blown sky-high.

Comparable stories could be told of others in similar circumstances but the Green and Winston families suffered worst of
all. Yet Lil Green was constantly in the thick of the fight for
amnesty and against the Smith and McCarran Act persecutions.
This devoted and beautiful wife and comrade finally could take
no more and succumbed to the ravages of cancer. There was
the deepest sympathy with Gil and the family in their great
loss.

While still in Lewisburg I was ordered to appear before an
immigration department hearing dealing with the order of
deportation issued against me on February 10, 1948. After
several weeks of controversy, during which I refused to answer
questions because my lawyer was not present, the hearing finally
took place on November 19, 1952.

The reasons outlined for my deportation were couched in
very lengthy and repetitious legal language. Briefly, it was
charged that I was an alien who believed in the overthrow of
the government by force and violence; that I belong to an organization that held the same belief; that I wrote and caused to
be distributed articles that so advocated; and so on, *ad infinitum.*
The second series of reasons covered my membership in the
Communist Party.

I submitted a long statement, from which the following are
salient excerpts:

"I categorically deny that I am guilty of any wrongdoing, and
declare that deportation of me from the United States would be
contrary to the best interests of the American people. It would
be a violation of the Constitution and the Bill of Rights. It would

be contrary to our best traditions—before the McCarran epoch—in relation to immigrants. It would demonstrate to the peoples and nations of the world that those in control of our government have embarked on the well-known fascist path of trying to destroy political ideas and association by the force and violence of a government that represents the interests of five per cent of the people—meaning Big Business—that owns 87 per cent of the wealth of the country, through exploiting the majority.

"I have been in the United States for 39 years and consider myself an American in every way, except for the legal paper of citizenship, which has been systematically denied to all those of my political convictions who have been in the public eye.

"Specifically, I deny the allegation that I am 'an alien who believes in, advocates, advises, and teaches the overthrow by force and violence of the Government of the United States.' What I believe in, advocate and teach has been an open book all my life, and since 1918 has been well known to any agency of the government that was interested.

"During the last 39 years, since arriving in the United States, I have contributed to the well-being and to the wealth of the country—through my employment in industry; my payments of taxes; my participation in the political life of the country, expressed in helping to build trade unions, to establish a system of social security, by fighting for equal rights for the Negro people, by enlisting the American people in the struggle against fascism and for a policy of peace based on co-existence of the socialist and capitalist sectors of the world. I have even sacrificed my personal liberty—dear as it is to me and my family—rather than betray the interests and traditions of the American people by bowing to the fascist concept of relinquishing my right to working-class ideas and membership in a working-class political party."

In a routine manner, I was ordered deported that day. It is interesting, however, that they rested their order of deportation *solely* on my being "a member of the CPUSA" and declared, "It is further concluded that the respondent is not deportable from the evidence of record on the additional charges contained in the warrant providing for his arrest or on the additional charges lodged during the course of his first hearing on November 5, 1952."

The time neared for our release on March 1, 1955, on what is called conditional release (CR) — during which period (till the end of your sentence) you are under the direct supervision of a parole officer who tries to control your every move, decides where you can be employed, where you live and where you go. Now, the papers had new headlines: "Lost Indictment Hangs Over Jailed Reds — U.S. May Seek Double Terms for Commies."

This referred to the second Smith Act indictment charging membership in the party, for which we had not been tried in 1949. This had not been forgotten but deliberately left in reserve precisely for this purpose, and it carried a ten-year sentence. We felt it was quite possible that the government would not even release us, but would try us again.

Before we entered prison in 1951, it had been agreed by the national committee that if I was ordered deported and Britain agreed to accept me, there would be no legal way to avoid deportation. In such circumstances, if deportation was inevitable (unlike the case of non-citizens whose country of origin refused to accept them), we further decided that the sooner I left and started to develop a world campaign against the pro-fascist persecution in America, the better.

Therefore, during 1954 an effective and broad campaign was developed in Scotland and a John Williamson Defense Campaign Committee established. This was sparked by the Scottish District of the National Union of Mineworkers. In this campaign, Charlie and Mickey Doyle, who had just been deported to Britain, also played an important role.

The first aim of the campaign was to get me paroled so that my deportation would take place before the end of my five-year prison sentence. When this failed — and with the threat of a new trial and ten extra years in prison, still to be followed by deportation — the campaign for my release was intensified. At least 15 members of parliament raised questions in the House of Commons and it became a public issue. These MP's placed the main emphasis on the threat of "double jeopardy," a violation of the sacred common law of England.

Side by side with this splendid campaign to which the Communist Party of Britain contributed so much, I wrote two letters from prison to the British ambassador, Sir Roger Makins, and one to the home secretary, Sir D. Maxwell Fyfe. I knew these would all be copied and sent to Washington.

Since the double jeopardy issue was now being raised in parliament about me, it became a subject for discussion in the American papers, because it affected all Smith Act prisoners. While the campaign in Scotland did not result in my being released from prison any sooner, it perhaps contributed to the government's decision to avoid risking a trial on the second Smith Act indictment for any of us—because of the possible world protest against double jeopardy.

When we were finally released from prison on March 1, 1955, the three non-citizens—myself, Stachel and Potash—were put under bail in connection with the deportation order, as well as the second Smith Act indictment. This involved, from the outset, daily reports to the immigration office. The pressure continued from Britain and, after much legal maneuvering, the second indictment was dropped to allow me to be deported. The aim of the American Committee for the Protection of Foreign Born, which was handling that end of my case, was to get agreement for Mae and the two boys to accompany me. They felt this was necessary to avoid any vindictive move that might prevent them from leaving the country later (they were all United States citizens).

The government refused any such commitment and told me I could be deported at any time. During these weeks I always had a bag packed in case I was forcibly taken to a ship by myself. While my first letters to the British ambassador had received a polite brush-off, later on I received unsolicited visits from British consular officials offering me help. They also interceded with Washington demanding the entire family travel to Britain together. This reflected mass pressure, especially in Scotland and in parliament.

Finally it was agreed I would be deported on May 4. Before leaving, there was a "private" farewell in a hall where 250 comrades gathered. It was, of course, a very emotional affair. I said in my speech:

"In preparing to leave the United States, it was dramatized to me that I am a very rich person. Don't get me wrong—these riches are not in material wealth, but in those values that really count in life.

"I have in mind the warmth and sincerity of the goodbyes of hundreds of party actives throughout the country, in New York, and in our own community. Of particular significance were the expressions of neighbors, storekeepers, schoolteachers and friends of our children in the neighborhood. And these riches of mine were further shown in the hundreds of New Year's cards sent to me in Danbury but which were only given to me in March. Another example of these riches came to light when I unearthed from a closet some 700 letters sent to me in 1948 while I was on a hunger strike on Ellis Island. In a different, but still significant way, was my finding a share of stock—not sold on the stock market—but among the industrial workers of the Midwest. This was a $10 share of stock to help launch the *Daily Worker* in January 1924. . . .

"But these tid-bits about my riches have roots in raw ore. I think of how these 37 years have been packed with abundant experiences of working-class activities and struggles, out of which I have learned much and contributed my best. . . .

"If I made a small contribution to the many activities and struggles previously referred to, it has all been due to our party. . . .

"Upon my return to Britain I will continue to devote myself, as I have done these last 37 years, to advancing the interests of the working folks of both Britain and the USA."

When May 4 arrived, I was practically encircled by FBI men until we got on the *Queen Elizabeth*. Our tourist cabin was on the bottom deck and the steward told me later that FBI men had come and counted all my baggage and watched the cabin, and that some of them had stayed on the ship and only gone off with the pilot.

On the ship was a flock of reporters, photographers and TV men. Our departure was front-page news, with pictures in the papers the next day. That night, our departure on the ship and an interview with me on the deck of the *Queen Elizabeth* appeared on TV. In my statement to the press and on TV, I said:

"I am being deported for the same reasons I have been jailed and persecuted these last years—for my working-class activities and ideas. My ideas are simple: I hold that the interests of Americans demand co-existence—not war, cold or hot. I hold that McCarthyite reaction endangers the liberties of all Americans and that the majority must unite to restore the Bill of Rights for all. I hold that true Americanism calls for a relentless struggle for the unconditional equality of the Negro people. I favor a society where production is for use, not for profit—namely, socialism.

"These are my ideas. These are Communist ideas. These are American ideas. I didn't bring them with me from Scotland as a child of ten. I brought no foreign ideology except perhaps the democratic heritage represented by the immortal Robert Burns."

Between 50 and 60 comrades had come to the ship to see us off. We took over one of the public rooms and had a farewell party. My closest co-workers, who had been released from prison at the same time, could not take a chance and attend either of these affairs, because one of the regulations prohibited any association with ex-prisoners during conditional release. However, we found appropriate means of saying goodbye to each other. We were accompanied to the ship by one of Mae's brothers and his wife.

The full meaning of being torn up by the roots and isolated from your adopted country, its people, your comrades, friends and family does not strike you till weeks, even months later. But, as we stood on the deck of the *Queen Elizabeth*, my eyes instinctively turned to Bedloe's Island. Passing the Statue of Liberty I no longer saw the historic symbol of democracy that greeted each new immigrant with the words: "Give me your tired, your poor, your huddled masses, yearning to be free."

While the form of the famous statue was there, the McCarrans and McCarthys had succeeded temporarily in piercing the heart and blinding the eyes of Liberty in their drive to destroy the traditional forms of democracy associated with the United States. They had replaced its torch of liberty with the sword of war; its book of law with the new code of the frame-up and the informer.

I knew there was nothing voluntary in my departure. It was the end of a seven-years fight to defeat deportation. But in my heart and mind were the words of two letters I carried with me. One was from the group of political refugees, headed by Henry Winston and Gil Green, which I will always treasure. After giving warmest greetings on our release and sorrow at their inability to be there, they wrote in part:

"The aim of reaction was to keep you behind bars for many years. If they were unable to do it, thanks are due to the growing pressures of democratic opinion at home and abroad, as well as the beginnings of a changing climate in our country. Enormous and new possibilities are opening up which enable us to look confidently toward successful struggles which will check and defeat reaction, fascism and war. . . .

"Your release at this time is definitely connected with, and is a reflection of, these new winds. In the same way the postponement of action on the second indictment is not without its significance. . . . The past period, a period of ebb, is giving way to new and heightened levels of struggles by our class and people. . . .

"It is in this same sense, Johnny, that we view your deportation, not as something that is permanent, only a temporary separation from the American working class which you've served so long and so well. We will miss you no matter how brief the period. . . . Your dynamic qualities of leadership must be restored. . . .

"Our estimation of you is as it always has been, namely, as a worthy and outstanding leader of our party. . . . a fighting son of our class. . . . Our party is proud of you."

The other letter was from Comrades Foster and Dennis to Harry Pollitt, the general secretary of the Communist Party of Great Britain. It cited my record in the party and then made this extravagant estimate:

"He has been a tested leader of the YCL, of our party, and of the American working class for over 25 years. He is a devoted, experienced, and capable leader in mass work. He has political and organizing initiative, and is a firm and skillful party organizer, as well as trade union organizer. He combines stability with extreme conscientiousness, loyalty, fearlessness, and dependability. . . .

"Remember, Harry, in saying all this we don't relinquish our first claim on Johnny."

16

Return to My Native Land

The ocean voyage to Britain should have served as a rest. But after having been locked up in prison, then uprooted and going to what in effect was a new country—even though it was returning to my birthplace—neither mind nor body would rest. Running through my mind was what lay ahead, how would we live, how would the family take to Britain and what was I going to do. My thoughts kept returning to my comrades, to the people and to the homeland we had just left. Many people in the rest of the world might view it as McCarthy's "mad America," but it had been our home and we knew the American people would cleanse it eventually of McCarthyism.

When we were a day away from landing, I began to get phone calls on the ship from British newspapers. At Southampton, there were more reporters and photographers. Once through immigration and customs we received a warm welcome from a party delegation headed by John Gollan, then national organizer and now general secretary. In the delegation was my old friend Charlie Doyle, who had been working hard in Britain as a member of the Defense Committee. After driving to London, where Mickey and Charlie Doyle accommodated all four of us in their flat, I had a press conference.

That day's London *Daily Worker* had an editorial entitled "His Ain Folk," in which I was welcomed home. After telling of the bitter struggles in America, it declared that I was now free to be at home among my "ain folk" and "it is to them and their kind, both in Britain and America, that he owes his right to walk and speak in freedom," and not to the British foreign office.

The next day we were off to Glasgow to see my 81-year-old mother, who lived in a one-up room in the small village of Eaglesham where her mother was born and raised. At Glasgow

Station we were met by a hundred or so comrades, headed by Comrades Gallacher, Peter Kerrigan and the officers of the Scottish Defense Committee that had been set up on my behalf. Flowers, singing and Willie Gallacher's "Welcome to Bonnie Scotland" made it a wonderful heart-warming welcome for all of us.

We were then rushed out to Eaglesham. I had not seen my mother since she left America in 1934 to return to Scotland. Mae and the boys had never met her. It was a very emotional moment. The press insisted upon being in on it. The next day's Glasgow papers carried pictures and write-ups. Typical was the Glasgow *Record*, with a picture and a headline, "'I'm Proud of My Deported Son,' says Mrs. Williamson," It wrote. "Scots-born Communist John Williamson came home last night . . . deported from the United States . . . to tears in his old mother's eyes. But they weren't of shame or reproach: "I don't care what they say about my son. He's a good boy and I'm proud of him. His views are his affair . . . and I admire him for sticking to them.' Of the two grandsons she had never seen, Mrs. Williamson said, 'They are two grand boys. If they grow up like their father, they'll do well.'"

It was a well-deserved pleasure for my mother. The doctor told me privately she was not far from the end but, by supreme will power, had kept alive these last few months. In addition to poverty and old age, she had suffered several heart attacks. The first of them followed a visit from the FBI, when she was frightened and intimidated by interrogations about me. There were six of these visits. At one of them she was asked 82 questions and made to sign her answers. The interrogators walked off with my birth certificate and a picture of me as a boy. Allowing the FBI to question an old sick woman was made an issue in the local press and raised in parliament.

The day after my arrival in Glasgow, I had another press conference. Later, all of us except my mother, who was bed-ridden, were given a big Communist reception in a restaurant above the Gaumont Odeon theater: 250 comrades, including Pollitt, Gallacher, Kerrigan, Finlay Hart and Bill Lauchlan had taken valuable time off from the general election campaign to attend. Gifts were presented to each member of the family by the Defense Committee. In a short speech I expressed deep appreciation, told of events in the United States and appealed

for continued efforts to help the fight for freedom and democracy over there.

During the next ten days, we met comrades and friends and
all the members of my mother's family in and around Glasgow.
I was meeting some of the younger ones for the first time. In
the months that followed, I visited and kept in close touch with
my mother, but her health deteriorated, and in November
1955 she passed away peacefully—as she had spent so much
of her life.

On one of these first days in Glasgow, a worker struck up a
conversation with me as we both waited for a tram. Sensing
from my clothes or speech that I was from the United States, he
casually commented on the political atmosphere there. "I see
where they have just deported some trade union chap for being
a Communist. His mother lives here in Glasgow. Did you hear
of him?" To his surprise, I informed him that he was talking
to "the chap." He expressed the usual Clydeside warm welcome,
insisted upon paying my fare, and when he got off waved vigorously goodbye till the tram was out of sight. The response
of this worker, whom I had never seen, was in accord with the
warmhearted welcome that my family and I received everywhere.

As I traveled around, I became more and more aware and
appreciative of the work so many had done on my behalf. The
British party at its 23rd national convention in 1954 adopted
an emergency resolution which saluted the fight of the American party, sent greetings to all who were in prison and called
upon the trade union and labor movements to fight for my
immediate return to Britain without a new trial and possible
second prison sentence. Mae had been asked to send letters to
some 70 members of parliament and many editors, which she
did. She has on file many replies.

After much publicity in the Scottish press, the adoption of
resolutions by hundreds of trade union branches and other
labor organizations, and questions in parliament, there was
established in Scotland "The John Williamson Defense Committee," headed by William McLennan, publisher, and Dan
Wilson of the Amalgamated Engineers Union.

Its members included James Reid and William Lambie, the
provost and treasurer of Saltcoats, respectively; David Wright,
the provost of Kirkcaldy; Councillor A. Hamilton of Fifeshire;
William Pearson of the National Union of Mineworkers; Tom

Bell of the Construction Erectors Union; Donald Carson, Amalgamated Society of Woodworkers; William Crombie, Electrical Trade Union, and others.

This committee conducted widespread activity through leaflets, press statements, letters, petitions and delegations among trade unionists, co-ops, local Labour party branches, churches, and others. The members and branches of the Miners Union in Scotland responded magnificently. It had a number of MPs raise the question of my release from prison in parliament.

It also issued a petition addressed to the United States Embassy, on which thousands of signatures were collected. The Scottish Miners Union conference again took up my case and, as a result, the Scottish Trades Union Congress voted to raise it with the foreign office. The moderator of the Presbyterian church did likewise.

As the campaign gained momentum, the tone of the replies of the foreign office gradually changed. From the original brusque "no interference" note, the home secretary finally wrote Miss Jennie Lee, MP, that "We are at present considering whether valid grounds exist for approaching the United States authorities in order to secure Mr. Williamson's deportation as soon as he is released, thus avoiding his re-arrest and trial on the outstanding indictment." In Danbury prison I was even visited by the vice consul from New York together with the law officer of the United Nations British Delegation, who assured me they were ready to "offer me all assistance," and told me that there were no Smith or McCarran Acts in Britain.

The activity of the Defense Committee had obviously gotten under the skin of the United States Embassy in London. It wrote several letters to the committee, full of lies and half-truths, and circularized them to all MPs from Scotland, to the provost of Glasgow and all the Glasgow area press.

During my first days back I wrote letters of appreciation to the main participants in this campaign.

Back in London after election day, I was welcomed at an enlarged executive committee meeting of the party, and the committee held a reception for us in the evening, with speeches, singing and drinks. All of these warm welcoming activities confirmed my feeling that international solidarity permeates the work of the party in Britain. They also made the transition to our new home easier.

The late Harry Pollitt had the knack of combining his acute political leadership with personal warmth. His eyes twinkled when he could inject some *apropos* jest into his remarks. Being from Lancashire himself, he always jokingly complained that Scots were dominating the British party. When I was first introduced to him, he said, "Now we get another Scot via the United States. Thank Christ, you have an American accent, even though you come from Glasgow."

With the pleasantries out of the way, I had to arrive at a serious decision. Was I going to consider myself an American Communist in exile, working in Britain or elsewhere but awaiting the day of return to the United States, or was I to sink new roots, adjust myself to the conditions of my native land and carry on there for the foreseeable future?

Despite earnest requests I had received to live and work in the Soviet Union, China and Czechoslovakia, I decided that though there would undoubtedly be problems of adjustment in Britain and while I knew that leadership status could not be transferred from one party to another, I felt that my place as a Communist was in the midst of the struggle in Britain. Mae fully agreed with this conclusion.

This in no way reflected a lack of appreciation for the kind offers of the comrades in t e Socialist countries. No doubt, things would have been a lc easier economically, but as each year went by and my contact with America became more remote, my usefulness would have declined.

I have now been active in Britain for more than 11 years. During the first year I spent much time speaking at meetings up and down the country and writing articles about the struggle against McCarthyism in the United States. While the majority of the meetings were organized by the party, I also spoke before more than 50 trades union branches and wrote articles for several trade union papers and journals. The Defense Committee in Scotland wound up its affairs by printing a pamphlet I wrote about the struggle in America.

These propaganda efforts had to lead to other activity. Our aims were to organize two broad movements: one, to help Paul Robeson get his passport and his freedom to sing again in Britain and elsewhere; the other, to try to bring pressure from Britain and other European countries against the Smith and McCarran Act presecutions in the United States.

To advance these objectives, an enthusiastic conference of 153 delegates and 44 visitors from the labor movement was held in Scotland. The speakers were President Abe Moffat of the Miners Union and myself. Following this meeting various committees were set up in support of Paul Robeson's fight for a passport. I attended the Trade Union Congress in Southport and helped get dozens of signatures, including those of general council members, to send a cablegram to Eisenhower. Later, a national committee was established in Manchester, with Will Griffiths, MP, as chairman, and Frank Loesser as secretary. On this committee Cedric Belfrage and I were very active. In London a separate committee was established, with wide support and numerous activities.

Activities in support of the victims of the Smith and McCarran Acts and for the repeal of these laws did not get the same broad support as the campaign for Paul. However, valuable work was done, individual people of prominence spoke out and a committee was established. This group collected statements, initiated a petition and released much publicity material.

Indicating its concern to develop maximum solidarity, the party, before I arrived, set up a United States Advisory Sub-Committee of its international department, headed by R.P. Dutt and Idris Cox. I became a member of it, just as Charlie and Mickey Doyle had done before me and, later, Claudia Jones, when she was deported from the United States.

My other activity during this period was extensive writing for party publications. The London *Daily Worker* initiated a weekly column, "The American Scene," which I have continued to write (it became fortnightly in 1959).

Reflecting the concern of the socialist world at the heroic fight-back of the democratic forces in the United States, especially by the Communists who suffered the worst attacks of McCarthyism, I received many invitations in 1955 and 1956 to come and explain what was happening, as well as to tell about the experiences of the 11 Communist leaders who had been imprisoned.

Together with Irving Potash, I visited the Soviet Union, Poland and Czechoslovakia. He went on to People's China. I made two visits to Western Europe, meeting with other well-known figures of the Left. A few months later, a separate two-day conference of representatives of the Communist parties of

France, Belgium, Holland, Switzerland and Luxemburg took place, where I reported on the American scene.

Because of events in Britain and an assignment to specific work, these visits abroad had to be curtailed. Articles by me appeared regularly for at least a year in the party press of Sweden, West Germany, France, India, Belgium, China and Czechoslovakia.

At home (for Britain was now my new and permanent home), I was asked to work in the central organization department. For the next two years, I helped John Gollan and then Bill Lauchlan, successively national organizers of the party. During these two years I had the opportunity to become acquainted with the functioning of the party and its leadership in every district.

In the last months of 1958, it was proposed that I accept election as the party district secretary of South Essex district. This was a county adjacent to London, north of the Thames. It was an important industrial area that included the big Ford Motor plant at Dagenham and many other large plants. It also had within it two new towns—Basildon and Harlow, and eight or nine of the largest London county council overspill housing estates. It covered a rather large territory, had had its own well established towns as well as the overspill of London's East End, and was expanding.

For me, it was a challenging assignment. It combined everything—industry, electoral work, struggle against United States nuclear air bases (Wetherfield) and foreign capital investment (Ford's, May & Bakers, Shell, Esso, Proctor & Gamble) and it offered unlimited room for party growth. I also felt the challenge to show that despite my uprooting from the United States, I could still sink roots in a new country and a party with its own established leadership and its own style of work, even though I was past 55 years of age.

During the next four and a half years until my serious heart attack on April 1, 1963, I worked more doggedly than in all my previous years. I had always been a hard worker, but the physical and economic difficulties here were enormous—32 miles daily travel between home and office, difficult financial position, no technical help, and no means of transport for the first 18 months.

During those years the South Essex district membership grew

from 810 to 1076; the membership in our key factory branch, from under 50 to over 100. Local electoral contests mounted from nine to 34, including all nine wards in Dagenham, where we also nominated a prospective Communist parliamentary candidate. A strong collective leadership had been established; several large and successful public meetings for Harry Pollitt and John Gollan had been held; and important contributions had been made to the economic struggles and peace activities of the area.

During my work in South Essex I tried to cultivate a spirit of criticism and self-criticism in all our work and all of the leadership. Firm friendships were established that will always remain with me. It was at the 26th National Congress, Easter 1959, that I was elected for the first time to the national executive committee. Reelection followed in 1961 and 1963. At the 29th congress, in November 1965, I retired from the executive because of restrictions imposed by my health.

For one whose only previous serious illness had been two bouts with a slipped disc in the United States, my heart attack—without any warning—was a great blow. While on the critical list for the first week, I survived due to good medical care in the hospital, Mae's devoted and loving attention, the great consideration from all ranks of the party, starting with the general secretary who visited me regularly, and the mountain of letters and cablegrams from Essex, Britain, the United States and the Soviet Union. I was out of all activity for seven months, during which time the party of the Soviet Union again demonstrated its humane concern by inviting me to one of their sanitoriums, together with my family.

The most difficult thing for me was to accept and adjust to the doctor's final conclusion that I must not return to my post as district secretary or to any comparable post with long hours and little opportunity for rest. The chief hospital consultant on heart disease—a good doctor but conservative in outlook—told me, toward the end of the seven months: "The biggest problem with people like you, whether Right or Left, is to learn to live with your trouble. Your outfit should make you a glorified office boy and you should adjust yourself to it, if you are interested in living." I have been and am interested in living another 20 years, but I hope I have been more than a glorified office boy, even under conditions of restricted activity.

Since the end of 1963, I have been organizing party cadre training, especially at branch leadership level, teaching at some of the schools, speaking and carrying out other responsibilities. I have been employed part-time as librarian in the Marx Memorial Library and organizer of its educational activities. In my spare time, my work on this book, my column in the *Daily Worker* (now the *Morning Star*), book reviews and other articles have kept me busy.

It might be of interest to make some observations contrasting Britain to the United States. The great majority of visitors, even of working-class and progressive background, still limit themselves to the tourist sights — central London, the castles and palaces, St. Paul's, Tate Gallery, Stratford, etc. — and seldom see the real Britain. It is said, with a good deal of truth, that the further north you go, the colder the weather and the warmer the people. And that applies also to the party in Britain.

To fail to see Scotland, Wales, or the big industrial areas like Birmingham, Glasgow, Manchester, Leeds or Liverpool (and to learn something of the labor movement and its great history) is unforgiveable. To visit London and attempt to form an impression of it from the tourist hotels, restaurants and guided tours, is to miss the London of Dickens, Marx, Bernard Shaw or of Jack London when he visited the city. One should see the houses, schools, parks, factories, and, above all, meet the people. To know anything about Britain is to compare wages, rents, prices, factory conditions and union influence with those in the United States.

Comparisons that don't take account of history and recent developments can be very superficial. To the average American, the British trade union movement will appear politically developed and super-democratic, compared to the American trade unions, but to the Britisher there are a host of issues and policies in which they feel they still have room for improvement.

When it comes to the Communist Party, there are also a few significant ways in which it differs from the American party. In Britain, the party has stronger roots in the factories and unions; its members are publicly known in factories, unions, mass organizations, the arts or public life. It has a singleness of purpose during elections, when everything else is literally neglected and there is a solid concentration of time, effort and forces on the elections. Its leading committees are composed so as to guarantee a permanent contact with the workers in the key industries, factories and workers' organizations. Its style of journalism is such that the *Morning Star* is considered a model of all-round balance of features and news is praised by typographic experts and is the most widely read paper at all trade union conferences.

However difficult it was for Mae and myself to adjust ourselves to a new country—and for Mae it was especially bewildering—the younger members of the Williamson family acclimated themselves quite easily. Bob's first year at Cooper Union in New York was not recognized here, and he had to go to a grammar school and take his general certificate of education examinations. He then went to the university, where he has received his B.Sc., M.A., and his Ph.D. in biochemistry. At present he is a lecturer at the University of Glasgow, is married, and we have two grandchildren.

Neil, who was only eight when we arrived, passed his general certificate of education examination with flying colors and is attending Leeds University, where he is studying mathematics. To our great satisfaction, both our sons are politically progressive and forward-looking.

During these years in Britain, I have been asked hundreds of times, "Would you like to go back to live and work in the United States, if you could?" In the early years it was a commonplace question, but even now it still gets asked. The questioner asks it in good faith, without knowing that it opens an old wound.

People in their own country, even Communists, forget that whatever the political climate of another country, it is home to its people. In my case, America was my home for 42 years, starting as a boy of ten. There I went to school, got my first job, participated in my first strike, joined the Socialist and Communist movements, participated in the class struggle and in the leadership of the party, got married and raised a family. Does anyone think it was easy to push these 42 years to one side, to deny their existence? True, I was born in Scotland. But when I returned at 52 years of age, it was essentially a new country.

A realistic estimate convinced me that since my return to the United States was not in the cards in the foreseeable future, my duty was to get into the class struggle and party activity in Britain. While my comrades in Britain have been generous in helping us to settle in, the depth of the problem that confronted me was never fully appreciated; and maybe it is expecting the impossible that it should be.

A Communist's allegiance is to the working class of his own country and he strives to win over its people to the struggle for a socialist society. I must admit that I truly feel as if I belong to two countries, the United States and Britain. Those 42 years of my life, the best years, cannot be wiped out. But this feeling does not cancel out my immediate allegiance as a Scot and a British Communist to the working class and party of Britain.

Our home, our family and our roots are now here — even if the roots have not yet reached a proper depth since their transplanting, and even if the gardeners themselves are occasionally frowned upon by insular compatriots because they have not been able to shed all the Americanisms acquired during a lifetime.

Therefore, if the opportunity arose to return to the United States, I can only answer as of today: for one or more visits, working or otherwise, I would welcome the opportunity; if for good, that would have to be decided on the basis of political and personal circumstances.

I take pride in my activities in the United States, but I hasten to add that whatever contribution I may have made to the development of working-class consciousness and organization was due to the Communist Party. When we speak of the party as the vanguard, the organizer and political leader of the working folk, we are uttering the simple truth.

But the party is also the molder of people. It took me as a young industrial worker of 19 years of age, with no schooling beyond the eighth grade, who had started work at 13, and it taught me everything I know. It developed in me whatever qualities I have. It gave me some challenging tasks that I didn't always fulfill successfully, although I always did my best. And the party membership, over a 25-year period, expressed confidence in me by reelecting me each time to the national committee.

My pride in the party has grown even stronger these past years, as it has battled against and survived the many and varied onslaughts from the strongest bastion of world imperialism. The American party has suffered great losses in leadership through the years of struggle, harassment, prosecution and imprisonment. It has never been easy to be a Communist in the United States. Since 1948 it has become many times more difficult, but the American Communists have proven worthy.

Years of membership and activity in the party is one's most valuable possession, not "wasted years," as some moaned when they spewed forth their venom and ran from the battlefield in 1956-57. If the working class, oppressed people and true democrats are to march forward to a socialist America, the party remains indispensable, as it has been in other countries of the world.

Most of the comrades who have been deported look back with the same pride in the party, while contributing their best in whatever country they may now find themselves. It has been my good fortune to meet or to correspond with many of these deportees. In Poland, one finds Dora Lifshitz in a responsible post and refusing to retire on pension; Bill Gebert is an ambassador; George Siskind and others are in other phases of work. In Bulgaria, George Pirinsky is secretary of the peace movement. In Hungary, there are Joe and Ann Peters, one in publishing, the other in radio, as well as Emil and Grace Gardos. In Czechoslovakia there are John and Evelyn Vaffiados. In Italy, we find Fred Brown and another comrade who became editor of an important daily paper. In Denmark, there is an old-timer from Chicago, Nels Kjar, as well as Andy Overgaard. And after many years in the German Democratic Republic, Beatrice Johnson went to Cuba. Among those in Britain are Charlie and Mickey Doyle and Harry Carlisle. All those whose names are omitted will, I'm sure, understand why.

These former members of the American party who engaged in activity of a new type in a dozen different countries could each tell his own story. But none of them ever forget the battles of the American class struggle in which they participated, nor the lessons learned there. All of them, without detracting one iota from their present loyalties, are fervent propagandists for the American party.

The Communist Party in the United States is the only inheritor of a great tradition of early American working-class militancy and socialist sentiment. The course of history has made its present-day development and growth an especially difficult one. There are many objective factors, among them the relative prosperity of many workers and the ideological corruption of some, to which has been added the pall of fear rising from the unparalleled and sustained campaign of anti-Communist hysteria and persecution.

Faced by these conditions, many dropped their active membership because they and their families could no longer live under such pressure. They will return. But some have left in a different mood; as they relish the temporary windfalls of capitalist affluence, they justify their own escape from the struggle by denigrating the half century of party activity. Despite all this, the Communist Party of the United States stands solid, and its ranks will soon swell with new recruits to bring it to a size never before achieved.

Thomas Paine, that revolutionist, who called three countries — England, America and France — "my country," wrote:

"Tyranny, like hell, is not easily conquered; yet we have this consolation with us, that the harder the conflict, the more glorious the triumph. What we obtain too cheap, we esteem too lightly."

History will record that the 17 million-strong trade union movement, the efforts over the years for independent political action by laborers and farmers, and the great freedom movement of the Negro people, all owe much to the never-ceasing activities of the small but active Communist Party.

To a question that one gets asked in Britain and Europe over and over again, "What hope can there be that the American working class will ever fight for socialism?" my reply has been and remains: However long and difficult the path, the American workers will achieve socialism. They are second to none in their militancy and they fight courageously at their level of understanding for their demands. When they comprehend the great liberating influence and ideals of socialism, they will fight equally well and victoriously for a socialist America based on Marxist principles.

Among the tens of thousands who will become Communists in the years ahead and help influence and lead the American working people to this glorious future will be many of America's youth. The well-known British leader, Tom Mann, an associate of our own Bill Foster and Elizabeth Gurley Flynn and, like them, an early syndicalist who later became a Communist, said on his deathbed in 1941, "Tell the comrades to have good courage. Go on with the work. There will be setbacks, partial success and then final success. The young people will have a lot to go through, but they will succeed in the end."

If the experiences recorded in these pages help in any small way the young people of the new generation who must carry forward the great liberating banner of socialism and communism to victory in the United States, I will feel well rewarded.

And when America's new generations read about Lincoln and Douglass, Sylvis and Debs, Ruthenberg and Foster, Flynn and Bloor and Dennis and Davis, I commend to them these beautiful words of Eugene Victor Debs, when he had just received a ten-year sentence in a federal court in Cleveland, Ohio, in September 1918:

"In the unceasing struggle between the toilers and producers and their exploiters, I have tried to serve those among whom I was born, with whom I expect to share my lot until the end of my days. . . . I never more clearly comprehend than now the great struggle between the powers of greed and the rising hosts of freedom. I can see the dawn of a better day of humanity . . .

> *Let the people take heart and hope everywhere,*
> *for the cross is bending,*
> *the midnight is passing,*
> *And joy cometh with the morning.*